REAL
FOOD
GUIDE

JORDANS
REAL
FOOD
GUIDE

DAVID MABEY

Illustrations by Julie Mabey

Quiller Press
London

First published 1984 by
Quiller Press Ltd
50 Albemarle St.
London W1X 4BD
Copyright © David Mabey 1984
ISBN 0 807621 35 X
Phototypeset by Hobson Street Studio Ltd, Cambridge
Printed by Richard Clay (The Chaucer Press) Ltd, Suffolk
Production services by Book Production Consultants,
Cambridge

Contents

Acknowledgements

This book is the result of many years' delving into the mysteries of British food, during which time I have contacted, spoken to and made friends with scores of producers, farmers, fishermen, shopkeepers and market traders. They are too numerous to mention by name, but they know who they are and I'd like to thank them one and all.

Of late, I have also had useful assistance from the following: The Farm & Food Society, The Soil Association, The Free-Range Egg Association, The Organic Food Service, The Bee Farmers' Association, Organic Farmers & Growers Ltd., The National Vegetable Research Station, the McCarrison Society, The British Herb Trade Association, Loseley Park Farms and The Maldon Crystal Salt Company.

I should also like to thank Drew Smith, Editor of the *Good Food Guide* for information on guinea fowl (and for sticking to his guns about real food in restaurants), and my brother Richard, as usual, was a mine of information and sympathetic criticism. Special thanks to Vivien Green who was a pillar of strength and encouragement when needed. I am also most grateful to Mary Knowler for her invaluable help and assistance.

Many writers and many books have inspired me, but I should like to mention in particular Susan Campbell's excellent *Guide to Good Food Shops* which was the source of countless leads and contacts.

Finally I should like to thank Bill Jordan and Jeremy Greenwood for making it all possible.

I should add that all the views expressed in the book are entirely my own and may not necessarily reflect those of organisations and individuals mentioned in the text.

How To Use The Guide

The book is divided into sections devoted to different types of food such as cheese, poultry, fruit and honey. Within most sections there is also a catalogue of specific items listed aphabetically. Each entry provides information about the history, availability and characteristics of the food, what to look out for and what to avoid.

The choice of items is biased towards those that have a British flavour, in other words those that are grown or produced here, have a specific 'home-grown season' and are available as such in our shops.

At the end of each section, in most cases, there is a limited directory of suppliers, producers and stockists etc. In this edition of the guide, the list is quite small, but it is intended to be a base from which we can develop a much more comprehensive directory of real food. To help us on our way we would be grateful for any comments or recommendations from readers, and hope they will take advantage of the tearout forms provided at the back of the book to give us information about real food suppliers and also to tell us if any of the present entries should be re-assessed for one reason or another.

About the directory Entries are listed alphabetically by town, beginning with England and following on with Scotland and Wales. It has not been possible to provide information about suppliers in Ireland in the present edition, although this may be possible in the future.

Some shops and suppliers appear more than once for different foods. This is quite common, since a maker of good pork pies, for example, is likely to have a reputation for sausages too. Also, while a number of the listings are for one item only, it's worth bearing in mind that they will probably offer many other types of real food that are acceptable.

For reasons of space, opening hours are only given when they are extraordinary. Readers should assume that shops are open normal hours (with half-day closing here and there); market days are normally listed, as are opening times of places such as herb farms, which are often very restricted and seasonal. In such cases it's always best to telephone before you set out, especially out of season.

The symbol M indicates that a particular producer or stockist operates a mail-order service. Always ring or write (enclosing s.a.e.) for details first.

While every effort has been made to ensure the accuracy of specific entries in the directory sections, circumstances can change and neither the author, the publishers nor Jordans can accept any liability for information that subsequently turns out to be incorrect.

Foreword

Eating patterns in this country have changed dramatically over the past hundred years or so and most people would agree that the health of the population has improved with each generation. So too, perhaps, has our understanding of the fact that good wholeome food and good health are linked inextricably in whatever environment you choose to live.

Today there are signs that many traditional values of simple food production are returning as consumers demand high standards and show a willingness to pay for them. More and more manufacturers are beginning to move away from chemical preservatives and additives, while major retailers compete on their respective 'freshness' campaigns.

Perhaps the last 20 years has seen the greatest changes in our dietary and shopping habits.

Soon after Jordans began its business as a family flour miller in 1855, bran was removed from the flour and was considered a waste product. Happily that situation has now changed and bran – a significant contributor to a healthy diet – is not only retained in Jordans flour but added to many of our cereal and snack food products. In the not too distant future, we are looking to include conservation grade grains in our products. These grains are grown on farms which are biologically based without the reliance on high cost inputs to the soil.

We believe this Real Food Guide is such an interesting and useful book because it sets out to explain, in simple terms, what good foods are all about, where to find them in specialist outlets and how to choose to suit individual tastes and pockets.

Any publication that promotes the qualities of good simple food and increases public awareness of its benefits deserves the support of all those associated with the food industry.

Bill Jordan
August 1984

Introduction

Take a walk down any high street or shopping centre and you can't fail to notice how much emphasis is put on food and food products. This book is about the kind of food we are being offered, how to improve it and how to make the best possible use of it. And it's a book aimed at consumers and shoppers, to help them understand what is happening to our food and also to give them information which they can use to exert pressure on sections of the food industry that really could be providing us with better food. There are signs that the climate is changing, people are more and more concerned about the quality of the food they eat, and some food producers *are* beginning to respond. But there is still a very long way to go.

The subject of the book is 'real food', particularly real British food. Of course it can be argued that all food is real: it exists, it isn't imaginary – yet some products are undoubtedly more real than others. 'Real' in this sense means natural, fresh food; food that is not highly processed or loaded with synthetic additives. It is the kind of food that has always been with us, but which is now finding a new lease of life.

Learning the language As consumers we are often baffled by the way our food is produced. It would be helpful if manufacturers explained their business more clearly and were encouraged to label their products more simply but also more comprehensively. Some are genuinely concerned to make the consumer aware of what they are doing, and are using advertising and promotion positively to educate rather than persuade. More manufacturers should follow their lead.

The whole subject of ingredients, additives and food labelling is still virtually unintelligible to most people. Do shoppers know, for instance, the order in which ingredients are listed on a packet (beginning with the most important by weight), or what the term 'meat' means when applied to a sausage or a pie? And how many can decipher the complex code of additives, all those substances included in food products as preservatives, emulsifiers, stabilisers, anti-oxidants, colouring, flavouring, etc, etc? Without a degree in chemistry, the memory of a Mastermind champion or a list of additives in your shopping basket, you are likely to be none the wiser when you real the label (Would you realise, for instance, that E304 is actually the anti-oxidant 6-O-Palmitoyl-L-ascorbic acid?) This is important because we need to be able to understand what some manufacturers are putting into our food and why they are doing it. There must be ways of explaining this in language that is comprehensible to everyone.

Additives are now beginning to dominate the style and direction of some sections of the food industry and we are being obliged to consume more and more of them. Way back in 1975 it was calculated that we took in more than 4 pounds of additives each year, or the equivalent of 12 aspirin-sized tablets each day. It's anyone's guess what the current figure is.

We are being bombarded by an array of potentially toxic substances which must be a frightening prospect. But at least packaged foods do have labels and the list of ingredients can be helpful, if only to tell you roughly what the products contain. But what about unpackaged food? If these have a label at all it may only give the vaguest description of contents, and behind this facade lurks a second barrage of chemicals: pesticides, growth promotors, hormones, antibiotics and many more which are put into the earth, sprayed onto crops and injected into livestock. Much of our fruit, vegetables, eggs, meat and dairy products is affected by these practices, which pose an insidious threat to anyone concerned about the quality of the food they eat.

But alternatives do exist. An increasing number of farmers, growers and producers are rejecting pesticides and other chemicals and are working hard to produce more wholesome food, more safely, more humanely and with greater awareness of the wishes and needs of the consumer.

Signs of the times In his editorial for the 1984 edition of the *Good Food Guide*, Drew Smith made a good case for real food in restaurants, arguing that it was outrageous and indefensible for chefs to pass off pre-packed foods as fresh and also that the whole business of restaurant catering depended far too heavily on highly processed food of one kind or another. It is, after all, one of the marks of a good chef that he chooses and selects his raw materials with care and understanding. But in far too many restaurants cutting corners is accepted practice: meals come complete in plastic bags and only need to be dropped into a pan of water, soup is 'home-made' if a few pieces of chopped carrot and onion are thrown into the saucepan of re-constituted powder, and frozen vegetables are preferred because it takes time and effort to prepare fresh ones. No wonder so much of our restaurant cooking has such a bad reputation.

The reaction of the catering industry to all this was predictable: how dare the Editor of the *Good Food Guide* suggest that there was anything wrong with short cuts, economies or highly processed food; he clearly didn't understand what catering in Britain was all about. But Drew Smith was right, restaurants should be showcases for the very best food and cooking we can offer, not second-class establishments where portion control and labour costs are more important than the quality of the food.

While only a few of us regularly frequent restaurants, all of us have to eat, and it was the controversy surrounding a report about our diet which proved to be the real bombshell. Some years ago, the Department of Health commissioned a report from NACNE (National Advisory Committee on Nutrition Education) on the relationship between food health and disease. The findings and recommendations, which might simply have been more reading matter for the academics in fact created shock waves through whole sections of the food industry, and as a result publication of the report was blocked by the DHSS for two years. That in itself was a fatal mistake, a scandalous cover-up, and eventually the news did leak out, thanks to a forthright piece of journalism by Geoffrey Cannon in the *Sunday Times*. As a result, a watered-down version was released in 1983 through the Health Education Council.

But what was all the fuss about? Briefly, NACNE concluded that the British diet put us all at risk from heart disease, cancer and diabetes in particular, but also put forward some far-reaching recommendations which should be achieved by the year 2000. These included a reduction in fat of 30% of total energy intake, a 50% cut in sugar, salt to be cut by half and fibre intake increased to at least 30 grams per day. Such recommendations weren't simply cosmetic gestures, but signified nothing less than a complete re-think of our eating habits. No wonder the powerful food industry lobbies were desperate to keep the report under wraps, for it struck at the very heart of many of their products, which still rely on high levels of salt, sugar and animal fats.

In practical terms, NACNE's prescription for a healthier diet was less fat, less refined sugar and less salt. On the plus side there should be more fibre and starchy carbohydrates, more fish, fresh fruit and vegetables. The emphasis above all was on the quality of fresh produce, careful, sensibly planned shopping and the avoidance of highly processed food with synthetic additives.

Fighting for our food Changing our diet means changing our attitudes to food, but it would be foolish to make the whole approach too negative. In fact we should be *more* adventurous and interested in the food we eat, and *more* enthusiastic about it. Not constricting but expanding our diet. Not following the path of self-denial in the hope that a few well-chosen foods will prove to be our salvation (heaven forbid that we should be doomed to a diet consisting only of a few grains and pulses).

We should be making better use of the marvellous choice of natural produce that is all around us. Why eat breaded scampi when there is monkfish to be had? Why settle for soapy cheese cut from a block when you can enjoy full-flavoured farmhouse Cheddar as an occasional treat? Why buy insipid frozen duck when you can have rich venison or plump, juicy mussels? Why eat a battery-farm egg when you can get a free-range one?

In the end we will get the food we deserve. And we will only achieve better food by making better use of our resources and by actively encouraging producers and suppliers who are keen to offer us real food. At the moment there are signs that this is happening. Some supermarkets now sell free-range eggs and organic vegetables, and more and more have special cheese counters, help-yourself selections of fresh vegetables and fruit, was well as special departments selling fresh fish and meat. More market gardeners, growers and farmers are moving over to organic methods of production and all kinds of organic produce are getting easier to obtain. There are butchers who are prepared to make wholesome sausages from lean meat, fish smokers who are curing fish without resorting to dyes or smoke solutions, cheese makers who are keeping alive some of the finest cheeses in the world, but who also have the foresight and imagination to invent new cheeses for today's and tomorrow's needs. Add to the list herb growers, millers, mustard makers, fishermen, bakers, as well as a whole range of shopkeepers, market traders, and suppliers who are genuinely responding to the campaign for better food. A little more cooperative effort could work wonders; it could transform British food and our diet.

But it all depends on you, the shopper. You have the final say and you have the most powerful sanctions – your money and your custom. So keep up the pressure, encourage producers and suppliers (large and small) who *are* making an effort to raise their standards, but don't be afraid to criticise where there are shortcomings. Fight for real food and in the end you will win.

The Real Food Code

★ Fresh is always best.

★ Buy locally. Support your local producers and suppliers, but always check the true origins of your purchases.

★ Eat with the seasons.

★ Look hard at labels and packaging. Learn the language and learn to read between the lines.

★ Follow the NACNE guidelines: eat less fat, salt and sugar; eat more fibre, fresh fruit, vegetables and fish.

★ Remember that real food means making better use of our skills and resources.

★ Enjoy real food. It's one of the greatest pleasures we have.

Cereals, Flours & Bread

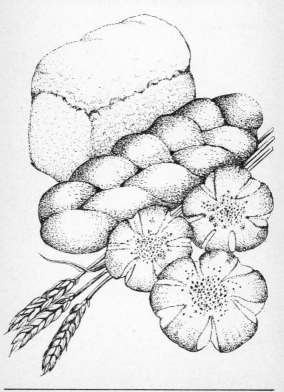

Cereals & Flours

The word cereal is a way of paying homage to Ceres, the Roman goddess of agriculture, and edible grains of one kind or another are the most important food crops for the populations of almost every country in the world. Cereals actually come from the family of cultivated grasses including rice, wheat, oats, barley and millet and the grains that we harvest are the fruits of these plants, storehouses of food and nutrients. Roughly half the world depends on rice, while the other half – Britain included – eats wheat, oats, corn and barley.

All kinds of wheat now dominate the scene largely because they yield a substance called gluten which is essential for bread-making. This gives bread dough its elasticity and holds the structure together when it is expanding due to the action of yeast. Without gluten, the bread would be flat and heavy.

The whole grain   A wheat grain really consists of three main parts. On the outside is the husk or bran, the central portion or endosperm, and the sprouting portion of the kernel, known as the wheatgerm. It is the make up of these different parts and the way they are handled that can result in nutritious or worthless flour and bread.

The outer bran is a vital source of dietary fibre – the name given to a whole range of complex plant substances which pass right through the intestines as 'roughage', without being absorbed; the presence of fibre helps digestion, prevents constipation and seems to prevent too much fat and sugar entering the bloodstream too quickly. Nutritionists agree that we need a diet with more fibre in it, and one of the best sources is the bran from wheat grains. Bran makes up about 15% of the grain and a valuable source of fibre.

The wheatgerm, which makes up 2½% of the grain, is a very concentrated source of nutrients, especially thiamin, nicotinic acid and vitamin B6, plus minerals such as potassium, magnesium, iron and zinc. It is also a source of essential fats.

The remaining part of the grain is the endosperm, which consists largely of starch with some protein.

Depending on the way the cereals are milled and turned into flour, various parts of this complicated grain can be lost. The most important difference is between wholemeal and white flour. In wholemeal flour, the whole grain is used and nothing is taken out. On the other hand, white flour is produced so that most of the bran and wheatgerm are removed, leaving only the starchy endosperm. As a result there's a difference between the nutritional value of bread made from wholemeal and white flour.

Today's flour and milling In the very beginning, grain wasn't milled at all; it was roughly crushed or pounded in something like a primitive pestle and mortar, and the results must have been very coarse indeed. By the Iron Age there were very basic rotary mills, the ancestors of most of our surviving stone mills. The grain was ground between two massive stones, which of course had to be turned laboriously by hand. But is was the Romans who pioneered the idea of powering these millstones using the natural forces of water. Mills disappeared for a time after the Romans left, but re-appeared before the Norman Conquest, and those powered by water were quickly joined by windmills drawing their energy from the air itself.

For centuries the miller was an essential figure in village life, grinding the farmer's cereal crops and in turn supplying bakers, as well as private individuals. His skills survived and there are still a few mills producing what is called 'stone-ground' flour.

But milling is now dominated by mechanically powered roller mills, invented during the 19th century. The clinical efficiency of these mills was perfectly described by Elizabeth David in her classic book *English Bread and Yeast Cookery*: 'Once the wheat is matured, blended, then dry-cleaned and wet-cleaned by a series of complex operations, the milling proper starts. Break rollers shear open the wheat berry, freeing the endosperm or starchy part of the grain. This is then separated from the bran and the rest of the 'offal'. The wheat berry has now become a granular semolina, to be pulverised into flour, graded through fine meshes, and ultimately chlorine-bleached, processed, 'improved' and packed into sacks or bags.' That in essence is today's white flour. If some of the bran and wheatgerm is subsequently re-added, the result is 'brown' flour.

There's nothing new in the desire to make bread whiter than it should be. Back in the 1850s loaves were frequently adulterated with alum, ground-up bones and white lead. Now we use other forms of bleaching agent. This doesn't simply make the bread look white but also instantly 'matures' the flour so that it can be handled easily in high-speed dough making machines.

Because white flour is deficient in vitamins and minerals (found in the bran and germ), millers are now legally required to put back some of these lost nutrients. So flour is 'fortified' with thiamin and nicotinic acid together with calcium (in the form of chalk) and iron. At the time of writing, there are currently discussions about a report from the COMA committee (Committee On Medical Aspects of food policy) which advises the DHSS and ultimately the Ministry of Agriculture, Fisheries and Food. This recommended that we should be encouraged to eat more brown and wholemeal bread but also that 'fortification' should be abolished. It seems likely that this will be overturned and that 'fortification' will remain standard practice – the theory being that white bread without fortification is even worse than the same bread with its quota of nutrients.

(NB: As we go to press, these recommendations have in fact been overturned).

Millers who care The milling trade is now dominated by three giants, Associated British Foods, Rank Hovis McDougall and Spillers, who between them supply something like 80% of Britain's flour. They are also bakers and have been systematically taking over smaller baking firms in recent years. As a result two out of every three loaves in Britain are produced by way of either ABF or RHM.

Fortunately there are millers who take a different view. They may use the old method of stone-grinding to produce wholemeal flour or, like Jordans, they may use roller-milling. What makes Jordans different is the fact that their rollers go slowly and so the grain isn't over-heated – thereby losing its essential nutrients – and there's no chance of the oil in the wheatgerm becoming rancid. It's a simple principle, but it shows how easily technology can be adapted to improve rather than ruin the food we eat. It's a shining example both of technology in its place, at the service of man, and of taking the best from the past and fitting it to today's needs.

Barley

One of the most important cereal crops in the Ancient World, barley was also extensively used in Britain, although by the Middle Ages it was already being replaced by wheat and rye. Heavy barley bread must have been a dismal prospect and it's not surprising that people took quickly to the alternatives. But barley has survived, because it is vital for brewing beer.

Guidelines Barley still has a very limited use in baking and you can buy both barley flour and barley meal. The flour is made from de-husked grain, while the meal is made from the whole grain. They can be added to wheat flour to give it a sweeter taste, although they are usually used on their own to make unleavened bread.

Pearl barley is the de-husked and polished grain, most commonly added to soups and stews in Scotland.

Barley flakes are widely available in health food shops and make delicious puddings and porridge.

Oat

The common cultivated oat (*Avena sativa*) was not established in Britain until the Iron Age, although it is known to have existed in Europe much earlier. For centuries oats were the staple cereal crop in Scotland and many parts of northern England where the climate was too inhospitable to grow wheat successfully.

Many of the classic regional recipes for oatcakes and breads have been lost, and much of the oat crop now goes to feed livestock, but interest in wholefoods has led to something of an oat revival, and they are now included in various kinds of muesli as well as in different types of 'alternative confectionery' and crunchy cereal bars.

Guidelines Oats are highly nutritious: they contain almost 17% protein, fibre, large amounts of thiamin as well as substantial amounts of iron and phosphorus.

There are basically three grades of oatmeal: fine, medium and pinhead (or small, middle and coarse). Oatmeal had innumerable uses in the past, from porridge to all manner of regional oatcakes, which were flat, unleavened breads baked on a cast-iron griddle or bakestone. A few of these breads have doggedly survived and you can still find them in bakers' shops in counties such as Yorkshire, Lancashire, Staffordshire and Derbyshire. Scotland's oatcakes are called 'bannocks' and tend to be either large round cakes, grilled on both sides, or little crisp biscuits. Oat flakes are also very versatile.

Rye

Rye doesn't have the long history of some other cereals, although it was found in Iron Age sites in Britain. It was once one of the most important cereal crops right up to the 17th century and was often mixed with wheat or barley to make 'maslin' or 'mixed' bread. Nowadays, though, its use is largely confined to north European countries such as Germany and Denmark.

Guidelines It is similar in composition to wheat although it doesn't possess as much gluten and so produces flatter, less risen bread. You can buy both light and dark rye flours (the light has been sifted and contains less bran) and they add a very distinctive, strong flavour to different kinds of bread dough.

The best known rye breads are pumpernickel and Scandinavian crispbreads.

Rye is subject to a fungus disease called ergotism, which can produce violent symptoms including hallucinations and trances similar to the adverse effects of the drug LSD. Ergot has virtually been eliminated in Britain.

Wheat

The most important of all cereal grains, synonymous with bread and our 'staff of life'. The first primitive varieties began to grow perhaps 10,000 years ago around the Eastern Mediterranean, and now there are literally thousands of different strains, although they fall into a number of important categories. First of all there are spring wheats, which are sown in March and April for harvesting early in the autumn; these are now overtaking the traditional long-maturing winter wheats sown any time from September to February. The other main distinction is between the colour of the grains and their hardness or softness. Most red and yellow wheats are high in gluten and good for making bread, while most white-skinned varieties have a softer, more mealy texture which is low in protein and high in starch; these are better for baking cakes and biscuits.

Guidelines Buying flour is really a question of understanding the language and terminology. These are the important words to look for:

White flour: this is flour made from 72–74% of the grain. The 28% or so that is removed is most of the bran and wheatgerm. What is left is a mixture of starch, some protein and a small amount of minerals and vitamins. Freshly milled white flour is actually creamy in colour, but most is now bleached to make it look pearly white. Always look for the word 'unbleached' on the label.

Brown flour: contains 81–90% of the whole grain with only a small amount of bran and germ removed. In theory the darker the flour the more bran it contains. By law, brown bread must contain at least 0.6% crude fibre. In some caramel is added to make the bread darker.

Wholemeal flour: this is literally 100% of the grain, with nothing removed, so it is high in fibre from the bran and vitamins and minerals from the germ. Wholewheat means flour made from 100% wheat. Wholegrain is another general term for wholemeal flours.

Granary flour: a specific type of brown flour to which malted wheat grains have been added. Similar versions may be known as malted flours.

Soft (cake) flour: low in protein and high in starch. Best used for producing cakes and other bakery products where a light texture is important.

Strong (bread) flour: high in protein and helps to produce the volume and texture needed in bread.

In general you should look out for wholemeal flour because this is the most nutritious; also go for unbleached flours as these are untreated with synthetic additives. An increasing number of independent millers are also now looking for sources of organically grown cereals, and many obtain them through Organic Farmers & Growers Ltd (see page 274) which acts as a clearing house and distribution centre for all kinds of organic produce. Organic flour will be labelled as such. Some flours may have unusual extraction rates such as 81% and these are normally listed on the label. Remember that the higher the percentage the closer to the whole grain the flour is.

Bread

We have relied on bread as our staple food for thousands of years and it has changed a good deal since the days of coarsely ground cereal mixed with water and heated over a fire. Bread was once made from anything that was available, from acorns, peas and beans to barley, oats, rye and wheat. In the past, white wheaten bread was the food of the privileged classes, while brown or black bread made from rye or barley was subsistence food for ordinary families.

Today's bread is still, broadly speaking, brown or white although almost all of it is made purely from wheat. But the roles have been reversed. Now white bread, processed, packaged and sliced is the common fare, while brown bread and its variations have assumed a more exclusive role – at least if price is anything to go by. Much of this is because most of our bread is produced by just three giant concerns (see page 20); independent bakers are diminishing in numbers and have to struggle to avoid competition and takeovers from the large companies.

Sliced white bread is the scourge of the land, it's not even worthy of the name bread. And yet people buy it by the ton. That anyone can actually prefer it when there are tasty, nutritive alternatives at the remaining local bakers is extraordinary. Considering that bread is such a fundamental part of our diet, we seem to care little about what we buy. Thankfully more and more people are supporting their local bakers or starting to make their own from some of the excellent flours now available.

The tide is turning. Sliced white bread is getting an increasingly bad reputation, we are starting to buy less of it and switch to more wholesome breads of one kind or another. And there's still plenty of interest in other aspects of our baking tradition – the oatcakes of the north of England and Scotland, home-made crumpets and muffins from the north west, fruit breads (like Wiltshire lardy cake and Welsh *bara brith*) and a whole host of different rolls and baps, in addition to loaves themselves.

General guidelines for buying bread (i) Support your local baker, even if some of his bread seems to be rather expensive. He will need both your custom and your encouragement to stay in business.
(ii) Buy wholemeal or genuine brown loaves where possible. These are high in dietary fibre and the best from a health point of view.
(iii) Bread made from unbleached, organic flour is the ideal, although this is still quite rare. (The flours themslves are readily available, so you can always make your own bread from them.)
(iv) Keep your eyes open for all kinds of local and regional types of bread.
(v) Eat more bread of the good wholemeal variety. And remember that real bread should be a pleasure to eat – full of flavour, texture and nourishment. Don't allow it to be levelled out, standardised or reduced to nothing more than a lump of cooked dough.

Making bread at home If you are thoroughly dissatisfied with the kind of bread being produced by the majority of the large baking firms, you can take matters into your own hands and make your own bread. Thankfully there are some excellent bread flours available from the independent millers and it's worth experimenting with some of the different types available. Always go for unbleached flours and those which have a high proportion of bran.

You can make loaves of any shape or size and it can be fun trying out many of the traditional shapes that have been devised over the centuries by country housewives and bakers.

By making your own bread you also ensure that it contains no additives of any kind, and you can also keep the salt content to a minimum.

For those people who are sensitive to gluten (see page 18) there are also a number of useful gluten-free flours on the market.

Millers

A small but thriving collection of independent millers are providing good quality flour as an alternative to the products of the milling giants. A good deal of the flour now comes from organically grown grain.

W. Jordan (Cereals) Ltd
Holme Mills, <u>Biggleswade</u>,
Bedfordshire
Tel: (0767) 318222

Dunster Water Mill
<u>Dunster</u>, Somerset
Tel: (064 382) 759

Neal's Yard Flourmill
8 Neal's Yard,
Covent Garden,
<u>London</u> WC2
Tel: (01) 836 1082

Doves Farm
Ham, <u>Marlborough</u>,
Wiltshire
Tel: (0488) 4374

Mayall Organic Farms
(Pimhill flour)
Lea Hall Farm,
Harmer Hill, <u>Shrewsbury</u>,
Shropshire
Tel: (0939) 290342

---

*Use the response form on page 287
to send in your suggestions and information.*

Dairy Products

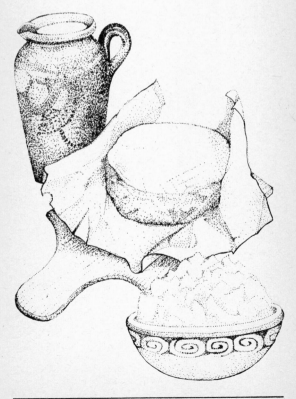

Milk

The milkman is such a familiar figure in British life that it's hard to believe that in the last century cows were kept in London and milking was done in the streets to prove that there was no adulteration with water. Milk – and by that we really mean cow's milk – has been one of our staple foods for centuries, but recently it has been the subject of some harsh criticism concerning the levels of saturated animal fat it contains. We consume far too much animal fat for our own good and one of the most important sources of this is the milk we drink. The richest gold-top milk contains something like 5% fat, of which about 60% is saturated. That may not sound a lot, but just think how much milk you drink in a week or a month and you'll see that it's a substantial amount.

Reducing the fat content of milk would involve drastic changes in both pasture and the types of cattle now preferred for dairy farming, as well as re-shaping the system of subsidies which are based on fat. At present more milk is produced with far too much fat in it at the same time as we are being urged to drink less for the sake of our health, and our children's health (for they drink more than anyone).

Guidelines Milk consists largely of water, together with calcium and albumen, casein (milk protein), lactose (milk sugar), fat and vitamins. But it comes in many forms and is processed in a number of different ways.

Condensed milk: normally available in tins. Processed so that about half the water is removed and sugar is added. It is thick, off-white and very sweet. Sold in cans.

Dried milk (powdered milk): milk from which almost all the moisture has been removed. Can be stored as a powder for up to a year and re-constituted by adding water.

Evaporated milk: similar to condensed milk, but has no sugar added. Sold in cans.

Homogenised milk: whole milk treated so that the cream is evenly distributed and does not separate into a distinct layer.

Pasteurised milk: this is heated (but not boiled) to destroy harmful bacteria, although some micro-organisms remain. This is our daily pinta. It's worth remembering that pasteurised milk goes off, but doesn't go sour.

Skimmed milk: this is milk from which most of the fat has been removed although all the nutrients (except fat-soluble vitamins) remain. Sometimes non-milk fats are added to it. Generally below 1% milk fat.

Sterilised milk: bottled homogenised milk that has been heat treated so that it will keep unopened for several weeks. Tastes like boiled milk.

UHT (ultra high treated) milk: homogenised milk subjected to very high temperatures (but for only one second!). Keeps almost indefinitely, hence its familiar name 'long life milk'.

Most of the milk we drink is pasteurised, and if you want to taste 'raw' milk that hasn't been treated in any way at all you will have to find a sympathetic farmer or keep cows yourself.

The best bet for anyone concerned about the fat levels in most milk is to switch to skimmed milk with its fat content of less than 1%. This is now readily available in supermarkets as well as health food stores.

Goat's Milk

More and more people are keeping goats for their milk and for the cheese you can make from it (see page 43). Goat's milk is very rich in fat (about 6%) and it also has high levels of casein or milk protein. The fattiness may be a disadvantage, but goat's milk is easy to digest and is a good alternative for anyone who is sensitive to cow's milk.

Goat's milk can be obtained from farmers and goat-keepers as well as from an increasing number of wholefood shops. It is also available frozen.

Cream

Cream is one stage removed from milk and its fat content is considerably higher. So health-conscious eaters should handle it with care. As milk cools the cream rises and this is literally 'creamed off', treated and packed into cartons.

Guidelines Like milk, cream is processed in a number of ways and the results vary a great deal.

Clotted cream: one of the West Country's most famous specialities. The milk is put into large 'setting pans' where the cream is allowed to rise. Then it is scalded to a temperature of 77–78°C for 40 minutes then left to cool. Slowly a wrinkled yellow crust forms which is skimmed off by hand and sold as clotted cream. Although it keeps well, some clotted cream contains added preservatives. Rich, thick and granular. Fat content is at least 55%.

Double cream: normally pasteurised. The colour varies from white to yellow. Has a thick pourable consistency but can be whipped. Fat content around 50%.

Extra thick cream: double cream that has been homogenised.

Single cream: the lightest of all types of cream. Normally pasteurised and homogenised. Will not whip. Fat content at least 18%.

Soured cream: prepared by introducing a lactic acid culture into a low-fat cream. Its slightly acidic flavour is used for salad dressings and various sauces.

Whipping cream: similar to double cream, but thinner and with less fat (minimum of 35%). Useful and economical, but is not very stable and doesn't hold its shape well.

AVOID synthetic cream or the new types that come in aerosol cans and can be sprayed on like shaving soap. They are full of sweeteners and additives.

Butter

One of our most ancient foods, which has been made in one form or another for thousands of years. We always associate it with cow's milk, but in other parts of the world it has been made from asses', ewe's, goat's and even camel's milk. In principle it could not be simpler: the cream is separated from the milk then churned until it forms a convenient and compact solid, which is butter.

Butter-making was one of the most important skills that country housewives had to master, and it was a rich and varied tradition. Everyone seemed to have their own way of doing it and the equipment they used, especially the churns themselves were wonderfully individual. Some were plungers, others were turned with handles attached to paddles, while in Wales there were wooden rocking churns that looked for all the world like a baby's cradle (and may even have served both functions).

Today, most butter-making takes place not in farmhouse dairies but in huge creameries that can handle something like 10,000 gallons of milk in an hour. Technology has taken over, although the principles of the process are still the same: the milk is spun in huge separators which trap the cream and separate it from the skim milk. The cream is cooled, allowed to age and then passed on to elaborate butter-making machines which can manufacture 2–3 tons of butter an hour.

Guidelines　(i) Butter contains about 80% fat, 60% of which is saturated animal fat, and it is this fact which has aroused a good deal of criticism recently. The butter industry is obviously in business to sell more butter and is desperately trying to make us eat more of it, even though every right-thinking nutritionist is recommending that we cut back on animal fats and foods containing them. The butter advertisers are quick to point out that butter is a completely natural product made without additives, that it is good for you and that it contains useful amounts of vitamins A and D as well as calcium and phosphorus. They are also ready to quote extracts from academic papers and research which confirm their view that there's no proven link between saturated fat, cholesterol and the incidence of heart disease.

Butter's main competitor, margarine seems to offer an alternative, as the manufacturers are only too ready to claim, because it is generally made from polyunsaturates which are not thought to be as harmful in terms of cholesterol build-up. In fact many 'block' margarines are made with animal fats and there are others containing what is called 'blended vegetable oils' which may contain palm or coconut oil, both of which are high in saturated fat. Your best bet is to buy soft margarines which are labelled 'high in polyunsaturates' but you should always check the ingredients of any margarine you buy.

Having said that it's really best to cut down on fats of all kinds.

(ii) Some butter is salted, some unsalted. In general it's best to go for unsalted. The more salt a butter has added to it, the longer is will keep. Also the further butter has to travel from where it is made to where it is sold, the more salt it will have.

(iii) Go easy on butter, use it sparingly and as an occasional treat. And if you do buy it, try to get locally-made farm butter rather than a block that has been scooped off some anonymous butter mountain. A little good butter from time to time will do you no harm, provided that the rest of your diet is low in saturated fat.

Buttermilk

This was originally the residue left after butter-making, although nowadays its is usually made from pasteurised skim milk. It is more easily digested than normal milk, although it still contains many of milk's nutrients.

Yoghurt

A wonderfully versatile, nutritious and useful food, made by allowing milk to go sour in warm conditions with the help of a friendly bacterium called *Lactobacillus bulgaricus*. Yoghurt has been a staple food for centuries in the Middle East, Eastern Europe and India, but we can thank one Professor Massal for identifying the bacteria involved and passing on his findings to the Russian Nobel Prize winner Ilya Metchnikoff, who, in 1904, began investigating the connections between yoghurt and the longevity of peasants in Bulgaria who ate vast quantities of the stuff.

Since then great claims have been made for yoghurt and in recent years it has become firmly linked with the trend towards healthier eating. It may not be traditionally British in character, but there are a number of dedicated British producers offering a good alternative to the bland, mass-produced versions which continue to flood into the shops.

Guidelines There's a lot of yoghurt about these days, but much of it bears little resemblance to the real thing. When buying 'plain' yoghurt there are several things to look out for. First, always buy 'live' yoghurt, that is yoghurt in which the bacteria *Lactobacillus bulgaricus* and also perhaps *Streptoccoccus thermophilus* are still active. This is because the bacteria are very useful indeed: they create a favourable environment in the intestine by knocking out harmful bacteria, they are also able to build up B group vitamins in the gut and replace natural intestinal flora that are depleted when antibiotics and other drugs are taken.

Don't assume that yoghurt is live, just because it is advertised as 'natural'. Most yoghurt produced by the large manufacturers is dead, processed and sterilised so that it will last longer. But who really wants yoghurt that will keep for ages: presumably the manufacturers do. However it doesn't have any advantages for the consumer.

Always choose yoghurt that is made from low-fat separated milk, rather than skimmed milk powder. This is easy to digest and is ideal for children and people who are sensitive or allergic to whole milk; and it's low in animal fat, which is another point in its favour.

Good yoghurt should also have plenty of texture. Most commercially-produced yoghurt is far too thin, runny and smooth; it also tends to be very acidic. Manufacturers no doubt think that this is what people want and that they will think they are actually eating the real thing, since they have nothing to compare it with. Fortunately this is no longer the case, and more good yoghurt is starting to appear in the shops.

The market for plain yoghurt is small when compared with that for fruit yoghurts, which have been agressively marketed by advertisers who try to convince us that these products are the most health-giving foods in the world. But the labels tell a different story. Almost without exception these fruit yoghurts contain preservatives, stabilisers, artificial colouring and flavouring; they are also loaded with sugar. Compare them with, say Loseley's fruit yoghurts – which are as good as you will get – and which have nothing added to them except a small amount of raw brown sugar.

Of course, if you want to avoid sugar altogether, you can make your own using live plain yoghurt plus any fresh fruits you like, in any combination you fancy.

Uses Plain yoghurt can be eaten as it is, and has innumerable uses in both sweet and savoury dishes. It's excellent with fresh fruit, honey and muesli, it is also the most pleasant and appropriate accompaniment for a whole range of spicy dishes, perfectly balancing their heat and fierceness and helping the digestion. Yoghurt can be used to marinade meat and poultry, it goes into soups and you can try it as a salad dressing and as a substitute for mayonnaise.

Cheese

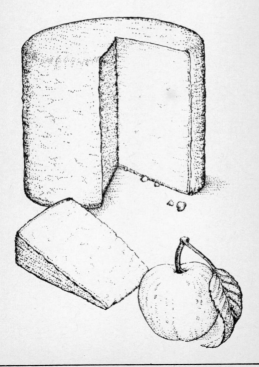

Cheese was being made and eaten in Britain more than 2,000 years ago, and it has always been one of our most important staple foods: nutritious, easy to store and transport, a neat compact way of producing concentrated food. For centuries it was a feature of farmhouse and country life, with almost every region and indeed every household having its own specialities. There was an enormous variety of cheeses of all types which were eaten at home and also despatched for sale at fairs and on market stalls.

The tradition survived quite happily until 1860 when disease killed off many thousands of cattle and the amount of milk – and therefore cheese too – dropped drastically. To save the situation and to prevent an influx of American cheese swamping the market, British farmers and cheese-makers banded together to form co-operatives and to open cheese-making factories or creameries, which could produce a great deal more cheese, more quickly and efficiently than any farmhouse dairy. In 1870 the first cheese factory was opened in Derby, and by 1875 there were six in operation. It was the beginning of the inevitable downhill slide for the farmhouse cheese-maker.

The First World War added to the problems since austerity restrictions and the need for quantity rather than quality meant that cheese-making had to become more standardised and there was little room left for local and regional variations. By the end of the Second World War, the situation was even worse: many of the old cheese-makers had retired or moved away, there was little sense of continuity or incentive for the traditions to be passed down the line to sons and daughters. Cheese-making in the traditional style was hard work; it needed time, dedication, patience. But in the depressed climate of post-war Britain these qualities were in short supply and the demand was for cheese that could be made and sold quickly without the care or ripening once lavished on it. As a result there was a further drastic drop in the number of cheese-making farms. In 1939 there were 405 farms in Cheshire; by 1948 this had dropped to just 44. Wensleydale fared even worse, and could only boast 9 farms as opposed to 176 before the war.

Although a handful of traditional cheesemakers did hang on, the market was increasingly dominated by the big creameries who were ready to respond to the supermarket boom of the 1960s. The old cheeses with their round shape, rind and months of slow maturing didn't appeal to the new breed of manufacturer, and so cheese was made in large rindless blocks. This had many advantages for producers and stockists: the cheese could be conveniently packed and sliced without any waste, it could be wrapped in hygienic transparent plastic and it didn't need maturing for any length of time (it was uneconomical to have whole cheeses sitting on the shelf for months on end).

But now the picture is begnning to change again and there's more and more demand for good cheese made and matured in the traditional manner. People are fed up with the blandness and lack of character of mass-produced block cheese, and want something better. Let us hope there are enough dedicated cheese-makers around to satisfy that demand. Patrick Rance, the undisputed hero and champion of British cheese summed up the situaton well in *The Great British Cheese Book* (a splendid piece of work about one of our finest foods): 'If Britain's cheese is to have a future, we must pay more attention to the cheeses our competitors cannot imitate, old cheeses made and finished in the traditional way.'

Types of cheese   Cheeses can be distinguished by their texture and fat content, and also by the way they are made. Basically there are five main groups:

Fresh cheese: as the name suggests these are unripened curds which are eaten soon after they have been made. Cottage cheese and cream cheese are good examples.

Soft cheeses: these are spreadable, briefly ripened and tend to contain a high percentage of moisture and fat. Not many British cheeses are in this style, although there are one or two exceptions such as Scottish caboc.

Semi-hard cheeses: these are matured cheeses with a high percentage of fat. They are easy to cut. Most of the classic British cheeses such as Cheddar, Cheshire, Derby, Gloucester and Leicester come into this category.

Hard cheeses: these are matured for a long time, and are very low in moisture, although they may be high in fat. Usually grated. British cheeses don't normally come into this category, which includes items like Parmesan.

Blue cheeses: blue or greenish veins in a cheese are caused by the infestation of harmless *Penicillium* bacteria which give the cheese a very strong distinctive flavour and texture. Originally cheeses turned blue by accident, but now the *Penicillium* spores are added deliberately to ensure that things go according to plan. Stilton is our best known blue cheese, but others such as Blue Cheshire and Blue Wensleydale are equally auspicious.

Cheese in our diet   Cheese has many virtues as a food, the most important being the fact that it is an excellent source of protein. Because it contains all the essential amino acids that the body cannot manufacture, it naturally figures highly in our diet. Cheese is also rich in calcium, phosphorus and various vitamins including A and B2 in particular.

But that isn't the whole story, because most British cheeses also have high levels of fat which is not a virtue in nutritional terms. Stilton contains 40% total fat, of which 60% is saturated, Cheddar has a total of 34%, while at the other end of the scale cottage cheese has a mere 4% fat. Clearly there's a case for going easy on these high-fat cheeses, and it's encouraging that one or two of the large manufacturers are now producing a range of low-fat cheeses. The point is not to ditch all of our finest traditional cheeses, simply because they are high in fat, rather to offer a choice of alternatives for those who wish or need to eat low-fat cheese. Good cheese is a pleasure to eat, provided you include it as part of a well-balanced diet.

Guidelines for buying cheese (i) Seek out a specialist cheese shop or a good delicatessen where whole traditional cheeses are on display. Lots of pre-wrapped pieces rather than the cheeses themselves is not a good sign.

(ii) Always try to sample a small piece of cheese before you buy. Although you can tell a great deal by the look of a cheese, there's no substitute for tasting it.

(iii) Many supermarkets now have good cheese counters where you can buy freshly cut cheese. Bear in mind the smaller the piece, the quicker it will dry out. Cracks in the cheese and a darker colour towards the outside are signs that it is over the hill.

(iv) It is always best to ask for a piece cut directly from a whole cheese.

(v) When buying traditional farmhouse cheese, look out for the presence of rind, and the number of the farm stamped on the side. Enquire whether it is a pasteurised or unpasteurised cheese. The heat treatment of milk to kill off harmful bacteria (pasteurisation) is said to destroy many flavour-enriching micro-organisms as well. So many cheese connoisseurs insist on unpasteurised cheese.

Applewood

One of the new breed of English cheeses, made by breaking up immature Cheddar curd, flavouring and re-milling it. Applewood is smoked – or smoke-flavoured – and has some of the texture and character of a processed cheese. Its other main feature is that it is coated in paprika. To me it always tastes like 'kipper cheese'.

A similar cheese goes by the name of CHARNWOOD.

Caboc

One of Scotland's most ancient cheeses, which was certainly being made in the 15th century by one Mariota de Ile, daughter of a Macdonald of the Isles. As Patrick Rance points out, this recipe has been passed down the line to her descendant Sussanah Stone, who has revived it at Blairliath on the southern shore of Dornoch Firth, Rosshire.

Guidelines Caboc is a sausage-shaped, full cream cheese with a mild buttery flavour. It is always rolled in pinhead oatmeal.

Caerphilly

Despite its Welsh name and its Welsh ancestry, Caerphilly is now considered to be an English cheese (at least by the English Country Cheese Council), for the sad reason that it is only made in large West Country creameries.

Caerphilly originated in little farmhouse dairies dotted across the rich pastures of mid-Glamorgan sometime early in the 19th century, and it was a great favourite with welsh miners, who appreciated its mild flavour and the fact that it was easy to digest (important if you spend much of your life bent double!).

As demand for the cheese grew, it was taken up by dairy farmers across the Bristol Channel in Somerset and Wiltshire. They were quick to realise its economic potential, and cashed in on the fact that it could be made and sold in a couple of weeks and didn't need to sit on shelves for months maturing like Cheddar and some other cheeses.

Guidelines A close-textured, flat round cheese, white in colour, and with a mild flavour suggesting buttermilk. Best eaten as it is, with bread and butter.

Cheddar

It's a disturbing fact that only about 1% of the cheese sold as Cheddar has the right to bear that name. Real Somerset Cheddar, a whole cheese made preferably on the farm from unpasteurised milk is incomparable, the finest cheese in the world, but much of the output of creameries from Ireland to New Zealand is a travesty of the real thing.

By the reign of Elizabeth I, cheese-makers around the village of Cheddar, Wells and Shepton Mallet were already renowned for their cheeses, so much so that most were 'bespoken before they were made', and the eminent 16th-century historian William Camden went so far as to say that Cheddar was 'an excellent prodigious cheese . . . of exceedingly delicious taste.' How right he was.

Cheddar's fame spread abroad as travellers to the New World took the recipe with them, but it was in England that it remained supreme. It owed much of its success in the 19th century to Somerset-born Joseph Harding who, in 1859, introduced a new system of cheesemaking that cut out many of the inconsistencies and errors associated with farmhouse cheesemaking and helped to standardise the process.

Guidelines Cheddar cheeses are no longer quite as 'prodigious' as they used to be, but good farmhouse versions are still magnificent, and more and more people are asking for them. And no wonder, because the alternative, as every supermarket shopper knows is the block of cheese, pressed and moulded into enormous edible 'breeze-blocks', not matured properly, wrapped in plastic and sold by the slice. The soapy taste and rubbery texture only serve to make things worse. In all it's a thoroughly disheartening spectacle and shows the extent to which we allow some of our finest foods to be ruined.

So, look for and ask for the alternative, which is a whole round cheese with a rind, wrapped in cloth and matured for at least six months to produce its 'bite' and incomparable nutty flavour. Cheddar is perfect with hunks of crusty bread and it's also a marvellous cooking cheese.

Cheshire

Probably the oldest surviving English cheese, Cheshire was mentioned in the 11th-century Domesday Book and is still made in the rich dairy farming country of north-west England.

Guidelines The most common form of Cheshire sold today is a young, crumbly white cheese with a mild, slightly salty tang; these cheeses are made early in the year – usually around April – and are sold quickly. But because of the high acidity and unpredictability of milk from cows turned out onto new rich pasture, it's a tricky process. Cheeses made later in the year can be matured to produce a more refined and exquisitely flavoured cheese. Some Cheshire cheese is coloured red.

Unlike Cheddar, all farmhouse Cheshire cheese is made from unpasteurised milk, and that includes cheese formed into blocks. Genuine cheeses are also stamped with the number of the farm they come from and the grading and the date they were made.

The favourite way of eating Cheshire cheese is with spicy cake or shortbread, and like its neighbour Lancashire it can be melted and spread on hot toast.

Blue Cheshire

A princely cheese with greenish-blue veins (known locally as 'green fade') streaked through its golden-yellow body. Blue Cheshire originated by accident since it is not uncommon for the occasional cheese to act as a home for mould during storage. But the cheesemakers didn't care for it, although apparently some found its way into the medicine cupboard to treat sores, earache and infected wounds. Nowadays the veining is done deliberately by introducing the harmless mould-producing spores into the cheese.

Blue Cheshire rightly has an increasing number of devotees, although it's still quite rare.

Colwick

A very rare and extremely localised cheese associated with Nottinghamshire and other parts of the Midlands. Nowadays it is made as a soft, skimmed-milk cheese with naturally a low fat content.

Cotherstone

Written off as a dead, or at least a dying cheese, Cotherstone still survives in the far north of England. It's a semi-soft full cream cheese with an unbound granular crust that is sometimes tinged pinkish-gold. Usually eaten very young, after about three weeks, although some cheeses will improve with keeping for a couple of months.

Cotswold

(See GLOUCESTER)

Cottage Cheese

One of the oldest and simplest forms of cheese, made from skimmed milk. Although the whey is drained from the curd it is not pressed, so it retains some moisture and has a distinctive granular texture. Usually eaten 2–3 days after being made. As it is a low-fat cheese, it is useful for those wanting to cut down on their intake of saturated animal fat.

Cream Cheese

Similar to cottage cheese, but made from full cream milk, or single or double cream. (Double cream cheeses have 40–60% fat, single cream cheeses 25–35%). It is white, soft and smooth in texture and needs to be eaten fresh. Some commercially produced varieties may contain preservative, so check before you buy.

Crowdie

Scotland's answer to cottage cheese, this ancient, smooth-textured crumbly cheese has recently been revived with great success by Sussanah Stone at Blairlaith in Rosshire. Crowdie, which has a delicate lemony flavour is also made with the addition of full cream.

Derby

Ambrose Heath, writing about English cheese in 1960 described Derby – with a certain amount of deference – as 'a good working-man's cheese', but added that 'the difficulty in obtaining it may yet make it an epicure's discovery'. He was right on both counts: Derby is a good, useful cheese – although not on a par with the finest Stilton or Cheddar – and it's increasingly hard to find.

Guidelines The original Derby cheeses were large round affairs, weighing up to 30lbs, but now what there is comes in the form of blocks or little rindless cheeses. It is creamy white in colour and generally has a mild flavour.

Sage Derby

Most Derby cheese now appears in this very distinctive green form. The cheese itself, originally made for Christmas and harvest festivities, gained its colour from the strained juice of pulped sage leaves, plus spinach leaves, although nowadays the curd is coated with sage steeped in chlorophyll. This produces the very characteristic marbled effect.

It was once the custom to decorate these cheeses with designs worked in fresh sage leaves.

Dunlop

Scotland's first and almost only traditional 'sweet milk' cheese, first made in the town of Dunlop, Ayrshire in 1688 by one Barbara Gilmour, who reputedly learned her trade in Ireland.

Guidelines   Traditional Dunlop cheese is now quite rare in Scotland. It is mild and quite moist, so it does not keep well, and it bears a passing resemblance to Cheddar in flavour. Indeed I hear that waxed Cheddar is sometimes passed off as Dunlop.

Ewe's Cheese

Sheep's milk was regularly used to make cheese in Britain until the Middle Ages. Since then sheep have been providers of wool and meat, while cows have been the source of our milk and dairy products. But there are signs that a ewe's cheese revival is under way. One to look out for, in particular, is Beenleigh Blue made by Robin Congdon at Harbertonford, near Totnes, Devon.

Goat's Cheese

There's a real boom in goat-keeping and goat's cheese-making. The milk of the goat is rich in fat (about 6%) and is high in casein, and the cheeses have a pronounced earthy quality about them. Most are made as soft or semi-soft cheeses, although a few are hard. In most cases the milk is unpasteurised.

Gloucester

Cheese has been made in Gloucestershire for hundreds of years, and developed into a cottage industry on the level heavy pasture lands around the Severn Valley during the 17th century. There were originally two distinct Gloucester cheeses, Single and Double, which were made using milk from different milking sessions.

Single Gloucesters were small cheeses made from the morning's milk or the skimmed evening milk and they were eaten on the farm quite young. Double Gloucesters, by far the most famous, were much bigger and were made from a blend of morning and evening milk. They were also allowed to mature and ripen for several months before being despatched and sold.

Guidelines All Gloucester cheese was originally made from the milk of Old Gloucester cattle, a breed that had almost disappeared from dairy farming until Charles and Monica Martell re-formed the Gloucester Cattle Society in 1974. They have been the champions not only of the the the cattle but of the cheese derived from their milk. Now they make both Single and Double Gloucester cheese at the farm at Dymock, south of Ledbury and sell their wares in local markets. I like this kind of enterprise. It's an enthusiastic and successful attempt to restore some of our better traditions of food and farming.

Double Gloucester should be a fine rich cheese with a delicate, silky smooth flavour. John Arlott, connoisseur of all the best things in life, celebrated it this way: 'Put a crumb no bigger than a pinhead on your tongue, and it will fill your whole mouth with its savour.' It is ideal for toasting and marvellous eaten on its own.

Unlike most versions of Double Gloucester, the Martells cheese is normally uncoloured.

Double Gloucester flavoured with chives usually goes by the name of Cotswold cheese.

Lancashire

The story of Lancashire cheese is one of neglect and decline both in quality and numbers. It has always been made on a small scale, often in farmhouse kitchens, and since 1913 when a dairy in Chipping began to make the cheese it has lived precariously. For a while its future seemed safe and, in 1939, 202 farms in the county were producing Lancashire cheese by traditional methods. Since then the numbers have dropped and now only four working farms are registered as Lancashire cheese-makers.

Guidelines 'A ripe (Lancashire) cheese, when toasted, has the consistency of a good custard and an unforgettably delicious taste. It is crumbly and cohesive, somewhat as icing-sugar is. Its richness of flavour is superb. It has the opulence of a fine old Madeira.' This is what Osbert Burdett thought about Lancashire cheese in his *Little Book of Cheese* (1935). Of course he was talking about the true Lancashire, a soft, loose-textured buttery cheese that is increasingly difficult to track down these days. But the experience of people like Singleton's Dairy at Longridge, north-east of Preston, proves that the demand for authentic traditional cheese is increasing and the market for block cheese and bastardised versions is shrinking. That, at least, is good news.

AVOID what is labelled as 'New Lancashire' or 'Single-acid Lancashire', the commercial cheesemakers alternative to true Lanchashire. It isn't worthy of the name cheese.

Good Lancashire cheese, as Osbert Burdett pointed out is a fine toasting cheese and was often known in the past as the Leigh toaster after the town not far from Manchester that once had a reputation for cheese-making.

Leicester

Big red Leicester cheeses were being made on farms in the county at the beginning of the 18th century and many acquired a fine reputation. But Leicester has suffered in this century, mainly because it has had to live in the shadow of Stilton, now the most renowned cheese of the region. As a result the firm of Tuxford & Tebbutt of Melton Mowbray was, until recently, the sole producer of whole Leicester cheese in the entire county.

Guidelines Leicester is rightly called 'Red' because it is the most vividly coloured of all English cheeses. It's actually more of a brilliant orange and it is shaped like a millstone, flat and round. It should have a soft, slightly grainy texture, in fact you should be able to spread it with a knife.

It can be eaten at 2-3 months old, although connoisseurs recommend 6–9 months. At its best the cheese should have a mild, sharp flavour with a slightly lemony tang. It is a good toaster, melting to a smooth velvety mass when put under the grill.

Lymeswold

To my mind the introduction of Lymeswold ranks as one of the great disappointments in the history of British cheese. Perhaps I have been unlucky, but I have always found it dull and uninteresting.

Guidelines Lymeswold is described as a mild-blue, full-fat soft cheese and was deliberately created to provide an English version of many of the famous cheeses from the Continent. In fact the name Lymeswold is imaginary, presumably dreamed up in an advertising agency, but it's curiously evocative; you might be foolled into thinking that it was a town in Thomas Hardy's Wessex!

As for the quality of the cheese, it seems always to be sold far too young. The blue veins are so mild and sparce as to be almost unnoticeable and the cheese is much too dry. It lacks that essential rich creaminess of Continental soft cheeses.

Stilton

The story of Stilton begins in Leicestershire and, more precisely, at Quenby Hall, where the celebrated 'Lady Beaumont's Cheese' was made early in the 18th century. One of the daughters of the Quenby housekeeper married Cooper Thornhill, who kept the Bell Inn at Stilton, on the Great North Road, in what was once called Huntingdonshire, and Quenby cheeses were sent there by Mrs Paulet of Wymondham, near Melton Mobray, who was the sister of the bride. The reputations of this cheese grew rapidly, its fame spread and it became known as Stilton. (After 20 years of desperate neglect, The Bell Inn re-opened its doors as a hostelry in August 1983, after seven years' patient and enterprising work on the part of the new owners.)

Guidelines Making Stilton is a delicate, painstaking and skilful task. It was originally the job of farmers' wives working long hours in the dairy, and in those days it took up to 18 months to produce a fully ripe mature cheese. Even today, with modern cheese-making methods it takes something like four months to transform 17 gallons of milk into a fine 14lb Stilton.

Stilton is unique among British cheeses in that it is the only one protected by a trade copyright. To be called Stilton, the cheese has to be made in its native regions – the Vale of Belvoir in Leicestershire, the Dove Valley in Derbyshire and also parts of South Nottinghamshire. Stilton-type cheeses made in other parts of the country have to be given a different name, such as Dorset Blue.

When buying a Stilton look for a greyish-brown, wrinkled crust, a mass of blue veins and a creamy texture. And when you come to serve it, don't be tempted to perpetuate the old habit of pouring port into the centre of the cheese. This is a pointless, messy exercise, guaranteed to ruin both the port and the cheese. Also don't scoop out the centre of the cheese as this is merely wasteful. Simply cut neat wedges from the cheese, working downwards in layers.

Excellent Stiltons originate from, among others, Webster's Dairy, Saxelby, near Melton Mowbray, and Colston Bassett & District Dairy Company, near Nottingham.

White Stilton

A White version of a blue cheese, rather than the reverse. It is simply Stilton that has not turned blue and is normally sold very young – about 20 days after it has been made. It has a pleasantly sharp taste.

Swaledale

Three farms now valiantly keep alive the tradition of Swaledale cheese, although only one at Daleside, Low Row, North Yorkshire offers them for sale. Like many other of our most interesting and localised cheeses, it does not figure in the list of nine promoted by the Milk Marketing Board. But that is no bad thing; it shows that the cheese can survive independently, and in fact the demand for it far outweighs the capacity of the farmers to make it.

Swaledale cheese is usually bound in cloth and has a greyish surface mould. It is a soft or semi-soft cheese made from unpasteurised milk and is normally eaten after about three weeks when still soft. However it can be left for months after which it becomes dry and crumbly.

Wensleydale

The original recipe for making Wensleydale cheese was brought to the Yorkshire Dales by monks following in the wake of the Norman Conquest. In the famous abbeys of Jervaulx, Fountains, Kirkstall and Bolton, they laboured away to produce a cheese that would brighten up their meatless diet. At first they made it from ewe's milk, but by the 17th century the cow had taken over.

The last farmhouse Wensleydale cheese was made in 1957. Since then production has been taken over by the Milk Marketing Board who operate two dairies in Yorkshire.

Today's Wensleydale cheeses are hard, white and cylindrical; those made at the Kirkby Malzeard Dairy are clothbound and marked with KM, rather than a number as in the old days. Traditionally Wensleydale cheese is eaten with slices of apple pie.

Buy locally. Support your local producers and suppliers. By-pass the chain of mass-production.

Blue Wensleydale

In the past Blue Wensleydale was almost as highly revered as Stilton and those made in the 1960s were said to be very fine cheeses indeed. Nowadays however the Milk Marketing Board sends white Wensleydale cheeses to be 'blued' at the Derbyshire Stilton-making firm of Nuttall's, so today's versions are something of a hybrid.

Windsor Red

A bright colourful cheese made by pouring red wine over Cheddar curd and then re-milling it. One version, made by the Tythby Farm Dairy, Bottesford, Nottinghamshire, uses elderberry wine from Merrydown at Horam, East Sussex. As Patrick Rance rightly points out there's a tradition of adding wine and other ingredients to cheese, so we shouldn't frown on these practices. (The effect, however, is very different to drowning Stilton in port.)

Cheese Shops

The number of shops stocking English cheese including locally made, farmhouse varieties seems certain to increase. Some sell a vast range, others perhaps one or two, but all are worth a visit.

The Cheesery
1 Regent Road, Altrincham,
Greater Manchester
Tel: (061) 928 0537

R. Morrell & Sons
82 Galgate, Barnard Castle,
County Durham
Tel: (0833) 37153

The Cheese Shop
14 Market Street, Bingham,
Nottinghamshire
Tel: (0949) 37409

The Cheese Shop
17 Kensington Gardens,
Brighton, East Sussex
Tel: (0273) 601129

Mrs M. Smith
Market Hall, Bury,
Greater Manchester
Open: Monday–Saturday

Chewton Cheese Dairy
Priory Farm,
Chewton Mendip, Somerset
Tel: (076 121) 560.   M.

Post Office Stores
Cotherstone,
County Durham

Curds and Whey
Dottens Farm, Baring Road,
Cowes, Isle of Wight
Tel: (0983) 292466

Dartington Farm Food Shop
Cider Press Centre,
Shinners Bridge,
Dartington, Devon
Tel: (0803) 864171

Loseley Farm Shop
Loseley House, Guildford,
Surrey
Tel: (0483) 71881

Mainly English
14 Buckingham Palace
Road, London SW1
Tel: (01) 828 3967

Paxton & Whitfield
93 Jermyn Street,
London SW1
Tel: (01) 930 0259

Neal's Yard Dairy
Neal's Yard,
Covent Garden,
London WC2
Tel: (01) 240 1154

The Cheese Shop
17 Church Street,
Market Harborough,
Leicestershire
Tel: (0858) 65729

The Cheese Shop
74 Beccles Road,
Oulton Broad, Suffolk
Tel: (0502) 64664

Wells Stores
Opposite The Bull,
Streatley-on-Thames,
Berkshire
Tel: (0491) 872367

The Real Ale
and Cheese Shop
9 New Bride Street,
Truro, Cornwall
Tel: (0872) 2091

Farmhouse
11 Chapel Street,
Aberdeen, Grampian,
Scotland
Tel: (0224) 51681

Comrie Cheese Shop
Drummond Street, Comrie,
Tayside, Scotland
Tel: (076 47) 408

The Cheese Shop
17 Market Street, Tain,
Highland, Scotland
Tel: (0862) 2258

Eggs

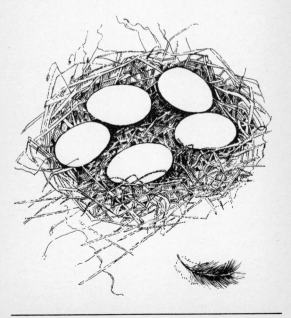

Wild birds' eggs were a useful and convenient source of nourishment for our prehistoric ancestors, who spent much of their time gathering food from the open countryside. Eggs appeared in the spring and early summer before much of the natural vegetation had ripened and animals had fattened themselves; they were also handy because they came sealed in a protective shell, which helped to preserve the contents and made the eggs easy to transport. In those days most eggs were probably eaten raw, sucked straight from the shell.

Domestic fowl started to appear in Roman times, and with a regular and reasonably reliable supply of eggs, it was feasible to add them to the list of kitchen ingredients. By the Middle Ages, even the poorest families usually kept a few fowls, although it was in the manor farms that they were reared most successfully. The medieval hen was expected to produce 155 eggs each year, plus seven chicks, three of which were to be made into capons. Eggs were a plentiful and cheap form of sustenance, both in the country and in the towns, where at the beginning of the 15th century you might buy up to 16 for a penny.

As eggs increased in popularity, farmers found ways of improving hens' productivity by feeding them on such things as hemp seed, buckwheat and 'toast taken out of ale with barley boiled'. But the egg trade was still dependant on the farmer's wife who did most of the selling and distribution.

Eggs today That situation existed until about 50 years ago, when today's egg industry began to develop. Gradually fewer and fewer eggs were produced and sold by farmers at the farm gate, and more from intensive battery farms. Until very recently the powerful egg industry seemed to be riding on the crest of a wave, and could boast about 96% of the total market. At present there are some 40 million birds crammed five or six to a cage, each one producing 225 eggs during its brief miserable life, kept in total darkness for hours on end, de-beaked (to stop it from pecking its neighbours), and pumped full of medications of one kind or another.

However, the situation has suddenly changed. Egg sales are continuing to fall, and not even a multi-million pound advertising campaign can persuade us to eat more. Not only are we wanting fewer eggs, but we are also demanding more choice, and in particular eggs produced in a more humane manner. Consumers are angry about the system which produces battery eggs and are turning to free-range as an alternative.

Free-range eggs For many years the egg industry has done all in its power to hide the realities of egg production from the consumer. Egg boxes have cosy pastoral scenes on them; advertising reinforces the natural, wholesome qualities of eggs, they may even be sold from straw-filled baskets. And the term 'farm-fresh' is used as a selling point, when it really means eggs fresh from the battery farm.

The free-range egg is the alternative, but there is a problem of definition. Legally there is no such thing as 'a free-range egg', and there's no legislation requiring producers to reveal how their eggs are produced. In an attempt to combat this, the Free Range Egg Association has devised its own definition: all hens should have at least 3 sq. ft per bird in their houses, they should have free access to outside runs, and they must never be de-beaked or fed antibiotics.

It's enormously encouraging that more and more free-range eggs are appearing on the market, in fact the demand is much higher than the capacity of farmers to produce the eggs. Some supermarkets are beginning to stock free-range eggs alongside battery ones, and even the big egg producers are starting to consider moving into the market. They know that we are eating less eggs and that the market is shrinking; they also know that there is increasing pressure to change the battery system and that it's bound to become more expensive to operate. The conclusion is obvious: abandon the costly and unacceptable battery system and concentrate on producing fewer but better eggs.

It's worth bearing in mind that producing free-range eggs isn't simply a small scale, cottage industry. Our biggest producer, Martin Pitt who runs a 40-acre farm in Wiltshire, now has 30,000 hens in his unique aviary system.

The nutritional value of eggs On the plus side, eggs provide a compact package of vitamins, proteins and minerals. On the debit side they are also the most concentrated source of cholesterol in our diet. As a result most unbiased nutritionists agree that we should eat only 3–5 per week.

Eggs are also rich in lecithin, a complex substance that also occurs in the body and has the ability to break up and emulsify fat into tiny globules which can disperse and not build up. This may help to balance out the cholesterol, although it's generally agreed that we should limit the amount of eggs we eat.

It is often claimed – even by some food writers who should know better – that there's no nutritional difference between battery and free-range eggs. But even the Ministry of Agriculture's own research has shown that battery eggs contain 70% less vitamin B12 and 50% less folic acid than free-range ones, and both of these compounds are essential nutrients.

It's also hard to believe that chickens living unnatural, captive lives, fed on an artificial diet and pumped full of drugs can produce eggs that are wholesome to eat.

> *Eat with the seasons.*

Guidelines for buying eggs (i) Always seek out and buy free-range eggs. Look for the yellow triangle sign which indicates that a shop or supplier has been inspected and recommended by the Free Range Egg Association.

(ii) Be wary of advertisements and phrases like farm-fresh, new-laid, country-fresh and so on. These are generally euphemisms to disguise the real origins of the eggs, most of which come from the battery farm. Always deal with a supplier you can trust.

(iii) Eggs are now classified under Common Market regulations, both for size and freshness. They range from size 1 (the largest, 2½ ounces) to size 7 (the smallest, 1¾ ounces). They are also classed A, B or C. 'A' represents fresh eggs; 'B' less fresh (they have usually been refrigerated for some weeks; 'C' are not generally sold to the public and are used by the food industry.

(iv) Although there's no nutritional difference between white and brown eggs, the latter look more wholesome. Commercial egg producers normally achieve this effect by adding a carotene derivative to the chickens' diet.

(v) Freshness is important in eggs. The less fresh they are, the less flavour they have. The freshest eggs are obviously those gathered straight from the farmyard while you wait, but if you are buying from a shop, find one with a good turnover. If you buy free range eggs that turn out to be stale, tell the supplier and also check their sources. Runny white, flat yolk and a foul smell are the classic signs of an old or bad egg.

AVOID battery eggs.

Other kinds of eggs

Duck Larger and richer than chicken's eggs. Must be eaten very fresh. Sometimes sold in health food shops, super-markets and some butcher's.

Goose Similar in size to duck eggs. Tend to have a rather oily taste and need to be eaten very fresh in briefly cooked dishes.

Pheasant Little eggs that often have white, buff or speckled shells. Not widely available, although they can be procured from pheasant farms. Useful hard-boiled or pickled.

Quail The growth in quail farming has naturally meant more quail's eggs. These tiny morsels are considered a delicacy and are usually served either soft or hard-boiled.

Producers and suppliers of free-range eggs

The number of producers and suppliers of free-range eggs now runs into hundreds, and readers should write to the Free Range Egg Association for details of their list of approved outlets, many of which are now concentrated in London.

Useful organisations

The Free Range Egg Association (FREGG)
37 Tanza Road, London NW3
Tel: (01) 435 2596

Chicken's Lib
6 Pilling Lane, Skelmanthorpe, Huddersfield, W. Yorkshire
Tel: (0484) 861814

Meat

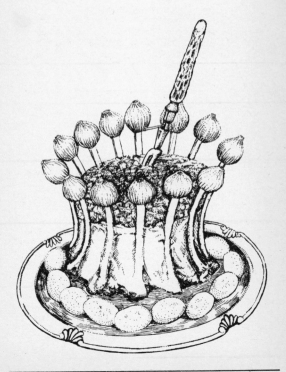

We began eating meat when we had the means with which to kill animals and cut up their flesh, so our carnivorous instincts are very deep-rooted. You might say that meat-eating is in our blood.

Most of the meat in the British diet comes from just three types of domestic farm animal: cattle, sheep and pigs (poultry and game are slightly different and distinct). It's worth remembering that until the last century, animals were not bred exclusively for meat. They were multi-purpose creatures that were only slaughtered for food when they were no longer productive in other ways: cattle and oxen were working beasts, pulling ploughs and wagons, sheep provided wool and leather skins, while pigs were all-purpose scavengers. By the time they were slaughtered their flesh was old, very muscular and tough; it also had a good deal of fat.

Selective breeding techniques and new systems of agriculture have changed all that. Animals no longer work as they used to, we have found alternatives to many of their natural products, and our tastes have changed too. So animals are now bred first and foremost for food and breeders aim to obtain the highest amount of lean meat from each animal in the shortest possible time. They want animals that will grow quickly and have a body weight that is 50–70% lean meat. The beasts should also be smaller and more compact than their forebears – the days of 50lb joints of beef are gone!

It's easy to be fooled by the cosy pastoral image of farming – cows grazing in the fields, pigs rooting about in orchards, the very essence of things natural. The reality is very different. The grass those cows are eating has been dosed with tons of fertiliser and sprayed with pesticides and other toxic chemicals, while the animals themselves are pumped full of growth promoters, hormones and antibiotics. Behind that now derelict orchard you might see the pig unit where animals are raised in confinement, fed on artificial foodstuffs and seldom if ever allowed to see the light of day.

All this is done in the name of productivity and efficiency but the result is meat that is increasingly unwholesome, both in the way it is produced, and in the kind of toxic residues that may well be present in the meat when it reaches the consumer, and in the actual quality of the meat itself. To be sure it is more tender and less fatty than meat in the past, but it's often virtually tasteless. Considering that it is the most expensive item in our diet, it really should be better than it is.

Meat in our diet   Meat is our major source of protein and a good source of many essential vitamins. Meat and meat products are also the top of the league when it comes to saturated fats in our diet. The NACNE report (see page 14) and most unbiased nutritionists agree that we eat far too much saturated fat for our own good, and recommend cutting our intake by up to 30%. Meat is clearly something we should be eating less of, particularly when you consider that a roast shoulder of lamb has about 26% fat, of which 50% is saturated. The quantities of saturated fat in products like this push up the levels of cholesterol in the blood, thus increasing the risk of heart trouble in people predisposed towards the disease.

Meat is also very expensive to produce, a fact that is passed on to the consumer every time he makes a purchase from the butcher's shop. So, the outlook for meat isn't good: it's uneconomical and wasteful to produce, the industry is propped up by chemicals, both in the animals themselves and in the food they eat. Many people now also have a moral objection to eating it.

The future We may all become vegetarians in the future; it may come to us all in the end. But that is a long way off, and meat is likely to be with us for quite a while yet. We will start to produce less as demand starts to decrease and the cost of production continues to increase (feed, drugs, fertilisers and energy for running sophisticated rearing units are all bound to become more expensive). It seems that meat will be next in line for the free-range, organic alternative. A small number of farmers already produce organic meat but as yet there's no organised system of distribution. In most cases if you want the meat you have to go to the farm to buy it, which is bad news if you happen to live fifty miles from the nearest producer. A handful of shops now specialise in organic meat, notably Wholefood Butchers, off Baker Street, London, and it would be encouraging to see more offering this service.

One scenario for the future might be of meat as a luxury item in a largely vegetarian society, produced organically on a small scale by specialist farmers. It would cater for the needs of a small proportion of the population who would no doubt be prepared to pay the price for it.

Guidelines for buying meat (i) The only way of finding out how good a butcher's meat is, is by buying it, but you should always try to find a shop that is clean, busy and well-stocked with fresh meat rather than sawn-up frozen pieces.

(ii) Much of today's meat is bred for tenderness rather than flavour, but generally the best meat comes from animals that have not been intensively reared. Organically produced meat is the ideal choice but this is very rare in shops.

(iii) Freshly butchered meat is bright red, while meat that has been hung for several days will take on a dark brownish-red colour. Beef in particular needs to be well-hung to make it both tender and full-flavoured, although many butchers are reluctant to do this nowadays. Always check.

(iv) Fat can vary in colour from white in young lamb to yellowish in mature, well-hung beef. Although fat content is a problem from a nutritional point of view, it is useful for the cook as it tends to stop meat drying out.

Beef

Beef, a roast beef in particular, is perhaps the most famous and enduring of all English foods, a meat that is cherished and revered across the land. For centuries it was the great treat, even though it was food for the privileged classes only. To say we are a nation of beefeaters is a long way from the truth, as the diet of any Victorian labourer and his family would show.

The ancestors of the beef cattle we hold so dear were the wild aurochs first domesticated in Greece around 6000 BC. We have come a long way since then. In the Middle Ages people kept pigs, sheep and cattle, and as winter approached – at Martinmas, precisely – they killed off part of their beef stock and salted it down to last through the winter months.

By the 18th century, though, fresh beef was all the rage. It was the age of John Bull, symbol of the English squire, a beefeater if ever there was one. It was also the age of 'Turnip' Townshend, who showed that cattle didn't have to be salted down for the winter months, but could be kept going on turnips. Robert Bakewell took up this idea, and in the process became England's first commercial stockbreeder. The results of his efforts were cattle that were far more productive and, to judge by contemporary animal portraits, were enormous beasts with huge bodies and slender legs. They were also immensely fat.

Times and tastes have changed since the days of Robert Bakewell and his massive beasts. Nowadays cattle are killed when they are younger with less fat and more lean to the meat. Intensive rearing is increasingly the order of the day with animals confined and fattened up very quickly in the space of a few months, no doubt with the help of growth promoters and specially formulated feed. Such meat may well be tender, but it has no flavour.

Even so there are breeds such as the Aberdeen Angus and the equally good Hereford that can produce superbly flavoured beef, particularly if it has grazed well and been allowed to develop at a more measured pace. Sadly such animals are the exception rather than the rule in today's livestock farming.

Guidelines Perhaps the most important key to good beef is hanging. Most beef nowadays isn't hung properly if it is hung at all. It is crucial, because only hanging will allow chemical changes to take place in the tissues, notably the production of lactic acid which softens the meat. Butchers often don't like hanging beef because they haven't the space, they know that storing meat without selling it is expensive, and they realise that the meat will drip and shrink during hanging, which is economically bad news. Always check whether the beef you buy has been hung, and for how long. It could make all the difference. Well-hung beef is dull-looking, rather than bright red and shiny.

Fat is another important factor. Most modern beef is bred for leanness and it's quite rare to see the classic fine veining of marbled fat within the meat, which is the renowned feature of good Hereford beef. Although 'marbling' is superb for cooking and prized by meat-loving gourmets, it is not the most desirable from a health point of view. Yellowing fat indicates age; white fat is a sign of youth.

One way of telling if steak is tender is to squeeze it. If it is soft and pasty it will be tender to eat, if resilient it will be tough. However most butchers would not take kindly to you squeezing their meat in front of their eyes.

Cuts of beef vary from the very tender to the tough and sinewy. Most tender cuts come from inner muscles or those muscles which do little work e.g. fillet, rib and loin cuts; hard working, well-developed muscles, particularly from the front end of the animal, need long, slow cooking eg. brisket and shin.

Don't confuse tenderness with flavour. Although fillet is by far the most tender cut, it is by no means the tastiest. It can be very bland and you end up simply paying for the texture of the meat.

Uses Different cuts have different uses. Steaks from the rump, sirloin or fillet can be grilled; joints of topside, rib and sirloin are favourites for traditional roast beef; fatty brisket is often salted or used for boiled beef. Cheaper cuts are used for steak and kidney pies, casseroles and stews, while off-cuts and very stringy cuts like skirt are made into mince.

Lamb/mutton

Sheep were some of the first animals to be domesticated in the Middle East, around 9000 BC, and since then they have been valued for their wool, their meat and their milk. Since the advent of the cow and the coming of the dairy industry, ewe's milk has gone out of fashion in this country, although a few people are beginning to revive the practice of making ewe's milk cheese (see page 43).

Selective breeding has robbed us of many of our traditional breeds like the ancient Soay from Scotland, big sturdy Romney Marsh sheep, the little marsh-grazing Welsh sheep, the tough resilient Herdwick from the Lake District and the plump South Down sheep of Sussex and Hampshire. They are still to be seen, but the efforts of sheep-farmers are now concentrated on new cross-breeds where meat comes first and wool last.

The decline of mutton is one of the sad losses from British cooking, but it is easy to see why it has fallen out of favour: the joints can be very large, the meat can be strongly flavoured and fatty, and there's a definite ring of austerity about phrases like 'boiled mutton' that can put people off. This is a pity, because good mutton can be superb to eat. Fortunately a few butchers, particularly in Scotland, are still in the habit of selling it.

Guidelines The best English lamb is sold as 'spring' or 'new season's' lamb when it is 5–7 months old. It is pale pink, mildly flavoured, sweet and tender, but it is also expensive. Older lamb from animals killed later in the year is darker, almost brownish-pink in colour, but the flavour is almost as good.

Lamb has fine white fat; it also has a very thin parchment-like outer skin called 'fell' which is left on joints to keep them in shape during cooking, but should be trimmed off chops. As the whole of the carcase is tender, lamb is only hung for a few days or a week at the most.

Mutton, when it is sold, comes from animals over one year old. It can be fatty and the meat is very much darker than lamb. It is less expensive than lamb.

Much of the lamb we eat comes frozen from New Zealand, and doesn't bear comparison to fresh English lamb. But, of course, you get what you pay for. Buying frozen lamb can be a problem as it is difficult to ascertain exactly what you are getting. Also there's no way of telling how long a particular joint has been frozen: it may have been in a cold store for years. When it comes to butchering frozen lamb, the electric power-saw has replaced the sharpened knife, and as a result pieces of meat tend to be sawn through indiscriminately, with little regard for the natural formation of the flesh. When thawed out the meat can be completely ruined.

Uses Shoulder and leg joints are excellent roasted, and the meat can also be used for casseroles; breast of lamb is fatty but can be stuffed and roasted till it is crisp on the outside; chops and cutlets are for grilling, scrag end for stews, Rosemary, mint, coriander and juniper berries are the most appropriate flavourings. In general lamb should be lightly cooked so that it is still pink.

Pork

For centuries, man's best friend was not a dog, but a pig. Indeed the cottage pig was the salvation of most farming families in Britain (and right across Europe) from the Middle

Ages until the 19th century when the Industrial Revolution began to change the face of the land and the livelihood of its people.

The virtue of all the old breeds of pig was their adaptability, they could live anywhere and feed off anything, all the while growing bigger and fatter. And every bit of the beast, from its snout to its tail could be used as food: the head was turned into brawn, the trotters were pickled, the blood was made into black puddings, the 'flitches' or sides were cured as bacon and ham, and much of the rest was either put into the pickling tub or eaten fresh.

Pig breeding has changed a good deal since those days; gone is the scavenging porker; now there are sophisticated pig units for rearing them. The animals are fed a controlled but artificial diet so that they grow quickly and grow lean, and they are slaughtered while they are still young.

Even so some sturdy outdoor pigs like the Gloucester Old Spot have clung on, thanks to a few enterprising farmers, and it may well be that they will be useful again in the near future. As the cost of feeding stuff continues to rise and the pig units become more and more expensive to operate, farmers may well turn to the all-purpose outdoor pigs that can fend for themselves as pigs always used to do. They could prove to be not simply nostalgic reminders of the past, but useful and valuable food animals of the future.

Guidelines Pork should look and smell absolutely fresh. It taints very quickly, especially in warm weather. The flesh should be pale pink, almost colourless in places, and definitely not red or bloody; the fat should be firm and white, and the skin pale and soft.

Most pork is prime, in other words it can be roasted or grilled, because today's pigs are slaughtered young and the meat is tender.

Don't be embarrassed or cautious about asking for odd bits from the pig such as ears and tails. You may not see them on display, but the butcher can usually arrange to get some for you.

Uses Fresh pork is vry versatile. The leg and loin can be roasted, there are chops for grilling or braising, and the belly provides full-flavoured if slightly fatty slices which can be grilled or baked. Some belly of pork finds its way into sausages, terrines and the like, and it can also be pickled. There are spare ribs for barbecuing and also the fillet or 'tenderloin': like beef this is not the best pork in terms of flavour but it is the most tender. Pork can be cured as bacon and ham (see page 68–78).

> *Buy locally. Support your local producers and suppliers, but always check the true origins of your purchases.*

Veal

No other form of meat, except perhaps *foie gras*, has such an emotive ring to it as veal. And many people simply will not eat it as a protest against the way much of it is produced. All forms of intensive rearing are unacceptable and need to be condemned, but some veal calves are extremely cruelly treated. If we wish to continue to eat meat, then we have to devise more humane ways of producing it, with some respect for the basic rights and well-being of the animals concerned. The alternatives do exist and they are viable, as the trend towards free-range eggs have proved. (see page 52–53). There are signs that a few veal producers are trying to find a better way, by using deep bedding, allowing the calves milk on demand plus room to move and access to natural light. This at least is a start.

Guidelines   There are two main types of veal, milk-fed and grass-fed. Milk-fed veal has the best flavour and is the most expensive. Its flesh is very pale, tender and delicate. Grass-fed veal is cheaper, tougher and more strongly flavoured, and its flesh is darker. It generally needs more robust treatment and slow cooking. All veal should look fresh; if it has a dry, brownish appearance it is stale. Very young veal has only the smallest amount of firm, pale fat, so the meat can be dry when cooked.

The best veal comes from calves 4–6 months old and much of this is imported from Holland, although there is some veal production in this country.

It is impossible by looking at a piece of veal to tell whether it has been intensively or humanely reared. All you can do is ask and hope that the butcher gives you a straight answer.

Uses   The best cuts of veal come from the hindquarters – in particular the leg, loin and flank. Whole joints can be roasted and slices can be cut from the fillet end of the leg for escalopes. Veal cutlets and chops are grilled or fried, breast or shoulder joints can be boned, rolled and stuffed, while assorted cheaper cuts can be used for pies, stews and casseroles.

Offal

The collective name for all kinds of edible internal organs from various animals, including liver, kidneys, heart, pancreas and the like. They are generally considered to be quite cheap – with a few exceptions – and highly nutritious. Many of them are good sources of vitamins and minerals,

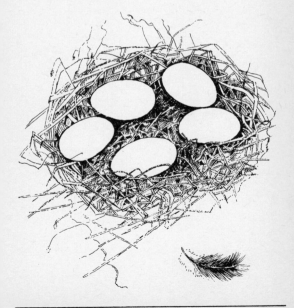

White pudding

Sometimes known as 'mealie puddings', these are black puddings without the blood.

Availability Good white or mealie puddings are produced in Wiltshire, Oxfordshire and parts of the West Country. Also very popular in Scotland.

Guidelines Usually shaped in a ring like a black pudding, but are light fawn in colour. They are normally made from oatmeal and pork fat with often a little minced lean pork, plus plenty of pepper.
  In Wiltshire and the West Country you may find 'hog's pudding' which is similar but sold as a monster straight sausage.

Uses The best way is to simmer them in water, then brown them quickly in bacon fat.

Sausage makers

While the mass-produced factory sausage dominates the market, there are a number of excellent butchers and sausage-makers producing real sausages of various kinds.

Black pudding

Albert Hirst
36, Queens Road,
Barnsley,
S. Yorkshire

Morris's Pork Butchers
120 Market Street,
Farnworth, Bolton,
Greater Manchester
Tel: (0204) 71763

Mitchell's
Kirkgate Market, Bradford,
W. Yorkshire
Open: Monday –
Saturday 8 am – 4 pm

E. Chadwick
Market Hall, Bury,
Greater Manchester
Open: Monday –
Saturday 9 am – 6 pm

Moffat & Carr
63 High Street, <u>Wooler</u>,
Northumbria
Tel: (066 82) 431

J. R. Mitchell & Son
40–44 Bridge Street, <u>Kelso</u>,
Borders, Scotland
Tel: (057 32) 2109

N. & D. Macleod Ltd
The Green, <u>Portree</u>,
Skye, Scotland
Tel: (0478) 2222

Cumberland sausage

John Watt & Son
11 Bank Street, <u>Carlisle</u>,
Cumbria
Tel: (0228) 21545

J. & J. Graham Ltd
Market Square, <u>Penrith</u>,
Cumbria
Tel: (0768) 62281

R. Robinson & Sons
4 Angel Lane, <u>Penrith</u>,
Cumbria
Tel: (0768) 2156

Fruit sausage

N. & D. Macleod Ltd
The Green, <u>Portree</u>,
Skye, Scotland
Tel: (0478) 2222

Haggis

Grierson Brothers
148 King Street,
<u>Castle Douglas,</u> , Dumfries
& Galloway, Scotland
Tel: (0556) 2637

John Grant & Sons
Cathedral Square, <u>Dornoch</u>,
Highland, Scotland
Tel: (086 281) 320   M.

Charles Macsween & Son
130 Bruntsfield Place,
<u>Edinburgh</u>, Lothian,
Scotland
Tel: (031) 229 1216   M.

Duncan Fraser & Son
22–24 Queensgate,
<u>Inverness</u>, Highland,
Scotland
Tel: (0463) 33066

Pork sausage

M. V. Crump
3 Mill Street, <u>Ashwell</u>,
Hertfordshire
Tel: (046 274) 2255

Bartlett & Son
10 Green Street, <u>Bath</u>, Avon
Tel: (0225) 66731

Eastwood & Son
15 Gravel Path,
<u>Berkhamsted</u>, Hertfordshire
Tel: (04427) 5012

Ye Olde Pork Shoppe
31 Salisbury Street,
<u>Blandford Forum</u>, Dorset
Tel: (0258) 52828

Edis of Ely
4 St John's Street,
Bury St Edmunds, Suffolk
Tel: (0284) 3297

A. Waller & Son
15 Victoria Avenue,
Cambridge, Cambridgeshire
Tel: (0223) 550972

Sole Butchers
1 Market Street,
Chipping Norton,
Oxfordshire
Tel: (0608) 2629

Kew's of Rudham
The Square, East Rudham,
Norfolk
Tel: (048 522) 236

J. G. Sweetland
10 Stortford Road,
Great Dunmow, Essex
Tel: (0371) 2868

C. A. Palmer
Bridge House,
1 The Thoroughfare,
Halesworth, Suffolk
Tel: (098 67) 2108

Bangers
105 Blatchington Road,
Hove, Sussex

Bellew's Butchers
5 Silver Street, Ilminster,
Somerset,
Tel: (046 05) 2502

Inkly & Son Ltd
18 Bailgate, Lincoln,
Lincolnshire
Tel: (0522) 23455

S. H. Edwards Ltd
340–344 Camberwell New
Road, London SE5
Tel: (01) 274 1427

Cobb, Butcher
5 Sloane Street,
London, SW1
Tel: (01) 235 5377

Curnick
106 Draycott Avenue,
London SW3
Tel: (01) 589 8452

Wainwright & Daughter
359 Fulham Road,
London SW10
Tel: (01) 352 0852/3

Druce & Craddock
24 Marylebone High Street,
London W1
Tel: (01) 935 3600

John Lane (Butchers) Ltd
6 Walkers Court,
London W1
Tel: (01) 437 8903

C. Lidgate
110 Holland Park Avenue,
London W11
Tel: (01) 727 8243

Butcher & Butcher
13–14 Saint Thomas Street,
Lymington, Hampshire
Tel: (0590) 73134

Musk's Sausages & Delicatessen
1 The Rookery,
Newmarket, Suffolk
Tel: (0638) 61824

H. F. Richards Ltd
Covered Market,
off High Street,
Oxford, Oxfordshire
Tel: (0865) 42089

R. J. Underwood
170 Bitterne Road,
Southampton, Hampshire
Tel: (0703) 25995

W. J. Hill & Son
119 Mount Pleasant,
Tunbridge Wells, Kent
Tel: (0892) 26870

Patrick Strainge
79 Corn Street,
Witney, Oxfordshire
Tel: (0993) 2244

Tomato sausage

Keith Boxley
14 Abbey Road,
Lower Gornal, Dudley,
West Midlands
Tel: (0384) 214515

A. W. Curtis & Sons Ltd
163–4 High Street,
Lincoln, Lincolnshire
Tel: (0522) 30802

Venison sausage

Wholefood (Butchers)
24 Paddington Street,
London W1
Tel: (01) 486 1390

H. F. Richards Ltd
Covered Market,
off High Street,
Oxford, Oxfordshire
Tel: (0865) 42089

John Strange
16 High Street,
Lyndhurst,
Hampshire
Tel: (042 128) 2659

White pudding

Bartlett & Son
10 Green Street,
Bath, Avon
Tel: (0225) 66731

Charles Macsween & Son
130 Bruntsfield Place,
Edinburgh, Lothian,
Scotland
Tel: (031) 229 1216   M.

Duncan Fraser & Son
22–24 Queensgate,
Inverness, Highland, Scotland
Tel: (0463) 33066

A. Urquart & Son
New Buildings,
Lairg, Highland,
Scotland
Tel: (0549) 2475

W. J. Webster & Son
112–14 South Street, Perth,
Tayside, Scotland
Tel: (0738) 22732

Useful Organisations

The Natural Sausage Casings Association
Gysin & Hanson Ltd
96 Trundleys Road, Deptford, London SE8
Tel: (01) 692 8217

Poultry

The word 'poultry' describes any bird which is reared commercially for food, as distinct from game, which is gleaned from the wild. Most of our poultry, including chickens, ducks and geese are descended from wild birds, but the rise of poultry farming as an industry has meant cheap, plentiful supplies at the expense of quality and flavour.

Intensive rearing, particularly of chickens and turkeys involves feeding the birds an artificial diet full of supplements, vitamins, antibiotics, growth-promoters and so on. The aim is to get the birds to grow as quickly as possible. It seems that the breeders have been successful: some chickens can now reach a weight of 5lbs in as many weeks, but at what a cost in terms of quality. Anyone who has a love of real food should avoid all frozen chickens and turkeys in particular, as well as by-products such as boned turkey roasts.

General guidelines for buying poultry   (i) Always seek out a butcher with a good reputation for selling fresh poultry, and always try to find out where the birds have come from. Genuinely free-range chickens are quite rare, but are well worth the hunt.

(ii) Nowadays most fresh poultry comes ready plucked and drawn and is normally sold by its plucked weight (ie. with giblets and innards intact). Frozen birds are sold by their oven-ready weight.

(iii) Most poultry can either be bought whole or in portions – anything from chicken drumsticks to quarters of duck.

(iv) Frozen chickens and most other frozen poultry are often sold without giblets, but if they are included they will be in a plastic bag inside the bird, and obviously need to be removed before cooking. If you are buying fresh poultry always make sure you get the giblets.

(v) You can tell the freshness of poultry by its pleasant slightly sweet smell, soft dry skin and plump flesh.

(vi) Age – and therefore tenderness – can be established by asking the butcher's advice, or by feeling the breastbone of the bird. In young ones this is pliable and gives slightly when pressed with the hand; on larger, older birds, only the tip of the bone bends.

Chicken

All our chickens are descended from the jungle fowl, *Gallus gallus*, a member of the pheasant family that was being bred in the Indus valley about 2000 BC. These days chicken is by far the most common and popular type of poultry, in fact in Britain we consume something like 600,000 tons of it each year. Chicken has been transformed from a luxury into a cheap source of protein, because of the clinical efficiency of the poultry industry. It manages to rear thousands upon thousands of birds using the deep-litter method (in which the chickens are confined in boxes filled with inedible litter and fed largely on a diet of bone-meal pellets).

Guidelines If ever a food has plummeted in flavour over the years it must be the chicken. Factory farming is the reason for this decline, and things are now so bad that English chicken is hardly worth eating, unless you manage to track down a source of genuinely free-range birds.

Frozen chickens are the worst of all, and should be avoided. Their contrived diet of concentrates, growth promoters, antibiotics and coccidiostats (drugs to prevent the poultry disease coccidiosis) makes them not only flavourless and insipid, but undesirable to eat as well. In most cases there is no problem in recognising a frozen chicken, although an unscrupulous butcher may occasionally thaw out frozen chickens, increase the price, and pass them off as fresh. If there is a lot of moisture on or around the bird, this may suggest that it has been thawed out.

Always buy fresh chicken. Some birds are genuinely free-range, and you should enquire when you make your purchase; most however come from small farms which can rear the birds commercially but do not have the facilities for freezing. Unfortunately there's no way of telling exactly how the chicken has been reared or what it has fed on unless you know the farmer. When buying a fresh chicken, go for a larger rather than a smaller bird, as this will have a greater proportion of edible meat to bone. The skin should be smooth and dry and the bird should smell faintly sweet. Make sure you get the giblets when you buy a chicken.

Most chickens sold are roasters, which are birds under 8 months old, weighing 3½–5 lbs. However there are others available: a *poussin* or baby chicken is generally enough for one person and weighs around 1–1½ lbs; *capons* are emasculated cockerels which can weigh up to 10lbs and are very meaty; *boiling fowls* are old birds, often of indeterminate age, which are too tough to roast or grill, but are excellent when put in the pot.

Cookery Whole books are devoted to chicken cookery but in general the age and tenderness of the bird will determine how you cook it. Young birds can be grilled, barbecued, fried or roasted, while older ones need to be casseroled, braised or stewed.

Smoked chicken is becoming increasingly popular.

Eggs see page 52

Use the response form on page 287 to send us your
suggestions and information.

Duck

The most famous of all domestic ducks must surely be the plump, snowy-white Aylesbury duck, and according to Mrs Beeton there was a real cottage industry devoted to these birds in the 19th century. 'In parts of Buckinghamshire, this member of the duck family is bred on an extensive scale, not on plains and commons, as might be naturally imagined, but in the abodes of the cottagers. Round the walls of the living rooms, and of the bedrooms even, are fixed rows of wooden boxes lined with hay; and it is the business of the wife and children to nurse and comfort the feathered lodgers, to feed the little ducklings and to take the old ones out for an airing.' How different from today's methods of rearing.

Guidelines In many ways duck is an uneconomical bird to buy. Domestically reared birds can be very fatty (much more so than their wild relatives, see page 116) and much of their weight is bony skeleton. So you will need to allow something like 2 lbs per person: young ducklings usually weigh 3–4 lbs, while older ducks average 4–6 lbs.

Frozen duck can be as dull and disappointing as frozen chicken, so buy fresh whenever possible. The bird should be well plucked and have clean dry skin; patches or sliminess suggest that it has been hanging around for too long.

Cookery Traditionally roasted with sage and onion stuffing and served with apple sauce and green peas. Salted duck with hot onion sauce is a Welsh speciality. Duck also makes a good pâté and the bones can be turned into excellent soup.

Duck eggs see page 54

Goose

Back in the 18th century it was quite a common sight to see great flocks of geese being driven along country roads from Lincolnshire and the Fens of Cambridgeshire to be fattened up by London's poulterers. The journey was long and hard, and the geese were often shod like horses to make the trek easier on their webbed feet. Fine geese still come from that part of the country, although they reach their destinations by different means.

Guidelines Large white geese are the most popular in Britain, and can weigh anything from 6–12 lbs. Young goslings or 'green geese' are birds up to 6 months old. Like duck, geese have a high proportion of fat and bone to lean meat, but a good bird of about 10 lbs makes excellent eating. Very large geese can be coarse and tough.

Generally fresh geese are better than frozen ones, although I hear that those produced by Button's of Redgrave, Norfolk are well worth buying.

Cookery Goose is rich, slightly gamey and strongly flavoured, so you do not need much of it. The bird is best roasted with a fruity stuffing and a garnish of sliced apples.

Goose eggs see page 54

Guinea Fowl

A native of the jungles of West Africa, the guinea fowl was the 'turkey' of Shakespeare's time, and up to the last war was found wild in England and shot as game. In the last 10 years we have started to rear guinea fowl on farms, but the growth of this new food enterprise has recently been cut short by a massive influx of farmed guinea fowl from France. At present only two farms – one in Aberdeen, the other in Norfolk – are producing guinea fowl to any degree, which is a sad testament to the way in which set ups of this kind are allowed to peter out almost before they have begun.

Guidelines Farmed guinea fowl is a lean bird with little fat and it can be rather dry. The flavour is a bit like strong chicken but the flesh has more texture. Unlike game, these birds are sold very fresh, and if you are buying 'in the feather' look for an abundance of healthy grey plumage spotted with white.

Cookery Can be roasted and served with fruit such as grapes, braised with cider, walnuts and mushrooms or marinated in lime juice and then grilled; the breast can also be stuffed with, say, diced leeks and watercress.

Turkey

Turkeys came to Europe from Central America in the 15th century, and were introduced into England in the first half of the 16th century. Today Norfolk is synonymous with turkeys, but more interesting is the fact that the original Norfolk Black turkey is being bred again in the native county by Valerie Green at Hockwold-cum-Wilton, near Thetford.

Guidelines   Always buy fresh turkey, even though it may be a little more expensive than the frozen variety which suffers from all the faults of frozen chicken. A good fresh turkey should be tender and succulent with a distinctive flavour.

Choose a bird that is broad and stocky, with a plump smooth breast and a layer of fat on its back.

Male turkeys, which are larger than the females, are said to have a slightly better flavour, although in practice the difference is hardly noticeable. Today's turkeys are fattened fast and can weigh up to 30 lbs, although most range from 10–14 lbs.

Make sure you always get the useful giblets with a plucked and drawn bird.

Be wary of so-called self-basting turkeys, which have additives as well as the butter which does the basting.

Cookery   Traditionally roasted with two stuffings, one of chestnuts, the other of sausagemeat, which help to keep the bird moist from inside while it is cooking. Younger, smaller birds are best for roasting; older ones can be casseroled, braised or made into pies and fricassées.

Game

First of all, a definition. We use the word 'game' to describe any creature that is hunted for sport as well as food. However, it isn't quite that simple, because birds and animals such as quail and rabbits, which are often reared domestically, are still counted as game. There are two types – the furred and the feathered, (although in the fish world, salmon and trout are also considered as game).

The virtues of game   All kinds of game have one supreme advantage: they are wild creatures allowed, for the most part, to live in their natural habitats, growing as nature intended and feeding off the land. As a result they are more full of flavour and nourishment than beasts doomed to the artificial environment of the intensive farming cage. This may seem obvious – a healthy creature ought to make good healthy eating – but there's more to it than that. Dr. Michael Crawford, one-time Director of the Nuffield Institute of Comparative Medicine, put it this way in his book *What We Eat Today*: 'The carcass from an animal free to select its own food produces three times as much protein as adipose fat; the carcass of an intensively reared animal produces three times as much adipose fat as protein . . . intensive high energy production is providing the community with adipose fat not protein.' In other words, wild game – high in protein, low in fat – is infinitely preferable to the battery chicken or the factory-bred pig.

Game is also seasonal, and that's an advantage too. Just as there's a time for asparagus and strawberries, so grouse and pheasant and partridge also have their season. This is their real attraction. Game should always be eaten fresh, not hauled out of the deep-freeze at any time of year for convenience.

Field and farm   In Britain the killing of game is strictly controlled by law: only certain creatures can be shot and the open season is restricted to a few months in the year. But it's impossible to say how much of the sportsman's bag ever reaches the shops or indeed the kitchen, which is a criminal waste; whatever game is shot should always be eaten or sold for food (provided it is in good condition). If we exported less of our own game to countries which already have plenty, and encouraged butchers and game dealers to stock more, the price of the most prestigious varieties would surely come down. Rabbit and pigeon have always been cheap and good value, and there's more venison than there used to be, but the rest is still very much exclusive.

One of the reasons why more wild game isn't offered for sale, is that there is less of it about. Birds such as grouse and partridge that once thrived on moors and in cornfields have been decimated by pesticides and by the depletion of their natural habitats.

Game farming offers some answers to the problem. It can be

a way of safeguarding the wild population; it can also provide a plentiful supply of food quite cheaply and efficiently, yet this is often at the expense of flavour and quality. You only have to taste the difference between a farmed and a wild rabbit to realise that.

General guidelines (i) Game birds are normally sold in a brace, a male and a female together, and are not bought by weight. They are either hung 'in the feather', or sold plucked and drawn ready for use. If the birds need extra hanging, they have to be bought 'in the feather'.

(ii) Hanging game: because of their general diet and lifestyle, wild creatures have enzymes which break down the tissues soon after the animal or bird is killed. This creates the distinctive gaminess of the meat, the softness, and the strong distinctive flavour. While this is happening, bacteria are also at work, breaking down the proteins in the flesh. Yet there's nothing unsavoury or indeed dangerous about well-hung game; like ripe blue cheese, it is perfectly harmless and can be safely enjoyed in an advanced state of putrification.

All wild game is greatly improved by hanging, but exactly how long for depends on your personal taste. Check with the butcher or game dealer exactly how long the game has already been hanging. Farmed game such as rabbits and quail can be eaten fresh.

Birds are normally hung by their heads; furred game such as hare are hung head downwards.

If you receive game by mail order, you will be told the date when it was shot, so that you can calculate how much longer it needs to be hung.

(iii) Always find out the age of the bird, as this will determine how you cook it. Every species is different, but there are some general pointers, such as size, downy feathers, clean soft-textured feet and pliable breastbones.

(iv) The choice and selection of game needs skill and experience, but it doesn't take long to work out if your game dealer is knowledgeable. If he is a man of reputation, you can safely trust his words and follow his advice.

(v) Always buy fresh rather than frozen.

Grouse

Lagopus scoticus, the red or Scotch grouse, is rated as one of the finest and most delicate of all game birds. Organised grouse-shooting didn't start until the 1850s, when breach-loading shotguns became available, but now trigger-happy marksmen eagerly await 'The Glorious Twelfth', the beginning of the season. The first grouse has the same elevated reputation as

Beaujolais nouveau, and invokes similarly ludicrous escapades and races to get the first on the table.

Availability   Red grouse is bred only in the British Isles and lives on young tender berries and heather shoots in Scotland, the Yorkshire moors, the west of Ireland and Wales. Ironically many more grouse die from lack of suitable food in their ravaged moorland habitats than from the gun.

In season: 12th August – 10th December.

Guidelines   Young grouse, shot between mid-August and mid-October are the most succulent. Look for soft downy feathers on the breast and under the wings, which should be pointed at the tips. Older grouse can be delicious but need special treatment. Ask your dealer about the age of the birds before you buy.

Can be eaten fresh, but is best hung for 2 days – 1 week, depending on age, fatness, the weather and personal preference. Check the vent end of well-hung birds for traces of maggots. Don't accept the birds if you see any.

Grouse are usually sold in a brace, but can sometimes be bought singly. Allow 1 bird per person.

Cookery   Delicate young grouse are superb roasted. They can be stuffed with wild moorland raspberries which dissolve and give the flesh a delicious fruity flavour. Or they can be served with rowan jelly, made from the berries of the rowan or mountain ash (see page 247). Older grouse need to be marinated and cooked very gently; best for casseroles, pies and terrines.

Hare

'A hare doth no harme nor displeasure to man . . . yet he maketh gentlemen good pastyme', so said Andrew Boorde, the 16th-century guru of dietary health, but he added that 'the Byble sayeth the hare is an unclene beaste and doth engendre meloncoly humours.' Certainly the hare was more popular for sport than eating in Boorde's day, and it is still an extraordinarily undervalued creature. The stigma of 'vermin' dies hard.

Availability   The greyish-brown English hare is widely available; the Scotch blue or mountain hare, is sold in the north.

In season: all year round, but can only be sold from early August to the end of February.

Guidelines Young hares up to one year old are known as 'leverets' and can be recognised by their size (they weigh up to 6 pounds), a softness of pad, ear and claw, and by their small sharp teeth. When cooked their flesh is as pale and tender as chicken. In contrast a fully mature male hare is an impressive creature weighing up to 12 lbs, with greying wavy hair and yellowing teeth, and its flesh is rich, dark and gamey.

Young hares can be eaten fresh, but older ones need to be hung, ungutted, head downwards for 7–10 days. The blood should be collected in a bowl as it is essential for enriching the sauces and gravies that go with the meat.

Get the butcher to skin and dress the hare if you are not keen on the gruesome business. Bear in mind that a dressed hare will lose something like 40% of its weight. A young hare weighing 6 lbs before dressing should feed 4 people comfortably.

Cookery Old and mature hares need to be marinated (usually in red wine or vinegar) for at least 24 hours; the older the hare the longer the marinade. Slow cooking is also essential. Young hares don't need to be marinated and can be roasted with great success. The most famous of all hare recipes is jugged hare, but hare pie and potted hare are also traditional favourites. Redcurrant jelly is the classic accompaniment, but there is currently a fashion for serving hare with bitter chocolate sauce.

Partridge

Two main species of partridge live in the British Isles: the indigenous grey partridge, and the French or red-legged partridge, introduced into Britain during the reign of Charles II. This 'coarse red-legged infantry', as one ardent British writer called it, is considered inferior to the delicate grey bird. Partridges live mainly on corn and rely for cover on gorse, scrub and hedges. Bigger fields, grubbed-up hedges and the increasing use of pesticides have greatly reduced their numbers in recent years.

Availability Found throughout the British Isles. Grey partridge are most common in the arable farming regions of East Anglia, while many red-legged partridges have settled in Essex and Hertfordshire.

In season: 1st September – 1st February.

Guidelines Partridge are at their best during October and November, and you can tell a young bird by the pointed tip of its first flight feather (in older birds this is rounded), and its yellowish-brown feet.

Young partridge can be eaten without hanging although most older birds benefit from being hung for 2–4 days, depending on the weather.

Generally weigh ¾–1½ lbs. Usually sold in a brace. Allow one bird per person.

Cookery Young partridge are superb roasted or grilled: the flesh is plump, light-coloured and has few bones. They are traditionally garnished with watercress and breadcrumbs or game chips. Older birds can be potted, casseroled or braised; they are delicious with apples or stuffed and served on a bed of cabbage.

Partridge stuffed with mushrooms was a 19th-century favourite, probably gleaned from gypsies who cooked the bird with woodland fungi.

Pheasant

Perhaps the most beautiful and mysterious of all game birds. Its Latin name (*Phasianus colchicus*) derives from the Ancient world, when it was the 'bird of Phasis' – Phasis being the river which flowed through Colchis, the country which divided Asia from Europe.

Pheasants were originally bred in China and may well have arrived in Britain with the Romans. They have never been domesticated, although they are the only game bird that is hand reared, and many are so tame that they can be fed by hand, living off berries, fruits, nuts and grass.

Availability Widely available throughout Britain.

In season: 1st October – 1st February; best November – January.

Guidelines A large cock pheasant has spectacular plumage, with its irridescent green neck, speckled body and long curving tail feathers; the hen, which generally makes better eating, is smaller and duller in appearance.

Young pheasants are the best, but all need to be hung (usually for 7–14 days) to develop their true flavour. An unhung pheasant is like dry, dark chicken.

Sold in a brace, the male and female together. Normally one pheasant will feed two people, although a large cock bird may be enough for three.

Cookery Young pheasants should be roasted; it is important to baste or lard the bird well as it can become dry. Serve it with bread sauce and game chips; celery and hot roasted chestnuts are fine accompaniments too. Older birds are excellent casseroled or braised, and the carcase of a pheasant makes delicious rich soup.

Pheasants' eggs see page 54.

Pigeon

Detested and shot by farmers as vermin, wood pigeons gorge themselves not only on corn, but on beech nuts and acorns, and are particularly fond of Brussels sprouts. So they can be plump, full-flavoured little birds which make excellent eating. The stock dove, rock dove and turtle dove (a summer visitor to Britain) are also sold, although the wood pigeon is by far the most common.

Availability Common throughout Britain, especially in areas where there is arable farming.
In season: all year round; best March – October.

Guidelines Young birds, known as squabs, are the best, and can be recognised by their soft downy feathers and small pinkish legs.
Pigeon can be eaten fresh, although if it is hung for a day or two, the blood will drain away from the breast meat, which is dark, lean and full of flavour. Generally only the breast is eaten, as there's little flesh on the legs and thighs.
Relatively cheap and very good value compared with other game. Allow one pigeon per person.

Cookery Roast a young pigeon, and protect the breast with bacon. Older birds can be casseroled in lots of different ways, in which case they should ideally be wrapped in large vine leaves. Pigeon pie, enriched with pieces of steak, is also a great treat.

Quail

Not a truly English bird, although it appears every summer on its migratory visits from its native India and Africa. The Romans condemned it because they believed it fed on hemlock and other poisonous plants, but by the 15th century it was already being sold by English poultry and game dealers.
It's now illegal to kill or sell wild quail in Britain, although the birds are reared commercially on quail farms.

Availability Farmed quail are increasing in popularity.
In season: all year round.

Guidelines Very similar in character to the partridge. The birds have greyish-brown, soft feathers streaked with white. Choose a bird that is plump.

Quail don't need to be hung, and can be eaten straight away. Because they are farmed they can be rather bland, and even a large 6 oz. bird is really no more than a couple of mouthfuls. Allow 1 or 2 per person.

Quail is often sold ready dressed and frozen direct from the farm, and it can also be completely boned.

Cookery Most commonly roasted on a spit, but can be cooked in any way like partridge (see page 112).

Quails' eggs see page 54.

Rabbit

The spectre of myxomatosis inevitably colours our attitudes to eating rabbit, especially the wild kind. However there is nothing to fear and no chance of eating infected meat, since the disease immunised those rabbits that survived it.

Rabbits are one of the most efficient converters of vegetable matter into protein, so it's not surprising that rabbit farming is a tempting and potentially lucrative proposition. In fact the breeding of rabbits for the table is fast becoming big business.

Availability Both wild and farmed rabbits are common.
In season: all year round.

Guidelines Farmed rabbits are generally sold young and plump and should have smooth, furry coats. They are usually quite bland compared with their wild relatives, but if they are fresh, they can make tasty eating. A great deal of commercially bred rabbit comes skinned, jointed and frozen.

Wild rabbits on the other hand can be delicious and full of flavour, especially if they have been living on a diet of green leaves and sprouting corn. But if old and in poor condition they are likely to be almost inedible. If you are buying a wild rabbit, choose a young one, and look for soft ears, small white teeth, and sharp claws not roughened or rounded with age.

Rabbits are hung already gutted and should be eaten fresh whether they are farmed or wild.

Allow one large rabbit for two people.

Cookery Young rabbits can be roasted with a coating of mustard, grilled or fried. They can be turned into a pie, stewed in cider or used to make a kind of brawn, since their stock is very gelatinous. Old rabbits will need marinading and slow cooking to bring out the best in them.

Venison

Originally all game was venison, indeed the word itself comes from the Latin meaning 'to hunt'. Nowadays it is restricted to the meat of various kinds of deer, which, in Britain, means red deer, roe deer and fallow deer in particular. A great deal comes from culls on parks and estates, deer farming is on the increase and there is also a fair amount of venison from the wild. And yet it is still hard to get.

Much goes to the hunters, landowners and restaurants who have contracts with estates, and something like three-quarters of Scotland's venison is shipped abroad, mainly to Germany. When it does find its way into the shops it is often overpriced and poorly presented. This is a crazy state of affairs. Venison could rival beef if the trade was properly organised; if more was available and more people bought it, the price would come down. And venison could provide a good natural alternative to beef, especially as it comes from a wild animal, not intensively reared, or pumped full of hormones and antibiotics, as much of our livestock is.

Availability The great centres for venison are Scotland, especially the Highlands, and also the New Forest in southern England. Other forest areas and estates provide spasmodic supplies for shops.

In season: close seasons vary for the different breeds in Scotland and in England and Wales, but as a general rule bucks (males) are in season from late June – end of September; does (females) from October – December.

Guidelines Opinions differ about the quality of different breeds but most agree that roe deer is the best, then fallow deer and red dear. The meat from young bucks 18 months – 2 years old is generally better than that from does, whatever the breed.

Deer are lean, athletic animals – as lean as Olympic runners, someone said – and they have almost no fat on them. Consequently their flesh can be dry, tough and coarse if not handled properly. First of all it needs to be hung well, for at least a week. If the meat looks shiny and wet and doesn't smell gamey when you buy it, it is too fresh and needs more hanging. (Wipe the meat dry, dust it with pepper and ginger and hang it up in a well ventilated spot.)

Unlike most other game, venison appears in the shops already butchered, so you can only guess at its age, or ask your butcher or game dealer. Large joints naturally come from large mature animals. Most fresh venison doesn't reach the shops until late October, by which time the animals have put on some fat; venison sold early in the year is likely to have been frozen.

Venison should be dark red in colour, fine-grained, and what fat there is should be white. The most common cuts are the fillet, haunch (the top of the hind leg) and the loin – often cut into chops. Cheaper cuts like scrag-end are also sold, and venison liver is gaining in popularity.

Cookery The secret of cooking venison successfully is to marinade it first; it should also be well larded or basted with fat during cooking to keep it moist. Tender fillet can be sautéed as steaks; the haunch is normally roasted after marinading; cutlets and chops can be grilled, while other cheaper cuts are ideal for slowly cooked casseroles, stews, pasties and the like. Redcurrant, cranberry or rowan jelly is the appropriate accompaniment.

Venison sausages see page 96.

Wild duck

Domesticated, commercially reared duck counts as poultry (see page 104), while wild duck is classed as game. The most common wild duck is the mallard, but other species such as teal, pintail and widgeon find their way into the shops too.

Availability Mallard is very common, while other species appear mainly around Christmas time. Particularly common around marshy coastal areas such as Norfolk and Lincolnshire.

In season: 1st September – 31st January, although the season may extend to 20th February in areas below the high water mark of ordinary spring tides.

Guidelines Compared with domestic ducks, wild ducks are leaner, less fatty and more strongly flavoured. Those living around coastal areas normally feed on green vegetation, although when times are hard they often resort to fish. This can give them a slightly 'fishy' taste, which is off-putting to some people.

Wild duck need 2–3 days hanging to be at their best, and may be drawn before hanging. Plucking can be a messy business, so it's best to ask the butcher to do it for you unless you're skilled and patient.

A large mallard drake will feed two or even three people; smaller birds such as the teal are only enough for one.

Cookery Lean wild ducks are best roasted or braised. A little marinading will help to tenderise and flavour the meat, which should be basted or larded with pieces of fat during cooking. (a potato or an apple stuffed inside the bird will help to absorb any fishy flavour.) Wild duck is delicious served with a bitter orange sauce; flaming in brandy is also a common practice, although this doesn't impress me. For best results slightly undercook the flesh so that it is pink and tender.

Wild goose

It is illegal to sell wild goose, so you won't find them on display in any shop, however you may occasionally be given one by a friendly wildfowler.

Woodcock

Highly esteemed among connoisseurs of game, the woodcock comes to Britain every winter during the mating season. Its strong flavour is said to heighten the appreciation of the equally rich wines served with it.

Availability One of the most exclusive game birds. Not widely available except in a few specialist shops.

In season: 1st October – 31st January; best November and December.

Guidelines An easily recognised bird with speckled brown plumage and a long beak. Traditionally sold without being drawn, because the 'trail' or entrails are considered a delicacy. Best hung for a couple of days before using.

With most game birds, breast is best, but those who enjoy woodcock prefer the thighs and wings.

After plucking, the head is left on and the beak is used as a kind of skewer to truss the bird: it is thrust through the thighs and into the body. Although this may sound like a neat trick, it looks distasteful and nasty.

Allow one large or two small birds per person.

Cookery Generally roasted with the entrails intact; alternatively grilled. The 'trail' is removed after cooking, mashed and spread on a croûton to go with the bird.

Note: **Snipe**, a tiny relative of the woodcock, can be treated in a very similar way.

Game dealers and suppliers

Most game dealers are also butchers or fishmongers and are often equally skilled and knowledgeable about both types of food. Most also sell a wide variety of game in season, much of it procured locally.

General

C. E. Evans & Son
7 The Soke, <u>Alresford</u>,
Hampshire
Tel: (096 273) 2477

W. Fenn
27 Frith Street,
<u>London W1</u>
Tel: (01) 437 3181

J. R. Hayward
57 High Street, <u>Beaulieu</u>,
Hampshire
Tel: (0590) 612211

John Lane (Butchers) Ltd
6 Walkers Court,
<u>London W1</u>
Tel: (01) 437 8903

A. J. Leggett & Sons
35 Blyburgate, <u>Beccles</u>,
Suffolk
Tel: (0502) 712192

Derek Fox
25 Market Place,
<u>Malton</u>, North Yorkshire
Tel: (0653) 2528

B. & J. Hall
5 Wellgate Fisheries,
<u>Clitheroe</u>, Lancashire
Tel: (0200) 23511

Harvey's
8 Tombland,
<u>Norwich</u>, Norfolk
Tel: (0603) 21908

Smiths
183 South Street,
<u>Dorchester</u>, Dorset
Tel: (0305) 3707

Murray's
26 Melton Road,
<u>Oakham</u>, Leicestershire
Tel: (0572) 3370

H. Taylor & Sons
1 Cornmarket,
<u>Faringdon</u>, Oxfordshire
Tel: (0367) 720149

R. W. Gillham
27 Church Street,
<u>Oswestry</u>, Shropshire
Tel: (0691) 3187

C. A. Palmer
Bridge House,
1 The Thoroughfare,
<u>Halesworth</u>, Suffolk
Tel: (098 67) 2108

Pettitts of Reedham Ltd
Camp Hill, <u>Reedham</u>,
Norfolk
Tel: (049 370) 243   M.

H. Hodgkiss & Son Ltd
115 St Leonards Road,
Windsor, Berkshire
Tel: (075 35) 65844

F. Pitts
31–33 Oxford Street,
Woodstock, Oxfordshire
Tel: (0993) 811435

G. F. Dimmock
Carsluith,
Kirkcudbrightshire,
Scotland
Tel: (067 182) 354

Geo. Campbell & Sons
18 Stafford Street,
Edinburgh, Lothian,
Scotland
Tel: (031) 225 7507

J. R. Mitchell & Son
40–44 Bridge Street,
Kelso, Borders,
Scotland
Tel: (057 32) 2109

Quail

Claxby Quail Farm
Claxby Hall, Alford,
Lincolnshire
Tel: (052 12) 2350

Goldesburgh Quail Farm
Clements Farm, Wheatley,
Hampshire
Tel: (042 04) 3174

Venison

John Strange
16 High Street, Lyndhurst,
Hampshire
Tel: (042 128) 2659   M.

Wholefood (Butchers)
24 Paddington Street,
London W1
Tel: (01) 486 1390

Warner & Hurst
Grainger Market,
Newcastle-upon-Tyne,
Tyne & Wear
Tel: (0632) 22847

Duncan Fraser
8–10 Queensgate Arcade,
Inverness, Highland,
Scotland
Tel: (0463) 32744

Useful organisations

The National Game Dealers Association
1 Belgrove, Tunbridge Wells, Kent
Tel: (0892) 41412

Fish

The waters around the British Isles are filled with all kinds of fish, and yet we have become a nation of meat-eaters, preferring a chop or a joint of beef to a herring or a salmon. But it's easy to see why fish has such a bad image: to many people it is slimy, smelly, bony and inconvenient, and it always seems to pose problems. What do I do with it when I have bought it? Surely it won't be as nourishing as meat? Why does it all taste the same? And behind the questions there's always the lurking memory of fish as an institutional food: the watery boiled cod of the school dinner, the steamed plaice of the hospital bed.

The truth about fish is very different. Because fresh fish is a natural food from a living creature, completely unprocessed, it doesn't immediately *look* like food. However any competent fishmonger can quickly transform it into a manageable fillet or steak, which neatly takes care of head, skin and bones. If a fish smells at all it should smell only of the sea. And fish is just as nutritious as meat, in fact it's actually better for you. (see later).

There are more kinds of fish available than ever before, and yet we are still notoriously conservative about which ones we choose to eat and how we decide to cook them. Cod, haddock and plaice are safe enough, we might even try skate or sole, but it takes tremendous persuasion to lure us into uncharted waters and explore the less familiar fish on display these days. Although we do see lots of frozen fish from abroad – tuna, swordfish, grouper, octopus and many more – the number of different types of fish caught in British waters and sold fresh is also on the increase, so we have a golden opportunity to take full advantage of them.

And when it comes to cooking fish, we can experiment too. Fish cookery is the most delicate and refined there is, and it's also best when it's kept simple. But fish needs careful handling and perfectly timed cooking: Somerset Moore, one of the best fish chefs in the country put it this way: 'When it comes to cooking fish a minute is like a lifetime'. Yes, fish and fish cookery is a challenge, but it's well worth the trouble.

Figures published in 1984 suggest that we are actually eating more fish, although the amount is still very small, just over five ounces per person per week. Frozen fish edged up slightly, but sales of the ubiquitous fish finger are falling. There are signs too that we are seeking out more fresh fish and becoming more adventurous. Perhaps, at last, the tide is turning.

Fish farming Obtaining food from the sea is still largely a matter of hunting: fish is caught by dangling hooks or dragging nets through the water. The idea of farming the sea is still in its infancy even though on land we moved over to organised agriculture centuries ago.

Some forms of fish farming have been with us for a long time: the Chinese bred spawn for fish 2,500 years ago, the

Romans cultivated oysters in special beds and medieval monasteries all had special 'stews' or fish ponds for breeding carp, pike and other freshwater fish.

In Britain there are already cultivated beds for mussels, oysters, clams and crayfish and a proliferation of hatcheries and fish farms for salmon and trout. (In 1970 there were just 40; the estimated number in 1982 was over 400.) As a system of producing food, fish farming seems to have nothing but advantages: it can offer the most highly prized fish at prices everyone can afford, all year round; it is less labour intensive than fishing and it's less dependant on the whims of the climate.

But at the moment it's difficult to find out what is actually happening down on the farm. There's no record of exactly how many there are and how they operate: the whole business of artificial feeding, unnatural growth rates and the overall quality of the fish must be watched. A lot of farmed trout seems to be going downhill and farmed salmon may well follow while, at the same time, river pollution, unscrupulous poaching and general neglect are putting our wild salmon at risk. If we are not careful we may soon have no choice *but* to eat farmed fish.

The big step however is to make a success of farming sea fish. This has been tried and experiments have been continuing for many years, but as yet there's been no real breakthrough. It is relatively easy to breed fish like plaice, sole and turbot, but eventually they have to be moved out of the hatchery into the open sea, and there they are prey to all manner of predatory creatures. In due course the problems will be solved, and sea fish farming could make a tremendous difference to our diet and food supplies. Providing, of course, it is managed with care and good sense.

We have plundered the resources of the sea for hundreds of years and are now beginning to pay the price: the West Country pilchard industry has gone; herrings are now almost an endangered species, the sea is polluted with chemicals and spillage from oil tankers, and fish now represents nothing more than profit, taking as much from the sea and putting as little as possible back. One can only hope that tomorrow's sea fish farmers have more respect for our food and resources.

The nutritional value of fish   Fish are highly nutritious, but under-rated. First of all they all contain plenty of protein, and some can rival the best lean meat on that score: steamed halibut has 24% protein, while a grilled herring has about 20–22%, both of which compare very favourably with lean beef.

Fish can be divided up into two categories: white and oily. White fish do contain fat, but it is largely confined to the liver: cod, haddock, halibut, sole, plaice and whiting come into this group. Oily fish have their fat distributed in their flesh, and include herrings, sprats, salmon and mackerel among others.

The great thing about fish, however, is that their fat is very largely unsaturated, unlike meat with its high percentage of saturated fat. So, in that respect fish is a better choice than meat on health grounds alone. Most fish also contain useful amounts of vitamins, especially A, B group, D and E, as well as valuable minerals such as iron, calcium and iodine.

This, of course, applies to fresh fish. Frozen fish is nutritionally acceptable, although B vitamins tend to be lost during thawing. However, for flavour, texture and quality it can't match the fresh article. Unlike some other types of frozen food, eg. poultry, frozen fish doesn't contain additives, although frozen food *dishes* of the 'cod in parsley sauce' variety are loaded with them.

So, we should be eating more fresh, unprocessed fish. In nutritional terms how fish is cooked and what it is served with can make a difference. Grilled and steamed fish are naturally the best on health grounds, but there's no harm in frying in oil – or even, occasionally, in unsalted butter – and a well-made light sauce is unlikely to do you irreparable damage.

General guidelines for buying fish (i) Get to know your local fishmonger, but shop around, too. Pick a shop that does good business, has a wide selection and where the fishmonger is on good terms with his customers.

(ii) Be inquisitive, ask questions, make requests for unusual fish. A keen fishmonger loves to talk and appreciates interested customers. Remember to give him some feedback and thank him when the results are successful.

(iii) Most fresh fish comes from the wild, so supplies can be seasonal and will often depend on the weather and the time of year. Stocks can even vary from week to week. The advantage of this is that the pick of the catch appears when it is in its prime. Freezing may allow us the luxury of eating any fish at any time, but there's nothing to beat a fresh, locally caught specimen cooked and served in its rightful season.

(iv) Freshness is the key to buying fish, and there are a number of signs to look for. The fish should appear healthy, with full bright eyes, red gills, closely packed scales and firm flesh with no hint of flabbiness. In other words, it should look as if it has just come out of the water.

Your nose will do the rest. If there's any trace of unpleasant odours, don't buy. (There are exceptions, such as skate, which always has a tinge of ammonia about it.) The fish should smell of the sea or river and be slippery to handle.

All of this needs a certain amount of self-confidence on the part of the shopper. But it's your money and you have a right to examine the goods before buying.

One tip about freshness: fish kept on ice are likely to be good. Indeed the presence of ice is usually a reliable indicator of a fishmonger's worth.

(v) A fishmonger will happily skin or fillet a fish if you ask him. Don't forget to take the head and bones with you: they are essential for making fish stock.

(vi) By wary of names and labels on fish. They can be misleading and have nothing to do with the fish itself. Either they are local nicknames which often need explaining, or they can be inducements to conceal the true nature of an unattractive fish: rock salmon is far more appealing than dogfish!

(vii) Fresh fish is best cooked the day it is bought, although if it is in very good condition, it will last in a refrigerator for 24 hours.

Saltwater Fish

Anglerfish (See Monkfish)

Bass (Sea Bass)

Greatly favoured by the Romans and highly prized on the Continent for years, the European sea bass is at last beginning to gain popularity in Britain. Until recently it was better known to anglers than to cooks.

Distribution Lives in large shoals close to rocky shores and large estuaries, especially around the south and west coasts of England and Ireland. When it ventures close inshore it is often landed by fishermen with rod and line.

Availability Increasingly common in good fish shops, especially in the south and west.
In season: May – October.

Guidelines A beautiful, elegant and slim fish, bright silver when it is alive; its back has a bluish sheen and its underparts are tinged yellow. Young bass are occasionally spotted. Easily recognised by its very spiky front dorsal fin. Large bass can weigh to to 12 lbs, but most sold in shops are around 3–5 lbs.

Bass appear whole on the fishmonger's slab, and it's worth checking to see if they have been locally caught. If the fish *has* been caught nearby and has not had to endure being transported it should be in good condition – silvery, bright-eyed and firm.

Cookery   Sea bass is sometimes known as 'salmon bass' or 'white salmon' although it has nothing to do with the salmon family.

Its moist, delicious white flesh doesn't taste much like salmon, but it can be cooked in the same ways – stuffed and baked in foil, poached, grilled and barbecued. And, like salmon, it can be eaten hot or cold. Depending on the size of the fish it can also be filleted and served with a delicate sauce of, say, fennel or cucumber.

Coley (Coalfish, Saithe)

No British fish has more vernacular names than the coley: Francis Day, the Victorian fish expert and naturalist, listed 57! It's also an unlucky creature. Although it is caught in huge numbers it is often treated carelessly and ends up being advertised as food for cats. However, in the Orkneys and Shetlands they have more respect for it: it's used with cunning and imagination as an essential part of the islanders' diet.

Distribution   Live in shoals which migrate to feed and spawn (they hunt herring and sprats and often follow their shoals). Mainly caught in northern waters, especially in the far north, although they are found around the whole coast of Britain.

Availability   Widely available.
   In season: all year round; best June – February.

Guidelines   Coley is a member of the cod family, but is much cheaper. Large specimens can be 2–3ft long and can live for more than 25 years. It looks rather like a cod although its greenish back is often charcoal-coloured (hence the name).

Most coley appear in the shops as fillets which have been frozen or chilled on ice. Don't be put off by the murky grey-pink colour of the flesh; it turns white when cooked and tastes delicious – far better than insipid cod.

Frozen coley is a fact of life, but it is always better to buy the fish in a fresh state because it has more flavour and the flesh is firmer.

Cookery   Coley can be used like cod, and has the advantage that it often has a more distinct flavour; its only disadvantage is that the flesh is sometimes rather coarse. But, in fish pies and robust dishes with sauces, this is not too important.

Cod

Once nicknamed the 'beef of the sea' because of its thick, meaty, protein-rich flesh, cod has been the most important and abundant of all British food fish for hundreds of years. In the Middle Ages, salt cod with mashed parsnips was a dish familiar to rich and poor alike, while during Victorian times the fish was valued for its massive head, which was elaborately dressed and extravagantly garnished with prawns and lobster.

Distribution   Inhabits the cold northern waters of the North Sea and the North Atlantic, living at a depth of 20–300 fathoms and only approaching the coastline during the spawning season.

Caught mainly by deep-sea trawlers which are often at sea for weeks; as a result most of the catch (especially from waters around Norway and Iceland) is frozen in huge blocks as soon as it is landed. Some is caught by inshore boats working off the coasts around the north of Britain, but even this is chilled on ice.

Availability   Widely available. Most of the catch is landed and distributed through major ports like Scarborough, Grimsby and Fleetwood. At a number of small fishing ports, local fishermen will sell part of their catch fresh from huts on the quay or the seashore.

In season: all year round; best September – March.

Guidelines   Fresh cod is now a rarity, but is the only cod worth eating. It's a massive white fish that can occasionally weigh as much as 80 lbs; its greyish-green back dotted with yellowish spots is very distinctive. The flesh should be perfectly white and firm, with no tell-tale signs of greyness or flabbiness. It is normally sold as fillets or as steaks with a bone in the middle. Always ask for a steak freshly cut from the thick 'head end' of the fish.

Best of all are delicious sweet *codling*, small specimens weighing up to 4 lbs. These are caught using a rod and line baited with lugworms or whelks. Always seek out and ask for fresh, inshore cod.

Cookery   Cod often suffers from dull, unimaginative cooking. It can be rather bland, but is extremely versatile and calls out for strongly flavoured sauces and accompaniments – tomatoes, garlic, cheese, ham and the like. But the finest fresh cod or codling should be cooked in the simplest way possible – either grilled, fried or poached. Otherwise the fish is excellent for everything from pies to fish and chips.

AVOID the cod in batter offered by some of the fast-food fish and chip shop chains. They process the fish, reconstitute it and reshape it, so that it appears in unnatural but identical triangular portions, which have neither the flavour, nor the texture of the fresh fish.

Smoked cod fillet page 161
Smoked cod roe page 162

Conger Eel

Conger eel was not an uncommon sight on fishmongers' slabs back in the 14th century, although it would only have been sold fresh in coastal towns. Otherwise it had to be preserved in some way, and the favourite method in later years was to pickle or souse it in vinegar after it had been split and rolled. One 18th century recipe used a mixture of beer and vinegar and flavoured the whole thing with green fennel leaves. Today, the conger eel is a sportsman's fish, a daunting challenge for adventurous anglers.

Distribution   Once nicknamed the 'evil eye', the fiercesome and terrifying conger eel patrols the waters around the south west of England, especially off Devon and Cornwall.

Availability   Not uncommon in large fish shops, especially in Devon and Cornwall, although a good proportion of the catch is caught by private anglers.
   In season: March – October.

Guidelines   A massive creature up to 8ft long, without scales and with a dorsal fin stretching almost the whole length of its body. Despite its name and shape it should not be confused with the *freshwater* eel, and can't be substituted for it in cooking; the freshwater eel is delicate and smooth, the flesh of the conger is meaty and rather coarse, but still well worth eating in its own right. Always buy a piece or steak of conger eel cut from the middle or head-end of the fish. The tail is a mass of sharp bones.

Cookery   The flesh of the conger eel is excellent for enriching fish stock and for making soups and stews. (Conger eel soup has been a speciality in Cornwall and the Channel Islands for many years.) Conger eel is also traditionally cooked in local west country cider and can be roasted like a joint of meat.

Fresh is always best.

Dab

Opinions differ about the virtues of the dab. For some it has always been the inferior member of the plaice family (the very word 'dab' is a term of contempt in Lincolnshire); to others it is the most highly prized member of the family. Assuming that the fish is really fresh, the latter view is undoubtedly the truth.

Distribution   Particularly abundant in the North Sea, living mainly on sandy ground in shallow water. Normally caught in trawl and seine nets by fishing boats. Little dabs lurking over the cockle beds in the shallow waters off the north Norfolk coast are sometimes speared with long bamboo poles.

Availability   Widely available. The best are those caught off the East Anglian coast and sold by local fishermen.
   In season: April – February; best June – December.

Guidelines   A relative of the plaice and the flounder, 8–10 inches long, with a brown, freckled back. Quite unmistakable because its skin is as scaly and rough as a file (its Latin name *Limanda limanda* actually comes from *lima*, a file).
   Buy whole fresh dabs, rather than fillets. The whole fish have more flavour and are easier to handle than small fillets, which can easily disintegrate during cooking.

Cookery   Dabs can be cooked like plaice (see page 141), but are at their best when gently fried whole in butter and eaten with new potatoes and fresh spinach. Or try the delicious Norfolk combination of dabs with local marsh samphire. Very small dabs can also be dipped in egg and breadcrumbs and deep-fried.

Dover Sole

Dover is not the exclusive home of the exquisite Dover sole, although great numbers are caught in the English Channel, and the white-cliffed port has traditionally been the best source of freshly caught soles destined for the London market.

Distribution   Caught in large numbers from the Bay of Biscay to the south of Norway, but most of the British catch comes from the waters of the southern North Sea.

Availability   Widely available. Fresh, locally caught soles can be had from most ports around south and eastern coasts of England.

In season all year round; can be scarce during spring and early summer.

Guidelines *Solea solea*, the true Dover sole, is the most highly esteemed of all flatfish. Can weigh up to 2 lbs, although most are about 13 oz. Easily recognised by its subtle elliptical shape and its fins which extend the whole length of the body.

It goes without saying that the flavour and texture of fresh Dover sole is incomparable, but it's a curious fact that the flavour actually improves a day or two after the fish has been caught. This is a quirk of chemistry not shared by other flatfish, and is due to decomposition and the formation of chemical substances which bring the flavour of the sole to perfection. Fish without roes have the most delicate flavour.

In Ireland, Dover soles are called 'black soles', and very small soles are known everywhere as 'slip soles'.

Cookery The sole has inspired the creation of a whole repertoire of elaborate dishes, sauces and garnishes which are the pride of classical French cuisine. These elaborate culinary feats are fine, but they can swamp the sublime flavour of the fish itself. Unless you are a master chef, it's better to cook the sole in the simplest way possible, either plainly grilled or gently fried in butter.

Flounder

This close relative of the plaice and the dab has never found great favour in Britain, although it is very popular in northern Europe (the Norwegians even dry and smoke them).

Distribution Although it is technically a saltwater fish, the flounder is most comfortable in water with a low salt content, so it is quite rare in the North Sea, and often spends the summer in rivers and estuaries.

Availability Not widely available, although some appear in shops from time to time. Around Flookburgh, Cumbria, where they are known as 'flukes' and are caught with stake nets, they are something of a local speciality.

In season: all year round; best February – September.

Guidelines Very similar in appearance to the plaice, although its dark side is dull brown, greyish or dull green, and it has only a few indistinct freckles. Usually about 12 inches long. Must be eaten very fresh otherwise it is dull and tasteless.

Cookery   The white flesh of the flounder remains firm when cooked, and it should be treated as other flatfish, eg. plaice (see page 141). Best fried or steamed.

Grey Mullet

Like the sea bass – which it slightly resembles in flavour and appearance – the grey mullet has never achieved the popularity it deserves in Britain. However its roe, dried and salted, has been a delicacy since Roman times and is still highly prized in France, Italy and the Middle East. It was also enjoyed by the English during the 17th and 18th centuries, under the name of 'botargo', and was a great favourite with the hard-drinking classes who used its salty flavour to provoke their thirsts.

Distribution   The grey mullet and its many close relatives live in temperate waters in many parts of the world, and appear in waters around the southern half of Britain. They are active fish that live in shoals in shallow inshore water, but often venture into brackish or fresh water. Because they are entirely herbivorous, extracting vegetable food from the mud, they have a reputation for tasting muddy.

Availability   Fresh mullet are not widely available, although shops in the west country, southern England and on the east coast may stock them, along with the adventurous London fishmongers.
In season: June – February; best July – October.

Guidelines   An elegant torpedo of a fish with a grey back and flashing silvery sides with dark stripes along its rows of coarse scales; it has a pair of fins which protrude from its head 'like the ears of a donkey'. Can weigh up to 5 lbs but most are 1–2 lbs.

Seek out a fish with its roe intact. This is rare but you may be lucky, especially if the fish has been locally caught and it is still 'intact'. The roe is a great prize. There's no need to be unduly wary about 'muddiness', provided you gut the fish and clean it straight away before cooking.

Grey mullet is still good value; a relatively inexpensive fish.

AVOID very small imported grey mullet which come deep-frozen in plastic bags from countries as far apart as Canada and Hong Kong. (They may be labelled by their American name of Striped Mullet). Once thawed and cooked they are dull and tasteless.

Buy locally. Support your local producers and suppliers, but always check the true origins of your purchases.

Cookery   The flesh of the grey mullet is rich, slightly oily, white and moist. The fish can be cooked in many ways like bass (see page 126). If it is large, it can be stuffed, wrapped in cooking paper and gently baked; smaller fish can be simply grilled.

Haddock

Next to the cod, haddock is probably the most well-known of British food fish, but it is not true to say that both are dull, undistinguished items with little flavour.

Haddock is a fish that the Scots have made their own. They were 'rizzared' or sun-dried and also cured by using the breeze, rocks and salty sea spray, when they were called 'speldings'. The Scots have also mastered the art of smoking haddock and produce two of our finest and most delicious specialities, the split Finnan haddock with its pale lemony sheen and the Arbroath Smokie, which is the whole fish with white flesh and dark, burnished skin (see page 157–58).

Distribution   Like cod, haddock is a fish of northern waters and lives mainly near the bottom in deep water water. It is caught mainly in the North Sea and out towards Norway. Like cod, haddock is also deep-frozen on board the trawlers or kept on ice. Some are also caught by long lining.

Availability   Widely available. Most of the catch is landed in ports such as Scarborough, Whitby, North Shields and Redcar.

In season: all year round; best May – February.

Guidelines   Don't underrate the haddock. At its best it is deliciously sweet and full of flavour. Small haddock, weighing around 8oz. are sold whole, but it is most common to find them as fillets. The whole fish resembles a small cod, but it has a *black* lateral line and a very distinctive dark 'thumb-print' behind its head (like the 'finger print of St. Peter' on the John Dory). These two features will always tell you if the fish you are being sold is haddock rather than cod or whiting in disguise.

The flesh of the haddock should be firm and opalescent white, and sometimes has a pinkish tinge. Don't buy the fish if it looks grey, limp and watery. And as a rule, settle for smaller rather than larger fillets (when the flesh can be rather coarse and lose its distinctive sweetness).

Cookery   Firm, white-fleshed haddock is superb grilled or lightly poached in milk and butter. It is excellent for pies and soups and is the outright favourite for fish and chips in the

north of England and Scotland. Like the cod it benefits from
strongly flavoured sauces.

Hake

The hake is a hunter, and a voracious one too, devouring
immense numbers of herrings, sprats and mackerel during its
forays. For a fish with such aggressive tendencies, its flesh is
soft and delicate: on Merseyside it is known as 'milky hake'. It
is easily digested, has few bones and makes an ideal choice for
invalids and children.

Distribution   Particularly abundant around the western
coast of Ireland, but also caught by trawl and long line in
waters off north-west England and Scotland.

Availability   Less common than it used to be. However it is
very popular throughout the north west where the main port
is Fleetwood, Lancashire.

In season: all year round; best June – January.

Guidelines   A close relative of the cod but more slender in
shape. Whole hake, up to 2ft long, are a daunting sight on the
fishmonger's slab with their large mouths brandishing rows of
sharp teeth. Usually sold as fillets, which are known as 'silver
fillets' in many parts of the north-west. Sometimes the fillets
are sold skinned. Small hake can be bought whole. The flesh
should be firm and white.

Cookery   With its delicate flesh and lack of bones, the hake
is a popular fish for poaching, baking, frying or grilling. Try
it the traditional way served with a sharp sorrel or gooseberry
sauce; alternatively there's an Irish recipe which involves
stuffing the fillets and covering them in a dish with mashed
potato. Hake was once popular in fish and chip shops,
although it seems to have rather gone out of fashion of late.

Halibut

By far the largest of all the flatfish, occasionally weighing more
than 100 lbs, although few could match the monumental 60-
year-old fish landed at Grimsby in 1959, which tipped the
scales at 504 lbs! The halibut is a most useful fish: not only
does it make good eating, but its liver is abundantly rich in oil
full of vitamin D, and even its skin was once used for leather
production.

Distribution Lives in deep waters off the northernmost coasts of Britain and in Icelandic and Norwegian waters. Caught with trawl nets or on hooks and lines baited with small plaice.

Availability The halibut grows slowly and is in danger of being overfished, so it is less common and more expensive than it used to be. Quite widely available.

In season: all year round; best September – March.

Guidelines A whole halibut is a most impressive creature, with a dark, olive-green back and a white belly. Very small halibut, weighing up to five pounds, are known as 'chicken halibut'.

Halibut is normally sold as steaks, and those from smaller fish tend to be the best. If possible, don't buy cuts from the tail end which can be very dry. The flesh should be firm, with a fine, close texture.

The Greenland halibut is a relative of the true halibut, but is much smaller and sometimes called the 'little halibut' (not to be confused with 'chicken halibut'). Its skin, on both sides, is grey-brown. Normally sold as fillets, but these don't match the true halibut in flavour.

Cookery The problem with halibut is that it tends to be rather dry, but the steaks are delicious poached with a light sauce, or grilled and basted with melted butter. It is also good cold with herb-flavoured mayonnaise.

Herring

From the Middle Ages until the 1950s, the herring was the most important fish caught in British waters. In fact the story of the herring is also the story of many of our greatest fishing ports; it shaped the lives of millions of people, it was the backbone of the economy, it was the object of bloody sea battles and it was so highly valued that it was used as currency (the worth of East Coast ports like Dunwich was estimated using the herring as a yardstick).

But overfishing has caused serious problems and as a result strict legislation has come into force in an attempt to conserve stocks and allow the fish to recover from years of exploitation. In 1977 a ban on North Sea herring fishing was introduced, however this was lifted in June 1984 and fresh North Sea herrings are once again in the shops.

Distribution The herring is a masterpiece of design, and speeds through the water in shoals to feed and spawn. They appear in different waters at different times of year: as well as the North Sea they are abundant off the coast of western

Scotland, and the Scottish North Sea coast towards Norway.

Traditionally they were caught with drift nets whose meshes allowed the very small fish through, but the advent of sophisticated trawls, which scoop up fish indiscriminately, has threatened the herring's chances of survival in many places.

Availability Less widely available than it used to be. Famous herring centres of the past like Great Yarmouth, Norfolk, have been superseded by ports such as Mallaig in Scotland since the decline of the East Anglian fishery.

In season: Scotch (Norwegian) May – September. (The East Anglian season is from October – December.)

Guidelines A beautifully streamlined fish, soft-finned and sleek, with a bluish-green back and silvery flanks. Its body is covered with flaky scales (they are described as 'deciduous' because they fall as easily as leaves from the trees). Herrings vary in size a great deal, depending on the time of year and where they were caught, but most are 8–10 inches long. Because they are landed no more than 24 hours after being caught, they should be very fresh. Look for the signs: a glint of brightness in the eyes, a firm body and a shiny silver skin.

Herrings are normally sold whole, although in Scotland it's common to see piles of the fish already filleted.

AVOID herrings that look tired and limp, with sunken eyes and a dull colour. They are stale and not worth buying. This is important because herrings are rich in oil and therefore deteriorate quickly.

The herring is the most nutritious of all fish: it's high in protein (22%) – on a par with lean beef; its fat content varies from about 5% when it has spawned in the winter to as much as 20% when it is feeding voraciously in early summer. The fat is rich in vitamins A and D as well as B group vitamins and valuable minerals like iron, calcium and iodine. No other fish can match the herring for pure natural nourishment. And it makes splendid eating.

Always look out for herrings which contain roe. Both the hard roe from the female and the soft 'milt' from the male are delicious in their own right.

Cookery Because the herring is so rich in oil, it's ideal for grilling. Filleted herrings can also be rolled in crunchy oatmeal and fried in dripping – a classic traditional Scottish dish; they can be served with a pungent mustard sauce, the English way, or stuffed and baked in the oven. Herrings can also be pickled and soused in vinegar and they are smoked to produce red herrings, bloaters and, above all, kippers.

Red herrings see page 161.
Bloaters see page 158.
Kippers see page 159–60.

John Dory

An extraordinary-looking fish, once seen never forgotten. In England it was originally called simply 'dory', from the French *dorée*, referring to the golden sheen of the scales. John seems to have been added later, in the 17th century, perhaps as a nickname. Whatever the origins it is one of the most delectable of all fish, ranking with the finest sole and turbot.

Distribution   Basically a fish of the Mediterranean, although it appears in the English Channel and the waters of southern England during the summer, later moving up into the North Sea to feed.

Availability   Not common. Mainly sold by specialist fishmongers in the south, although most of the catch is snapped up by restaurateurs; it's a fish fit for fashionable menus.

In season: January – April.

Guidelines   Instantly recognisable by its strange flattened body, huge head, feathery fins and a large black thumb print on each side, behind its head. According to legend St. Peter drew a gold coin from the mouth of the fish and his fingerprints remain, ringed with gold. Most John Dorys are about 1ft long and weigh around 4 lbs, although monsters up to 12 lbs appear occasionally.

For most dishes it is best to use the fillets with the thick skin removed. Remember that the proportion of flesh to bones, head, etc. is very low; the fishmonger will prepare the fish for you. The flesh is firm, white and very delicate.

The golden rule is, if you see a John Dory for sale, buy it.

Cookery   Best steamed or poached, although it can also be grilled whole. Like sole and turbot it is well suited to fine creamy sauces.

Lemon Sole

Strictly speaking, this is not a true sole, but a relative of the plaice. It may not have the aristocratic qualities of the Dover Sole, but it is well worth eating. Also goes by the name of Mary sole, merry sole, smear dab and sweet fluke.

Distribution   Like other flatfish, the lemon sole lives on the hard rocky bottom, and is abundant in the northern areas of the North Sea, as well as off the western and southern coasts of Britain. Caught by trawls and seine nets, and as by-product of other fisheries, eg. prawns.

Availability Widely available, particularly during the winter months.

In season: all year round; best July – February.

Guidelines Just as its names are confusing, so it may be difficult to distinguish the lemon sole from plaice, dabs and flounders. Look for the very small head and smooth slimy skin which is a rich yellow-brown colour with irregular markings and blotches of different colours from mahogany to green. Large lemon soles are 12–18 inches long and are quite fleshy; small fish can be rather thin. Equally good whole or filleted. Once again, fresh is best; frozen lemon sole fillets are thoroughly disappointing.

Cookery Although it doesn't have quite the exquisite flavour of the Dover sole, lemon sole can be used in similar ways: grilled, gently fried in butter and served with all manner of creamy sauces; it can also be cut in diagonal strips (or goujons) dipped in egg and breadcrumbs, deep-fried and served with tartare sauce.

Mackerel

In 1699, an Act of Parliament declared Billingsgate a free and open market for the sale of fish six days a week; on the seventh day, Sunday, mackerel alone could be sold before and after divine service. Mackerel was a special case because it was an extremely perishable, oily fish that deteriorated rapidly.

Mackerel is still a special fish, beautiful to look at, highly nutritious, and one of the finest to eat.

Distribution Wide-ranging and found in waters from the southern Mediterranean to Iceland and Norway. During the winter they hibernate in deep water, motionless and not feeding; then in the spring they move in shoals to spawning grounds south of Ireland and west of the English Channel. After spawning they move into shallow inshore water, feeding voraciously. And it is here, during the late spring and summer, that they are caught by west country fishermen with drift nets and also with hooks and lines.

Availability Widely available, although the best are caught and sold in Devon and Cornwall.

In season: April – September; best May – July.

Eat with the seasons.

Guidelines A beautiful streamlined fish with lovely iridescent markings; it should be, as Dorothy Hartley put it so memorably, 'so fresh that the light shines from it like a rainbow'. Mackerel is rich, fatty and nutritious, but it does deteriorate very quickly, especially in warm weather, and must be eaten absolutely fresh (the finest of all, it is said, are eaten on the boats, straight from the hook and into the pan).

In the 17th and 18th centuries, cooks were already aware of the mackerel's special qualities and gave detailed instructions for choosing the fish. Hannah Glasse, writing in 1747, had this to say: 'if they are new, their gills will be of a lively shining redness, their eyes sharp and full, and the fish stiff; but if stale their gills will look dusky and faded, their eyes dull and sunk down, and their tails limber.' Accurate advice indeed.

Mackerel can grow up to 16 inches long, although most are half that size, and generally the smaller fish make the best eating. Remember that the mackerel's flesh is rich, so you won't need too much. Mackerel are still one of the cheapest and best value fish on the market.

Cookery Whatever its size the mackerel is a fleshy creature with few bones. Small ones are best grilled; larger ones can be stuffed and baked. Mackerel was traditionally served with sharp gooseberry sauce – the best fruit and fish of early summer. Wild fennel was also a favourite in the past, but any sharp, tart accompaniment will do to counteract the richness of the fish. Mackerel is also soused or pickled in vinegar or cider and smoked mackerel is very popular indeed.

Smoked mackerel page 164

Monkfish

A grotesque monster of a fish, a weird creature with a massive devilish head and a thin tail which has wonderfully succulent flesh. Its other name 'anglerfish' refers to the fact that it carries with it a kind of fishing rod; in fact its dorsal fin extends and tapers into a thin rod in front of those frightening jaws. This lures all kinds of creatures, from small conger eels to unwary sea birds, into its vast mouth. An interesting fact: the first insulin was extracted from the pancreas of the monkfish.

Distribution Inhabits very deep waters down to 1,000 metres, and lives on the sandy and muddy bottom. Spawns around the north, west and south coasts of Britain between April and June. Usually caught in trawl nets.

Availability Becoming increasingly common and fashionable, and rightly so. Widely available.

In season: all year round; best during the summer months.

Guidelines   You are unlikely to see a whole monkfish on display; its head is normally cut off because it would surely frighten off customers, and because only the tail is eaten. Monkfish have dirty brown skin with an irregular net-like pattern, but again you are unlikely to see this as the tail pieces are nearly always skinned first.

The flesh of the monkfish is milky white and beautiful to eat – delicate, subtly flavoured, sweet and succulent. It resembles lobster and scampi – indeed it has been passed off as both of these, particularly in restaurants (see page 181). However, if you taste the two side by side, it's easy to spot the difference.

Generally the large pieces have the best flavour. But it's worth buying monkfish whenever you see it.

Cookery   The delicate, but firm flesh is enhanced by fine sauces: monkfish with lime sauce is a current favourite with chefs. It can be cut into chunks and grillled on skewers, braised or baked. Or, like scampi, breaded and deep-fried in pieces.

Pilchard

A close relative of the herring, but more delicate and soft-skinned. There was a prolific pilchard fishery around the Cornish coast during the Middle Ages, and vast numbers were caught during their late summer visits to the water off St. Ives and other ports; this trade continued well into the 19th century. Pilchard fishing and curing was a profitable local industry in which nothing was wasted: the fish were salted; the oil drained from them went to the leather tanners and was used as an 'illuminant'; the skimmings from the water in which the fish were washed was bought by soap boilers and any damaged fish were sold off as manure.

Distribution   Pilchards live in warm southern waters in the Mediterranean, the Bay of Biscay and off the coast of Cornwall and Devon. They are caught with drift nets and seines like other members of the herring family.

Availability   The pilchard industry came to an end after the First World War, when the fish suddenly began to disappear from west country waters. Now it is quite rare to find fresh English pilchards, although ports such as Brixham in Devon do sell them occasionally.

In season: April – November.

Guidelines Very much like a small herring in appearance, with a green glinting back and a silver belly. Up to 8 inches long. Small young pilchards are known famously as 'sardines'. Most now come frozen from the Mediterranean.

Like the herring, pilchards are rich in oil and highly nutritious, but they do deteriorate quickly – hence the habit of canning them in oil. Fresh pilchards should be bought locally and eaten the same day.

Cookery Pilchards can be treated like herrings, bearing in mind that they are less robust. The greatest of all pilchard recipes is the stargazey pie. The intriguing name of this pie refers to its design: the fish are put in whole, arranged like the spokes of a wheel, then a pastry case is laid over their bodies, leaving their heads exposed, as if gazing starwards. The point of this is to ensure that the valuable oil from the fish heads drains back into the pie during cooking. Surrounding the fish there might be pulp from the cider press, pickled rock samphire and pieces of bacon, all bound in a rich egg custard.

But for the simplest of all treats, grill the fish crisply in the open air, over charcoal or a wood fire.

Plaice

One of the most important British food fishes, certainly the most widely eaten of all flatfish. It can be excellent, although generations of invalids and schoolchildren might disagree, for it has been greatly abused.

Distribution Lives on the bottom in mud and sand, and is well distributed in the waters of the North Sea and the North Atlantic. Usually caught in trawl and seine nets, and marketed as fresh fish on ice. Some are caught with hook and line.

Availability Widely available, although the best plaice in the land come from Lowestoft, Suffolk.
In season: all year round.

Guidelines Plaice is an unmistakable flatfish which can vary a great deal in size. Its upper side is a warm brown colour with familiar bright orange spots; the underside is white. Plaice can be bought whole or as fillets; whole fish have the best flavour, and as a general rule, larger specimens are tastier than small ones. If you buy plaice fillets remember that fillets from the dark-skinned top-side are thicker and meatier than those from underneath.

AVOID frozen plaice fillets, especially those that have been breadcrumbed. There's no reason for buying frozen when fresh is so abundant; the fish is tasteless and the commercial breadcrumbs – as orange as the spots on the skin – are particularly unpleasant.

Cookery   Large plaice are best baked whole in foil; smaller ones can be poached or grilled. Fresh plaice can also be delicious in the hands of a skilful fish-fryer.

Red Mullet

The Romans were obsessed with the red mullet and valued it above all other fish. It was also a creature of distinction in Georgian and Victorian England, when it was common and plentiful. On one celebrated night in August 1819, 5,000 red mullet were caught off Weymouth Bay in Dorset, and it's said that the sea was as pink as a sunset.

Distribution   By nature the red mullet is a Mediterranean fish, but in summer it migrates to the waters off southern England, where it is caught in small numbers.

Availability   Fresh red mullet is quite rare in England; most of what we see on fishmongers' slabs comes frozen from abroad. Almost all of the fresh catch is sold locally in south coast ports like Weymouth.
   In season: May – September.

Guidelines   Not related to the grey mullet. Red mullet is actually pink, although its 'redness' is enhanced if its scales have been rubbed off and the skin is tinged with blood.
   Red mullet can also be mistaken for the red gurnard, although this is a much more angular, spiny fish with a tapered body and a pale, rose-coloured hue.
   Most red mullet sold in the shops weigh about 6 oz and are easily recognised by their colour, their twin beard-like barbels and the occasional yellow stripes along their flanks. They can be delicious, although they do tend to be rather dry and their bones can be troublesome. The liver of the red mullet has been prized since Roman times and is best cooked inside the fish.

Cookery   Can be grilled on a bed of fennel, fried or baked whole with herbs and butter. Small red mullet are also useful additions to fish soups of various kinds.

Follow the NACNE Guidelines:
Eat less fat, salt and sugar,
eat more fibre, fresh fruit, vegetables and fish.

Skate

People either love or loathe skate. For years it has had a rock-bottom reputation, partly because it looks strange (isn't there something faintly suspicious about those curious triangles of flesh on the fish slab?), and partly because it has a lingering smell of ammonia, even when really fresh. Fortunately we are now beginning to overcome our prejudices about this excellent fish.

Distribution   Found in waters all round the coast of Britain and generally caught on long lines.

Availability   Common in fishmonger's shops throughout the land.
In season: October – April.

Guidelines   We see only the wings of the skate on display; the complete creature belongs to the world of underwater nature films and science fiction, with its flattened kite-shaped body heavy accentuated tail, tough thorny skin and pointed nose.

It's a relative of the dogfish and the shark, which means that it doesn't have bones, only a soft cartilaginous skeleton. This is an obvious advantage when it comes to eating skate, because the long ribbons of delicate white flesh can be lifted from the fabric of cartilage holding them together.

When buying skate don't be put off by the odd ammonia smell, which might suggest that it isn't fresh. In fact it is always present, but miraculously disappears during cooking. More important, the fleshy wings should be firm and thick, and the flesh itself should have a pinkish tinge. The rough skin is torn off before cooking (this is a tougher job than it sounds).

Skate 'nobs', little nuggets of flesh from the tail are sometimes sold, and have a following in the north-west of England.

Cookery   The wings can be gently fried in oil or butter, or cut into strips, dipped in batter and deep-fried. Skate can be poached and served with butter cooked till it is nutty brown or with a garnish of capers. And it is delicious eaten cold as part of a salad.

Sprat

This diminutive relation of the herring makes excellent eating if really fresh, and like the herring it's highly nutritious. The fish are caught in huge numbers; they are cheap and very good value.

Distribution   Occur in waters all round Britain and are particulary abundant in the North Sea. Usually caught with trawls or seine nets.

Availability   Very common and sold in many parts of the country. However the finest are those procured straight from the fishing boats in East Coast towns like Southwold and Aldeburgh.
   In season: October – March.

Guidelines   Sprats belong to the same family as the herring and the pilchard, and look at first glance like small versions of both these fish. They are plump, silvery creatures with bluish-green backs and can be up to 5 inches long.
   They should be bought as fresh as possible, while they are still bright-eyed and glinting. Sprats that look limp, tired or damaged don't make very interesting eating.
   Like the herring, sprats are rich in protein, unsaturated fat, vitamins and minerals, and are a very cheap source of good nourishment.

Cookery   Small fish can be cooked whole without gutting, complete with head and tail. Grill them quickly or dip them in batter and deep-fry them. Larger fish can be cleaned through the gills; don't split them along the belly otherwise they tend to disintegrate. They can also be pickled and soused.

Smoked sprats see page 166

Turbot

Ranks with the Dover sole as the most princely of all flatfish, and is now sold at a price which reflects its elevated status. In Victorian times, before the invention of cooking foil and other useful culinary devices, turbot was cooked in huge diamond-shaped copper kettles, which were the only pans large enough to contain this often massive creature.

Distribution   An inshore fish living in waters from the Mediterranean to Norway. The main fishery is from the sandbanks of the North Sea.

Availability   By no means common. Most of the catch goes to restaurants, although smaller fish do find their way into the shops.
   In season: all year round; best March – September.

Guidelines   Turbot are very broad, some are almost circular in shape, they are thick, fleshy and have a mottled brown back which has little bony protrusions or 'tubercles', but no scales. Massive specimens weighing 20 lbs or more are occasionally caught, although most are 5-10 lbs. Small turbot weighing only about 2 or 3 lbs are known as 'chicken turbot'.

Large turbot are usually sold cut into thick steaks of manageable size, although you can usually order a whole fish for a special occasion. And small chicken turbot can always be bought whole and are just the right size for a family of four.

Cookery Turbot is always best cooked on the bone in the largest possible piece. It can be poached, grilled or wrapped in foil and baked, and should be served with simple accompaniments like a herb butter.

Turbot can also be filleted and served up with delicate sauces rather like sole.

Always keep turbot bones; they make rich gelatinous stock.

Brill a smaller, more slender relation of the turbot, is much in demand these days. It can easily be distinguished from the turbot because its' back is covered with scales, rather than bony tubercles. It can't match the turbot for flavour, although it can be delicious and seems to have found favour with restaurant chefs who stuff the fillets and serve them with watercress or leek sauces and purées.

Whitebait

Whitebait isn't actually a species of fish at all, but the collective name for tiny fry of the herring and sprat. Shoals of them were once caught in the Thames, around Blackwall, and great Whitebait Dinners were held regularly at Greenwich to the delight of 18th and 19th-century politicians who attended them.

Nowadays, the only reminder of the hey-day of whitebait is the annual Whitebait Festival held every September at Thorpe Bay Yacht Club, Southend, Essex; here the catch is landed, blessed and then summarily eaten.

Distribution Where there are herrings and sprats, you will also find whitebait, especially in the estuary around the North Sea.

Availability There's less whitebait around than there used to be, and most of the catch now appears as frozen blocks or bags, destined for restaurants. The deliberate landing of small herring and sprats in such numbers can't be good for the health of the fishery and the conservation stocks.

In season: all year round; best February – July.

Guidelines: It's been observed that whitebait seem to be getting larger every day, and it's true that the catch is now a very mixed bag, often including a lot of small *adult* sprats. If they are sold fresh, they should have all the qualities of the herring and the sprat.

Cookery   There's really only one way to deal with whitebait. Shake them in a bag of flour and deep-fry them till they are crisp and golden-brown. (The whole fish is eaten, so the bones provide useful amounts of calcium).

Whiting

Think of whiting and you imagine a fish with its tail stuffed awkwardly in its mouth. This curious Victorian device was probably nothing more than a piece of showmanship; it certainly added nothing to the quality or flavour of the fish.

Distribution   Found in waters all round Britain, although the majority are caught in the North Sea. They often live in shallow water and can be caught by inshore fishermen with a rod and line.

Availability   Very common. It goes without saying that the best and freshest are sold close to where they are caught.
   In season: all year round; best November–February.

Guidelines   Whiting is a relative of the cod, but has much softer, more delicate flesh. Its a long, compact fish with a greyish or olive-green back and white flanks. Most whiting are 8–12 inches long and weigh under a pound.
   Provided the fish is very fresh it can have an excellent flavour, but it quickly tires and goes stale, and there's nothing more insipid or boring than a stale whiting. The flesh should be flaky, milky white and soft.
   Can be bought whole or filleted. Frozen whiting is completely tasteless.

Cookery   Fresh whiting can be served in many ways, and responds well to poaching, baking and steaming. It can also be split open and grilled, and the flesh is useful for making stuffings.
   Very small, whole whiting can also be deep-fried in batter.

Look hard at labels and packaging. Learn the language and learn to read between the lines.

Freshwater fish

Carp

Related to the ornamental goldfish, tench and bream, the carp was introduced into England from Asia as early as the 14th century, and was the prize fish of the 'stews' or fish ponds that were a feature of almost every monastery in the Middle Ages.

Distribution Lives in slow-moving or stagnant ponds and rivers with a muddy bottom and dense vegetation.

Availability Most are landed by anglers and never reach the shops. Some are imported and there are one or two places where the fish is farmed.

Guidelines Noted for its size and its habit of living to a great age, (some reach 40). Wild river carp tend to be more slender in build than farmed specimens, which are often high-backed and humped in appearance. There are a great many varieties ranging from the scaled or 'king carps' to the 'mirror carps' which have irregular mirror-like scales of different sizes and the 'leather carps', which have hardly any scales at all.

Most carp offered for sale are farmed mirror carp sold when they are about 3 years old and weigh around 3 lbs. They should look bright, firm and lively.

Cookery The flesh of the carp is firm and sweet and the bones are easy to deal with. Needs to be cleaned well and soaked in vinegar before cooking. Can be poached, fried or grilled. Also stuffed with chestnuts and accompanied by all kinds of fruit.

The roe is considered a delicacy.

Char

The least known and least common members of the salmon family, although char pies and potted char packed into hand-painted delftware dishes were the delight of 18th-century tourists and travellers to the Lake District.

Distribution Confined to deep inland lakes in England, Scotland and Ireland. Most common in Lake Windermere,

Cumbria, where they are caught by fishermen using weighted lines with custom-built spinners attached to lure the fish.

Availability Still very localised. Most are sold in Lakeland fish shops or used by local restaurants.
In season: best May – September.

Guidelines The char is a handsome creature, looking rather like a trout, 10–12 inches long, with a dark green-brown back fading into silver and orange or deep red on the belly. Its flesh is creamy-white with sometimes a pinkish tinge to remind you that it is a relative of the salmon.

If you are lucky enough to find char for sale, the chances are that it has been freshly caught. It should appear firm, and should gleam on the fishmonger's slab.

Cookery Can be treated in any way like salmon or trout. Potted char, a buttery paste, is the speciality of one or two Lakeland restaurants such as Rothay Manor, Ambleside, and Tullythwaite House, Underbarrow, near Kendal.

Eel

Eels are mysterious creatures with extraordinary life histories which begin and end deep in the Sargasso Sea, although much of their life is spent in freshwater and this is where they are usually caught. Tiny young eels, known as elvers, are netted in the spring along the Severn estuary in Gloucestershire.

Distribution Eels spawn in the Sargasso Sea and finally reach the British coast after a three-year trip. They live in shallow brackish water, rivers and streams all round Britain.

Availability Young elvers are caught in the spring and sold in market towns along the River Severn, especially Gloucester. Mature eels are commonly sold in London as well as other parts of the country.
In season: all year round.

Guidelines Tiny elvers, looking like masses of thread-like transparent spaghetti, are a Severnside delicacy. You may need to take a sack or even an old pillow case with you when you buy them straight from the bucket. Most elvers are not eaten in this country, but are exported by the ton to Japan, where they are bred into full-sized eels. This has caused something of an elver crisis and the Severn River Authority is anxious to control catches.

Mature eels, long snake-like creatures, vary in colour depending on their age. Young ones are yellow and these are not really worth eating. Later, as they grow older, they turn dark-brown or black, with bright silver flanks and belly. These are the best eels of all and are caught in vast numbers before they embark on their journey back to the spawning grounds of the Sargasso Sea.

Female eels are larger and fatter than males and can reach up to 3 ft long, although this is exceptional in Britain. Most are half that size. They are often sold live from special tanks or trays, particularly in specialist eel shops like Cooke's of Kingsland Road in East London.

Eels are meaty and very nourishing although they can be quite rich due to the layer of fat just beneath the skin.

Cookery Eel is a versatile fish: it can be cut into chunks and fried, stuffed or poached; it can be made into stews and nourishing soups, while for lovers of traditional English fare there are always eel pies and jellied eels (poached, set in delicious jelly and sold in little pots).

Smoked eel see page 163

Perch

A 'daynteous and holsom' fish, better known to anglers than to cooks. Those who know their fish rate it as highly as the best trout and it is starting to appear on restaurant menus in this country. Even so, it is a rarity in most fishmonger's shops. Perhaps the time has come to add it to our list of available fish.

Distribution Usually found in lowland lakes, ponds and some rivers. Likes well-oxygenated water.

Availability Commonly caught, but rarely sold.
In season: all year round; best June – December.

Guidelines There are many species of perch, both fresh and saltwater kinds. The common freshwater perch is the most familiar to British fishermen, and is easily recognised by its erect, spiny front dorsal fin and vivid orange tail and pectoral fins. The spines and fins can give you a nasty prick if you are not careful.

The fish needs to be scaled as soon as it is caught and also needs thorough cleaning.

Cookery Treat like trout. Can be poached whole or filleted and turned into fritters. Large fish can be stuffed and baked.

> *Remember that real food means making better use of our skills and resources.*

Pike

When did you last see a pike for sale in a shop? Large numbers are caught in British waters every year and yet they never seem to reach the fishmonger's slab. Like perch they are undervalued and deserve more exposure.

Distribution Common in lakes and slow-flowing rivers, except where the water is very acid or low in oxygen. Tends to lurk in vegetation near the bank, waiting for its prey.

Availability A fish for restaurant menus, but almost impossible to track down in shops. Get to know an angler if you want to eat pike.
  In season: August – February.

Guidelines The pike has been called tyrannical and it's certainly a voracious predator feared by many inhabitants of lakes and rivers (including its own kind). It has a long, muscular body varying in colour from yellow to green, and a distinctive broad snout with powerful jaws. Pike can be enormous, up to 70 lbs in mainland Europe, although the biggest British fish are a good deal smaller than that. The largest pike are always females.
  If you do manage to find a pike, it will need to be well cleaned before cooking.

Cookery Pike recipes seem to have declined in number since the days of Izaak Walton, author of *The Compleat Angler*. Pike was obviously one of his favourite fish and he recommended stuffing it with an elaborate mixture of herbs, spices, oysters, anchovies and a pound of butter! Pike is the classic fish for French *quenelles* or delicate fish dumplings (although the word dumplings probably gives the wrong impression), and the fish can be poached or braised in stock and white wine.

Trout

Once a rare delight, trout is now very common and relatively cheap. The reason for this is the boom in trout-farming which has completely changed our attitudes to this excellent fish.
  It's important to make a distinction between the native wild brown trout and the ubiquitous rainbow trout. The latter was introduced to European fish farms in the 1880s and is now by far the most common farmed trout. There are also a number of cross-bred species and hybrids appearing in British waters.

Distribution Native brown tout live sheltered sedentary lives in many British rivers from Hampshire to the north of Scotland. Increasingly, farmed rainbow trout are being introduced into angling rivers to satisfy the needs of the fisherman. A large number of trout also come direct from trout farms.

Availability Thanks to fish farming, trout is now widely available. Wild trout, on the other hand, is much harder to find and is rarely sold in shops.

In season: March – September.

Guidelines The vast majority of trout sold in fishmonger's shops are now farmed rainbow trout, which are easy to recognise because they have a broad purple band along their flanks. Most rainbow trout are quite small, about 6 ounces in weight, whereas wild brown trout can reach 2–3 lbs.

The finest trout of all are those that are freshly caught and cooked within the hour. Compared with these exquisite fish, the products of the trout farm can seem very ordinary and even insipid. The great problem with all farmed trout is their artificial diet and the fact that they are forced to grow unnaturally fast (a farmed trout can reach 8–12 ounces within a year). The diet itself consists entirely of fish meal, often with antibiotics added to it.

There's now a fashion for so-called 'pink trout' which is baffling to say the least. The natural colour of trout flesh is white, but more and more farmers are adding colouring to the fish meal which causes the flesh to turn pink. It makes no difference at all to the flavour and presumably only serves to make the customer think he is eating salmon! However there seems to be a move back towards natural, unadulterated fish, and a few shops now only sell 'white' trout.

Fortunately not all farmed trout are dull. I'm thinking particularly of the fine fish that are released into Rutland Water, a vast man-made reservoir in the county once known as Rutland but now part of Leicestershire. These trout are allowed to feed and grow at their own pace for two years and the results are superb. Specimens weighing 3 lbs are not uncommon and, to my mind, they can almost rival the best salmon trout.

Always keep your eyes open for wild trout. Fishmongers who do sell them are happy to advertise the fact, if only to explain and justify the high price you may have to pay for them. All fresh trout, whether farmed or wild, should look as if they have come straight from the water and should still have a coating of slippery slime.

Cookery A fine fresh trout will respond well to baking in foil, grilling, frying or poaching in stock and white wine. Farmed trout (including frozen ones) can be brightened up with rich flavoursome sauces. The flesh will be firm, sweet-tasting and will part easily from the bone.

Smoked trout see page 166–67.

Salmon

Rightly called the king of fishes, the salmon is majestic, powerful, beautiful, but is at the mercy of man's thoughtlessness. Wild Atlantic salmon (*Salmo salar*) is born in freshwater, lives much of its life at sea, returning again to freshwater and the river of its birth, to spawn or be caught. Spent salmon, exhausted and out of condition after spawning, may die in the rivers or struggle feebly back towards the sea. All of this requires free access and many salmon are now prevented from getting to their spawning grounds by dams and irrigation systems. The fish can only live in the purest water, and increasing pollution has made more and more of our rivers out of bounds to wild salmon. The appearance and disappearance of the fish is a good indicator of the state of a river, so the much-publicised salmon landed in the Thames in 1983 may be a hopeful sign. In general, though, the outlook for wild salmon is bleak.

Distribution   Many British rivers have a reputation for salmon: the Severn, the Wye and the Avon in England, also the Solway Firth and the Tay in Scotland. The finest and freshest are locally caught.

Availability   Seasonal wild salmon is an expensive luxury, but there are increasing supplies of cheaper farmed salmon coming onto the market.
  In season: England and Wales, March – October; Scotland, February – October; Ireland, January – September.

Guidelines   A salmon in top condition should be steely blue on its back and sides, silver on its belly and have round black dots on its head and back. Huge fish weighing up to 60 lbs are occasionally landed, but the most common and useful are those between 3–10 lbs.
  The best wild salmon is expensive and far less common that it used to be. However it is unbeatable in simple dishes where the full flavour of the fish needs to come through. By contrast farmed salmon can be rather dry and bland, although it is a good deal cheaper.
  Wild salmon live on shrimps and similar creatures, from which they absorb carotenoid pigments which turn their flesh pink. Farmed salmon are fed an artificial diet and would be white-fleshed unless colouring was added to their food. It is

claimed that shoppers would not accept white salmon even if they knew how it came to be white.

There's no difficulty in distinguishing between wild and farmed salmon. Fishmongers normally label each type, and in any case the relative price per pound should be sufficient to tell you where the salmon has come from. Which kind you choose to buy will depend on your purse and on the way you want to deal with the fish. It is pointless paying vast sums for the best wild salmon, only to turn it into a pâté or mousse.

You can buy salmon whole or cut into steaks, depending on the size of the fish. Also don't neglect the tail piece, which may have more bones than other cuts, but will be cheaper and is normally delicious.

Frozen Canadian salmon, which are actually species of *Oncorhynchus* the Pacific salmon, are sold throughout the year and do have their uses in prepared dishes, although they can't compare with fresh wild Atlantic salmon when cooked.

Cookery If salmon does have a fault it's a tendency to become dry when it is cooked. The best salmon should be poached in wine or stock, or baked in foil and served with piquant or sharp sauces of cucumber or sorrel. It is superb cold with mayonnaise and new potatoes. Cheaper cuts or frozen fish can be used for quiches, omelettes, soufflés, mousses and pâtés.

Smoked salmon see page 164–65.

Salmon trout (Sea trout)

Salmo trutta, the sea-going version of the native brown trout of British rivers, is a migratory fish that spends much of its life at sea, but comes into freshwater to spawn and this is where it is normally caught. It is a fine fish – perhaps the finest of all – combining all the virtues of both salmon *and* trout.

Distribution Common around many parts of the British coast, especially in South Wales, north-east England and Scotland.

Availability Increasingly common and much sought after. Like, salmon, the best are caught and sold locally.

In season: March – August.

Guidelines Similar to salmon in many ways. Sold either as sea trout or salmon trout; in Wales it is called 'sewin'.

Salmon trout normally weigh no more than 4 lbs, although bigger fish are occasionally caught. So they are perfect for buying and cooking whole. The flesh is pink – slightly lighter than that of the salmon – and it is firm and wonderfully succulent. It doesn't have salmon's tendency to dry out. It is marvellous in every way; I think no fish can match it for flavour or quality.

Cookery Treat like salmon. Look out for smoked salmon trout, cured like smoked salmon.

Smoked fish

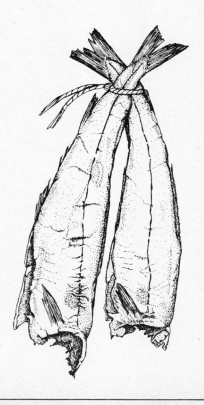

Fish-smoking is an ancient craft. The nomadic hunters and fishermen of neolithic times discovered that their catch would keep longer if hung up to dry in the open air, and soon found that they could achieve even better results by allowing the fish to cure over the smoke of an open fire. Smoking took less time than drying and it produced something that tasted rather unusual, although flavour wasn't as important as the valuable preservative effect.

For centuries the only people who ate fresh fish were those who lived along the coast. To transport highly perishable food inland was a slow and risky business with primitive vehicles and unmade roads, so to prevent the fish from going off it was always preserved, either by pickling in barrels or by smoking.

It wasn't until the 19th century when transport, roads and railways improved during the Industrial Revolution that fresh fish could be moved from place to place without it deteriorating. As a result the very strong, heavy cures which could preserve fish for months were no longer needed and milder cures were developed. Gradually smoking was used for flavour and texture rather than simply for preserving.

Today we produce some of the finest smoked fish in the world, and the range is enormous. Some, like kippers and Finnan haddock are split open, others such as bloaters and Arbroath smokies are whole fish; there are sides of smoked salmon, long strips of smoked eel as well as cod, sprats, trout and mackerel. Fish curers also turn their hand to other fish such as whiting and halibut, while from abroad there's smoked sturgeon and tuna.

Hot and cold smoking   Once the fish have been prepared – gutted, filleted or split – they are always put into brine or rubbed with dry salt. Then they are usually hung up to drip and dry before being smoked over wood chips and sawdust.

Most British smoked fish are 'cold-smoked'. In this case the temperature of the smoke doesn't rise above 85°F, and the flesh of the fish remains raw although it is impregnated with the smoke and dries out during the process. Kippers, Finnan haddock and smoked salmon are all cold-smoked.

Hot-smoked fish, such as trout, eel and Arbroath smokies are cured over hot fires. The temperature rises to around 180°F and as a result the flesh of the fish cooks as well as being flavoured by the smoke.

Real smoked fish should be cured using wood chips and sawdust which are allowed to smoulder. Hard woods like oak, beech, elm, and apple produce the best results; soft woods from coniferous trees contain resins which produce a bitter taste and coat the fish with a film of tar. However some commercial fish curers who are producing enormous amounts of smoked fish may make use of smoke solutions and dips which can create a kind of smoky flavour without actually using wood smoke at all. These manufacturers have no place in this book.

Dyeing fish 'There are manufacturers who injure the smoking business by manufacturing smoked herring which have not been near smoke, by curing the herring with a specially prepared yellowish-brown varnish or oil which imparts to the herring a little of a smoky flavour.' This complaint comes from an American fisheries report of 1884, although it might well sum up the situation today.

All the early dyes were natural in origin, the main one being annato, an orange-yellow substance obtained from the tropical plant *Bixa orellana*, although in recent years synthetic chemicals have taken over. Fish curers now use two in particular: tartrazine, a yellow dye used for colouring white fish such as cod, haddock and whiting, and Brown FK which gives kippers their reddish-brown hue.

There are two reasons why fish curers use dyes. First of all it's a disguise, used to cover up short-cuts in the curing process. By using a dye, in conjunction with a smoke dip, it's possible to create the illusion of a smoked fish without any of the time, patience and skill required to produce the real thing.

Secondly, curers claim that customers actually prefer fish that have been dyed and maintain that people are suspicious of, say, the light colour of undyed kippers, because they think that the fish has *not* been properly cured! Nowadays more people are rightly demanding undyed, properly smoked fish because they actually taste better than the false 'painted ladies' produced by some manufacturers.

Arbroath smokie

These hot-smoked haddock or 'pinwiddies' didn't originate in Arbroath, but in the nearby hamlet of Auchmithie on the road to Montrose. In the beginning they were smoked in cottage chimneys over peat fires but, by the 19th century, fishermen had devised another method. They cut old whisky barrels in two for the kiln, filled a kettle with chips from local birch trees to produce the smoke and covered the lot with a piece of canvas. It was a highly effective use of local raw materials. When some of the villagers moved to Arbroath they took their trade with them, and the fish became known as Arbroath smokies.

Preparation The fish are beheaded, gutted and salted, then tied in pairs by the tail with rope and hot-smoked so that the flesh is cooked during the curing process.

Availability One of the less common types of smoked fish, mainly produced and sold in Scotland by curers like R. R. Spink and Sons from Arbroath itself. But they do find their way into English fish shops.

Guidelines Smokies are instantly recognisable because they are always sold in pairs tied at the tail. They are headless but otherwise whole and unsplit, and the skins are the colour of burnished copper. Small haddock are used and each normally weighs no more than 8 oz. When the skin is peeled off the flesh should be white, moist and deliciously sweet, with a mild smoky flavour.

Cookery Ideal smeared with butter and warmed under the grill, to make a perfect dish for high tea or breakfast. They can be baked with cheese and tomatoes, and are delicious served cold.

Bloater

The word 'bloater' comes from the Norse *blautr*, meaning soft or plump, and 'bloated herrings' are mentioned in the plays of Shakespeare and Ben Jonson. By the 19th century bloaters were big business and it was estimated that Billingsgate alone was handling more than a quarter of a million baskets of 160 fish each year. Those days are gone and the trade is now much more limited, although bloaters are still worth looking out for.

Preparation Whole, ungutted herrings are salted or left in brine overnight. Then they are threaded on rods which are passed through the mouth and out through one of the gills, and gently smoked over smouldering oak sawdust for about 12 hours.

Availability Bloaters belong, first and foremost, to Great Yarmouth, Norfolk, and the finest still come from there. A small number of fish curers in other parts of the country also produce them.

Guidelines Good bloaters should be plump and silvery with just a hint of smoky sheen to them. You may see rows of them hanging up on rods direct from the smokehouse; these are the best to buy since they are likely to be the freshest. Because the fish are ungutted they have a very distinctive gamey taste which, together with the mild curing, makes them quite unlike other kinds of smoked fish.

Because they are mildly cured, bloaters will only keep well for a few days and are best eaten within 24 hours.

Cookery The best and simplest way to cook bloaters is to grill them and they are splendid eaten with scrambled eggs and a mug of tea. They can also be wrapped in foil and baked in the oven or filleted and used raw in salads.

Kipper

In 1843, John Woodger, a fish curer from Seahouses in Northumberland began to experiment with a new way of smoking herrings: he split the fish down the backbone, gutted them, soaked them in brine and then smoked them over oak sawdust. He had invented kippers, and these aristocrats are now the most popular and best known of all smoked fish. In Britain we now eat something like 2,800 tons of kippers each year, and spend £5½ million on them.

Preparation The best kippers are still prepared as John Woodger intended, although they are milder than their predecessors. Herrings with a high fat content are preferred by the curers, and they are split down the back, gutted and then put into brine for about 30 minutes. After that they are pinned up on 'tenter hooks' to dry before being cold-smoked for about 12 hours.

Availability There are four main centres for kippers: in Northumberland, around Seahouses and Craster, along the west coast of Scotland around Loch Fyne, on the Isle of Man and, to a lesser extent, in Great Yarmouth and Lowestoft.

Guidelines Good kippers should be plump, fatty and a bright pale golden colour. Don't be put off if the colouring is a little uneven, because that is a sure sign that the fish have not been dyed. It is illegal to dye kippers in the Isle of Man, but in other parts of Britain some curers may use this device to disguise poor smoking or short cuts in the curing process. Even in Craster, near the birthplace of the kipper, controversy still rages and it still divides the trade. (See page 157). You can always tell a dyed kipper by its dark mahogany colour and by the evenness of the dye.

Good kippers should also have a mild smoky flavour and should look oily. If the kipper you buy had all these attributes it will eat well.

Kippers vary a great deal in size, depending where they were prepared. Manx kippers, which are always made during the summer months, are small and delicately flavoured, and to my mind they are the finest of all. In contrast Loch Fyne kippers made from big Norwegian herring can be huge and very rich.

AVOID bony kipper fillets, which often come in frozen blocks. They are usually very salty and coarse in flavour. Even worse are canned kippers soaked in tomato sauce. And as a rule you should seek out undyed kippers because they have the best flavour.

Cookery Can be cooked by grilling, frying, 'jugging' (steeping in a jug of boiling water) or baking. Raw kippers can be filleted and marinaded for salads, and they also make a superb pâté.

Finnan Haddock

Finnan haddock get their name from Findon, a village a few miles south of Aberdeen where, in the 1820s, fishermen established a thriving business, smoking haddock over peat. However, it wasn't long before supplies were exhausted and special smokehouses were built and wood was used as a fuel. Gradually the curing process became more and more mild, until today, when Finnan haddocks are one of the most delicately flavoured of all smoked fish.

Preparation The fish are beheaded and split open along the abdomen, but the backbone is left in. They are soaked in brine then hung up to smoke. The process is one of cold-smoking, so the fish are cured but the flesh doesn't cook, and they are ready when they are pale straw-coloured.

Availability One of the most famous of all smoked fish which long ago ventured across the border into England. They are well-known in London, indeed some of the best smoked haddocks of all now come from Steve Hatt's shop and smokehouse in Islington.

Guidelines Easy to recognise. Look for the shape of the fish, fanned out like a lemon-coloured triangle; also notice the way it is split. In fact there are two methods: in the so-called Aberdeen cut the fish is split from head to tail so that the backbone lies on the right. But these days – perversely – it is more common to see the London cut, in which the backbone lies on the left and an extra cut is made along the side of the backbone so that the fish stands up and away from it. The flesh beneath the backbone is the most sweet and delicious of all.

The haddocks should be pale lemon colour, rather than dark brown. If they are brown they have probably been too heavily cured and will be dry, tough and salty. True Finnan haddocks are never coloured with dye.

Don't confuse Finnan haddock with smoked haddock fillets (often called golden cutlets). These are very small split fish with the backbone removed so they appear as double fillets. Choose one that is very pale in colour and quite thick and fleshy, otherwise it may taste of little but salt.

Cookery Finnan haddock are always cooked before being eaten, unlike, say, smoked salmon. Poached in milk with a little butter, it makes a splendid breakfast dish, and topped with a poached egg it is even better. A thick soup of Finnan haddock called 'cullen skink' is a traditional Scottish speciality from the Moray Firth. It also goes into kedgeree – that Indian colonial dish of fish, rice and curry spices.

Red herring

The forerunner of the bloater and the kipper, produced by heavily salting and heavily smoking whole herrings. 'Reds' were the staple diet of rich and poor from the Middle Ages right up to the 19th century, when better transportation and changing tastes turned them into an anachronism. The heavy curing was no longer necessary to preserve the fish on long slow journeys inland, and people were beginning to appreciate the milder flavour of bloaters and the newly invented kipper.

Preparation   Originally the herrings were salted for up to six days, then washed and strung on 'spits' or rods before being loaded into the smokehouse. There they stayed for up to a fortnight.

Availability   Red herrings were best known in East Anglia, and the ports of Great Yarmouth and Lowestoft once vied for the title of red herring capital. Few are sold nowadays although the firm of Suttons in Great Yarmouth still makes them for export and local fish curers occasionally produce their own versions.

Guidelines   Today's red herrings are dry and salty, but are nothing compared with their predecessors. They are a golden rather than red in colour, the skins look tough and the flesh is quite strongly flavoured.

Cookery   Soak them first if you want them less salty. Then they can be grilled or eaten cold. If the herring has roe, this can be used as a kind of relish spread on toast.

Smoked cod

Enormous fillets of bright-yellow or orange cod are given far too much prominence on fishmongers stalls, and are generally not worth buying.

Preparation   The fillets are dipped in brine to which the yellow dye tartrazine has been added. This gives the fish its gaudy colour and if the dye has been used carelessly the fish comes out almost orange. It may be smoked, although much of what passed for smoked cod is simply dipped into a solution which can give the fish the impression of a smoky flavour. But it's a very poor impression. Having said that there are a few fish curers who produce authentic smoked cod, but it's hardly the most outstanding of smoked fish.

Availability Mock smoked cod is widely available; every fishmonger seems to sell it and people still buy it. Real smoked cod is harder to find.

Guidelines Make enquiries, and find out if the fish has been smoked on the premises. If it has, the chances are that it will be the real thing. If not, and it looks as if it has been frozen as well, don't waste your money on it. These dyed fillets are tough, stringy and dreadfully salty.

AVOID smoked cod that looks artificial and unnaturally colourful: it has been dyed (a sure sign is the way the colour permeates right through the flesh).

Cookery Smoked cod doesn't have a very distinguished flavour at the best of times, but is useful for fish pies and the like.

Smoked cod's roe

For hundreds of years cod roes were salted on board ship and used as imitations of caviare or botargo (the preserved roe of the grey mullet). Nowadays smoked cod's roe makes a relatively cheap and marvellous food in its own right.

Preparation The roes have to be handled very carefully to ensure they do not burst; they are washed, packed between layers of salt and left for 6–8 hours. Then they are washed again to get rid of all excess salt; and finally they are put into the smokehouse and left for some 12 hours until they are dark red and firm.

Availability Still quite scarce, although most curers and fishmongers who have access to a supply of roes smoke them well.

Guidelines The roes should be dark red on the outside, but not have a charred appearance, and should be pinkish inside. They ought to feel firm too. Little lumps of blackened, shrivelled roe have been badly handled and will not be worth eating.

Cookery The classic use of smoked cod's roe is in the Middle Eastern dip taramasalata, but it is delicious simply cut into slices, seasoned with cayenne pepper and lemon juice and eaten with hunks of wholemeal bread.

Smoked eel

Smoked eel began to appear in the middle of the 19th century; before that if eels were preserved at all, they were usually salted or pickled. The Dutch are the great eel smokers (even their English rivals admit this), yet it is possible to eat the home-smoked variety on its home ground. But eel smokers are a secretive bunch, and catching eels is a closed trade. The men who go out on dark still nights hunting for eels in marshy creeks and dykes in Suffolk and Essex don't talk about their work. And when it comes to smoking the catch, they are improvisers, but skilled and enterprising. One I knew used a section of old drainpipe as his smokehouse, and the results were magnificent.

Preparation The eels are scrubbed and gutted, but left whole; then they are lightly brined, strung on rods passed through the throat and hot-smoked. Techniques tend to vary from place to place.

Availability Should be more widely available. Some of the best comes from East Anglian curers like Michael Rhodes at Cley Smokehouse, Norfolk, or the Butley-Orford Oysterage, Orford, Suffolk, where my very first taste of smoked eel still lingers in the mind.

Guidelines A whole smoked eel, lying like a stiff black rod on the fishmonger's slab, is an impressive sight. If it has been properly smoked the skin should be tough, but not charred, and the flesh inside should be creamy-white, slightly salty, moist and succulent without being mushy. The flesh should part easily from the bone.

Buy a piece of eel and divide the flesh up into fillets or chunks.

AVOID the thin, dried-up strips often left on display for hours at a time; they are tough and not worth eating.

Uses Smoked eel is very rich, so a little goes a long way. Lemon juice or horseradish is a good foil to the fattiness of the fish. Creamy scrambled eggs also do it justice without swamping its flavour, and it can be turned into a smooth pâté.

Smoked mackerel

For hundreds of years the rich fatty flesh of the mackerel was preserved by heavy salting or pickling, but about ten years ago, smoked mackerel burst upon the scene and has never looked back. Vast quantities are produced by some of the big seafood firms, but smoking mackerel is still a trade performed with great skill by West Country fishermen and fish curers.

Preparation The mackerel can be cured either as fillets or as whole fish, which are gutted and beheaded. They are put into brine, hung to dry and then hot-smoked so that the flesh cooks.

Availability One of the most common and popular of all smoked fish, now rivalling the kipper for supremacy. The West Country is the real home of smoked mackerel, where it is produced from locally caught fish. Fishmongers like Jackson's of Newton Abbot, Devon, are renowned for their smoked mackerel.

Guidelines If you are buying hot-smoked mackerel – either a fillet or a whole fish – choose a small one if you want real quality. Large fish tend to be very oily and the flesh becomes unpleasantly mushy. Some smoked mackerel – especially from large firms – is given the dye treatment as well as smoking, and comes out reddish-brown. Peppered mackerel fillets (coated with crushed black peppercorns) are quite popular, although it's not an idea that appeals to me: far too much pepper is used and it swamps the flavour of the fish.

Occasionally you will find cold-smoked mackerel, normally sold as fillets or double-fillets, but hot-smoked is by far the most popular.

Freezing is not good for smoked mackerel.

Cookery Hot-smoked mackerel can be eaten as it is, with lemon juice or horseradish; it can be grilled, or wrapped in foil and baked in the oven; and can be turned into a delicious fish pâté. Cold-smoked mackerel can be eaten raw, like smoked salmon, or warmed under the grill.

Smoked salmon

The Irish were smoking salmon back in neolithic times, judging by remains that have been found on the banks of the River Bann, and over the centuries, salmon curers have refined and perfected their techniques.

The great thing about salmon-smoking today is that each curer has his own way and the results are always subtle and distinctive. And unlike some of our other superb specialities, smoked salmon is widely sold for home-consumption, although a great deal naturally finds its way abroad too.

Preparation   Originally salmon was cured by splitting the fish open down the backbone (a technique later used for making kippers), but nowadays it is always cured as 'sides', which are simply whole fillets. They are rubbed with salt, and other ingredients (anything from sugar or molasses to rum and juniper berries), left for 24 hours, then washed, hung up to dry and finally smoked. In England oak is the most common wood used (gone are the days when wealthy clients insisted on cedar wood); in Scotland birch and juniper have been used, while the Irish have favoured peat. The fish is always cold-smoked.

Availability   Widely available. There are many famous names in the salmon-smoking business, from the Ritchie brothers in Rothesay, Scotland and Pinneys, who now operate from Annan, Dumfriesshire, to Spring's of Edburton, Sussex and Brown's of Fordingbridge, Hampshire; while in the London area, Jarvis & Sons of Kingston-upon-Thames have an enviable reputation.

Guidelines   Wild Atlantic salmon caught in British waters makes the finest smoked salmon of all, but it is, of course, the most expensive too. There is also a good deal of Canadian smoked salmon, as well as smoked salmon prepared from farmed fish. Both of these are cheaper than, say, the best Scotch salmon, but it would be churlish to reject anything except the authentic British wild product. However, once you have tasted the finest that the curers have to offer, you are unlikely to settle for second best, even if you do pay less for it.

Always buy smoked salmon cut in wafer-thin slices from a whole side, rather than pre-sliced pieces which may be dry. (Some pre-packed, pre-sliced smoked salmon is perfectly acceptable too.) The colour should be a delicate pink, rather than orange or red, which suggests that the fish has been dyed or too heavily cured. The flesh should be moist and succulent with a marvellously subtle flavour.

Don't forget to make full use of the off-cuts and scraps left after the prime slices have been carved from the side. These can be bought quite cheaply.

Uses   Sliced smoked salmon needs only a wedge of lemon, some wholemeal bread and unsalted butter. The scraps can be used for pâtés and mousses, chopped and added to omelettes or scrambled eggs and they make a lovely salad with avocado pears.

Smoked sprats

In 1724, Daniel Defoe recorded how he had seen sprats 'being made red' (i.e. smoked like herrings) in the Suffolk port of Southwold, and the tradition of smoking sprats in East Anglia has remained ever since, although it's not the organised trade that it used to be.

Preparation Sprats are cured rather like bloaters, although the process is much quicker because the fish are small and delicate. They are put whole into brine, for about 15 minutes, taken out and strung on thin metal rods or pieces of wire. Then they are allowed to drip, and smoked gently for about 4 hours. In practice this tends to lighly cook the flesh as well as producing the smoky flavour.

Availability Quite widely available, and still produced in East Anglian coastal towns like Aldeburgh, Southwold and Kessingland. If you're lucky you may find them offered as informal feasts in local pubs.

Guidelines Properly smoked sprats should have a light golden colour and moist, firm flesh. If they have been carelessly smoked they will become dry and shrivelled. They are some of the cheapest of all smoked fish, so it's worth buying lots of them and sharing them out generously. They are highly nutritious, tasty little morsels.

Cookery Can be eaten hot or cold. Put them under a very hot grill for a minute or two if you want them hot; otherwise eat them as they are (bone and beheaded them if you wish) with a squeeze of lemon juice and a sprinkling of spicy cayenne pepper.

Smoked trout

More smoked trout are now being sold than ever before, largely because of the productivity of trout farms. In fact many trout farmers are now smoking their own – although with varying degrees of success.

Preparation The fish are gutted and cleaned but left whole. After an hour or so in brine, they are strung up on rods threaded through the eyes or gills, and little pieces of wood are used to keep the belly flaps open. The fish are hot-smoked while still wet to ensure that the flesh does not dry out and harden.

Availability Now one of the best known, popular and widely available of all smoked fish. Produced by large firms, small firms, individual fish curers and fishmongers, as well as trout farmers.

Guidelines It's almost impossible to tell whether the trout you buy is a farmed or wild fish, but to ensure that you are getting a good one, look for plumpness, a golden-brown colour (some trout from large curers have a reddish-brown hue, suggesting that they have been dyed). Most smoked trout weigh about 4–6 oz. When the skin is peeled off the flesh should be creamy-white, firm and succulent, and definitely not dry.

AVOID frozen smoked trout. They seem to suffer even more than other smoked fish from freezing. The flesh becomes soft, mushy and watery. If the fish has been frozen, thawed and put in and out of the refrigerator it will also be ruined.

Cookery Best served cold with salad and a little *creamed* horseradish. (Most horseradish sauce is far too fierce for this delicately flavoured fish.) Smoked trout also makes a marvellous fish mousse and pâté.

Fish curers and suppliers

Most fishmongers provide a selection of smoked as well as fresh fish, but for the pick of the crop it's usually best to seek out a fish curer or a fishmonger with his own smokehouse. Some produce a whole range of different items, while others specialise in, say, kippers or smoked salmon.

General

H. Peck & Son
7 Wednesday Market,
Beverley, Humberside
Tel: (0482) 881582

Michael Rhodes
The Cley Smoke House,
Cley-next-the-Sea,
Norfolk
Tel: (0263) 740282

The Fisheries
129 Watling Street,
Gillingham, Kent
Tel: (0634) 51922

Hart & Son
52a High Street, Hastings,
East Sussex
Tel: (0424) 422273

A. E. Downing & Son
296 Nacton Road, Ipswich,
Suffolk
Tel: (0473) 78575

Hamburger Products
15 Charlotte Place,
London W1

Steve Hatt
88 Essex Road, Islington,
London, N1
Tel: (01) 226 3963

The Butley-Orford
Oysterage
Market Hill, Orford,
Suffolk
Tel: (039 45) 277

Fortune's
20 Henrietta Street,
Whitby, North Yorkshire

Pinney's Smokehouses Ltd
Newpark Farm, Brydekirk,
Annan, Dumfriesshire,
Scotland
Tel: (057 63) 275   M.

The Smokehouse,
Achiltibuie, Highland,
Scotland
Tel: (085 482) 353

G. F. Dimmock,
Carsluith,
Kirkcudbrightshire,
Scotland
Tel: (067 182) 354

Arbroath smokie

R. R. Spink & Sons
Brothock Bridge, Arbroath,
Tayside, Scotland
Tel: (0241) 73246   M.

Bloater

The Bloater Shop
Regent Road,
Great Yarmouth, Norfolk

Raglan Smokehouse
Raglan Street, Lowestoft,
Suffolk
Tel: (0502) 81929

Kipper

L. Robson & Sons
Haven Hill, Craster,
Northumbria
Tel: (066 576) 223   M.

John Curtis
10 Woodbourne Road,
Douglas, Isle of Man
Tel: (0624) 3875

Geo. Devereau & Son Ltd
The Fish Centre,
38 Strand Street, Douglas,
Isle of Man
Tel: (0624) 3257/3258/
6360   M.

T. Moore & Sons Ltd
Mill Road, Peel, Isle of Man
Tel: (062 484) 214

Raglan Smokehouse
Raglan Street, <u>Lowestoft</u>,
Suffolk
Tel: (0502) 81929

The Smokehouse
St Peter's Street, <u>Lowestoft</u>,
Suffolk

Ritchie Brothers
37 Watergate, <u>Rothesay</u>,
Bute, Scotland
Tel: (0700) 3012   M.

Smoked salmon

Springs Smoked Salmon
The Springs, <u>Edburton</u>,
West Sussex
Tel: (079 156) 338
M.   Tel: (079 156) 452

Brown's
High Street, <u>Fordingbridge</u>,
Hampshire
Tel: (0425) 53125

Gardiner's
13 King Street, <u>Hereford</u>,
Hereford & Worcester
Tel: (0432) 4343

A. H. Jarvis & Sons Ltd
56 Coombe Road,
<u>Kingston-upon-Thames</u>,
Surrey
Tel: (01) 546 0989

Ritchie Brothers
37 Watergate, <u>Rothesay</u>,
Bute, Scotland
Tel (0700) 3012   M.

Shellfish

People have been gathering and eating all kinds of shellfish since prehistoric times; indeed they were one of the prime sources of food for generations of coastal dwellers. And what nutritious morsels they were: high in protein, B vitamins and minerals such as sulphur, iron and zinc, with almost not fat at all. It's been estimated that an acre of good mussels could yield 10,000 lbs of meat in a year, which is far more protein at far less cost than a year's beef on good pasture. No wonder our ancestors thought so highly of them.

For culinary purposes there are really two main types of shellfish, the molluscs and the crustacea. Molluscs such as oysters, mussels and cockles are bivalves, living in hinged shells, while others like whelks and winkles inhabit a single shell. Crustacea, which all have a hard, jointed skeleton, include crabs, lobsters, prawns and shrimps among others.

Molluscs   These creatures feed by pumping water through their shells and filtering out plankton. If they happen to live in waters that have become polluted by industrial waste and sewage, they may build up high concentrations of dangerous micro-organisms and chemicals which can cause serious problems to anyone who eats them. So when buying or choosing molluscs, freshness and quality are vitally important.

On a commercial level, the preparation and sale of molluscs is strictly controlled. Some, like cockles, whelks and winkles, are always boiled before being sold which kills off any dangerous micro-organisms. Others such as oysters and mussels are sold raw, but are made safe either by 'relaying' – that is moving the creatures when they are young to a clean place where they can grow – or they can be allowed to clean and purify themselves in special tanks of sterilized sea water. A mussel, for example, can completely rid itself of any dangerous micro-organisms in 48 hours.

Crustacea   These are more complicated creatures which are less likely to be storehouses for dangerous micro-organisms and toxic chemicals. Even so, freshness is the key, and the safest thing to do is to buy, say, a lobster or a crab that has already been boiled (unless you have caught it yourself or are presented with one straight from the sea). Most crustacea are sold already boiled, although some are offered for sale fresh, or kept alive in tanks until needed. Apart from the cruelty of keeping creatures alive out of their natural environment, they can often be in poor condition by the time you come to buy them.

General guidelines   (i) Select and buy any kind of shellfish with care from a reputable fishmonger or local fisherman.
(ii) Avoid molluscs during the summer months. All are slightly out of condition during the breeding season, which

coincides with warm weather and a period when micro-organisms in the sea are at their most virulent. There is some truth in the old adage that you should eat shellfish only when there is an 'R' in the month. Remember that this has more to do with pollution than with any curious characteristic of the shellfish.

(iii) Examine all raw or live shellfish carefully. Throw out any that have damaged shells or are open. Occasionally a shell may appear to gape: if you give it a tap and it snaps shut then it is alive and well. If nothing happens, assume it is dead and throw it away. Avoid shellfish that have suspicious smells. Always throw out any that remain closed after cooking.

(iv) Cooked molluscs such as cockles and whelks should look plump and fresh and have no unpleasant odour.

(v) Cooked crustacea like lobsters and prawns should be intact with no signs of damaged shells or nasty smells. They should be firm and a good red colour. If they look pale and limp they are stale.

(vi) Whether you are buying raw or cooked shellfish, eat it the same day. They deteriorate very quickly and can rapidly become dangerous.

Cockle

One of the best known and popular of all British shellfish, the cockle has been harvested from parts of the British coast for thousands of years, and there's still a thriving cockle industry in England and Wales. Cockles are also one of the easiest shellfish to gather yourself.

Distribution   Live mainly in tidal sandbanks and mudflats, particularly around the mouth of large rivers. The most important areas for cockles are the North Norfolk coast around the Wash, in the Thames estuary around Leigh-on-Sea, Essex, and around the Gower Peninsula in South Wales.

Availability   Very common, widely distributed and not confined to its main fishing areas.
   In season: All year round.

Guidelines   A small mollusc with a rather dumpy, globular shell, heavily ribbed and ranging in colour from pale-brown to slate grey. Usually 2–3 inches across, although monsters are occasionally found. Inside, the meaty part is greyish white with a little yellow 'foot' extending from it.

   Cockles are always sold ready boiled or cooked, out of their shells. Traditionally they are also pickled in vinegar or brine, but this does little for their flavour and makes the cockles hard and rubbery. Pickled cockles shouldn't be used for cooking, as the vinegar imparts much too strong a flavour to any dish. Nowadays, fresh cockles are also individually frozen, which may be convenient but does nothing for the quality of the cockle itself.

Cooked cockles should smell sweet and look appetising, and need to be eaten straight away; pickled cockles will keep well for a week or so in the refrigerator.

Cookery Little dishes of cockles sprinkled with vinegar and seasoned with pepper are a great treat at seaside stalls, and cockles have many uses in the kitchen. They can be put into soups, made into pies or tossed in bacon fat and eaten with crispy bacon. In the past it was also common to stuff them into joints of lamb before roasting.

Crab

According to *The Book of Nurture* (1460), crab is 'a slut to carve and a wrawde wight (perverse creature)'. They have always been fiddly and awkward to prepare, but they are extremely good value, and a really fresh crab eaten at a leisurely pace on a summer's day is one of life's great pleasures.

Distribution The two most famous crab centres in Britain are Cromer on the North Norfolk coast, and Devon and Cornwall, especially ports like Brixham, Devon.

Availability Fresh crab is sold throughout Britain, although the best are those sold from shops and stalls near the fishing centres. Shops like R. Davies of Cromer specialise in crab, and very good it is too.

In season: May – October.

Guidelines There's no mistaking the common edible crab with its hard rigid shell or 'carapace' and heavy claws. Crabs vary in size enormously: Cromer crabs are quite small compared with the gargantuan armour-plated monsters caught in the West Country, but no crab can be sold if it is less than adult size (about 5 inches across) or if it is a female carrying eggs.

Crabs are occasionally sold fresh but it's much more common to see them already boiled. When you buy one there are several points to look for. First there should be no suspect smell. The shell should not be cracked or damaged and the crab should feel heavy for its weight; if it is light or seems as if it is full of water, you shouldn't accept it.

There's something immensely satisfying about the long process of dismembering the crab and extracting the meat.

The white meat comes from the claws in long, moist, succulent fibres; male crabs with bigger claws naturally yield more white meat than females. There is also some white meat in the body and smaller legs. The brown meat is more pasty in texture and can be spooned out from the carapace itself. Don't eat the head part, the stomach and attached organs, or the feathery, greyish 'dead men's fingers' (or gills). As a rough guide about one third of the body weight of the crab is edible meat.

Dressed crab – that is crab prepared with the white and brown meat neatly arranged in the carapace – does have advantages if you are in a hurry, but even when it's fresh and prepared on the spot by the fishmonger, it can quickly dry out and doesn't have the succulence of meat picked fresh from the crab.

Frozen or tinned crabmeat is a waste of time and money.

Cookery   Crab is delicious eaten with a salad or a crisp new loaf, but the meat can be devilled, made into soups and mousses or added to omelettes as well.

Crawfish

Sometimes known as the spiny lobster, this large crustacean is indeed a relative of the true lobster, and certainly rivals it in flavour.

Distribution   Mainly found in waters off south-west England and southern Ireland, where it is caught in pots like lobster.

Availability   Not very common. Most are despatched abroad (principally to France) or sold in local ports where they are landed.

In season: April – September.

Guidelines   There is one obvious difference between a lobster and a crawfish: the crawfish has no claws, only thin, whiplike antennae, which probably accounts for its lack of popularity. However it has as much, if not more, meat in its body and tail than a lobster of the same size.

Can be bought fresh or boiled. If it has been cooked enquire whether it has been freshly prepared, because there are instances of freeze-dried crawfish being thawed out and reconstituted by soaking them in water. In these cases the flesh is tasteless, the price high.

Cookery   Use exactly like lobster.

Crayfish

This delicate little freshwater lobster was once common in rivers and streams in many parts of England, from Kent and Hampshire to Yorkshire, but pollution has all but made it extinct. However, Ken Richards has pioneered techniques of farming crayfish at Riversdale Farm, near Gillingham, Dorset, so there's still an opportunity to taste this beautifully flavoured crustacean.

Distribution Lives by the banks of lakes, ponds and streams and can only survive in clean, well-oxygenated water. It avoids large rivers and doesn't like the cold of mountain streams.

Availability Now very rare and hardly ever seen in fishmonger's shops, but farmed crayfish can be obtained direct from Ken Richards' farm in Dorset.
In season: August – October.

Guidelines Freshwater crayfish are little creatures 3–4 inches long, which are green-brown when alive and red when cooked.

Cookery Serve simply to preserve the exquisite flavour of the flesh. Can also be prepared like lobster.

Lobster

Undoubtedly the most highly prized of all crustacea, the princely lobster now inhabits the world of expense-account eating. To be sure it is expensive, but it's worth bearing in mind that the price only represents the same one might spend on a couple of sirloin steaks, and lobster is as nourishing and rich in protein, without the fat.

Distribution Found in many parts of Britain from waters off the coast of Dorset, Devon and Cornwall, to Northumbria and the northerly outposts of Scotland, as well as Wales and the coast of Ireland. Caught in pots or 'creels', often one at a time; pots in the south are round wickerwork affairs with a hole in the top, while in the north they tend to be rectangular with a frame of hazel or willow covered with nylon netting.

Availability Most lobster is shipped abroad or snapped up by exclusive restaurants. But some does find its way into shops throughout Britain. Local suppliers are the best.
In season: April – October.

Guidelines An impressive creature with massive heavy claws. Live lobsters are dark blue or greenish; they only turn red when they are cooked.

They can be bought live from the tank or the fishmonger's slab or already cooked and ready to eat. It must be said that terrible things are done to lobster in the cause of freshness, profit and so-called good taste, and they often have to endure agony simply to provide customers with the dubious satisfaction of selecting their very own live specimen for the pot. I can't do better than quote Dorothy Hartley, who summed it up with great passion: 'Keeping lobster in huge floating tanks in the sea is permissible, but the claw-tied, mutilated, living creature, with sensitive feelers torn, eyes crushed in and cracked grinding carapace, nailed up in crates, and jolted miles by railroad to be shown, alive and quivering, on the fishmonger's slab, is a disgrace to civilisation. This senseless torture of animals must cease, before clean, wholesome food is safe for human beings to eat.' (*Food in England*, Macdonald 1954). There's no virtue in buying lobsters like this. Apart from anything else they are likely to be in poor condition. A freshly boiled lobster is a much better proposition in every way.

Like crabs, cooked lobsters should look fresh, have no suspicious odours or cracks in their shells and should feel heavy for their weight. Very small lobsters under 1 lb contain very little meat; very large ones, more than 4 lbs, can be coarse and dry. Female lobsters are larger than males, and have the advantage that they may possess a mass of orange-pink eggs or 'coral', which makes a delicious and attractive garnish.

Cookery Plainly cooked lobster, either served cold with mayonnaise and salad, or split open and grilled with butter is probably the best of all, but there are many classic dishes (particularly from French cuisine) like lobster bisque and lobster thermidor.

Mussel

Mussels have been gathered from shores and estuaries around Britain since prehistoric times. Early food-gatherers, who existed on what they could glean from the wild, would eat them raw or roast them on stones heated by bonfires on the shore. Up till the 19th century they were cheap and plentiful, but overfishing soon made them a delicacy, although they have now regained their position and are as abundant as ever.

Distribution Live in coastal waters all round Britain, preferring the intertidal zone. There are very prolific mussel beds of the north Norfolk coast, off the east coast of Scotland

and in south Wales. Kenmare Bay mussels from County Kerry, Ireland are also famous.

Availability   Very common and widely distributed. The best and freshest are always those caught and sold locally.

In season: September – April.

Guidelines   Mussels have familiar dark-blue or blackish shells varying in length from 2–3 inches. They are often encrusted with barnacles and have a protruding bunch of threads or 'beard' that needs to be removed before they are eaten. A lot of mussels these days are sold already cleaned, which saves some time and trouble.

They are nearly always sold fresh or raw, but you need have no worries about their safety, because they will have been cleaned in tanks of sterilised sea water before they are offered for sale. Even so, you should follow the basic rules for shellfish buying and select with care.

Like cockles, mussels are often sold cooked and pickled in vinegar or brine, which only serves to make them harsh and rubbery. Individually-frozen mussels are also becoming quite common, but are indifferent in flavour.

Cookery   Best cooked simply in a large pan with white wine, finely chopped onion and herbs. Can also be used for soup and put into fish pies.

Oyster

The Romans made oysters popular in Britain, and for centuries they were one of the cheapest foods available: in the 15th century they were selling for 4d a bushel when beef was 3½d a lb. They were devoured by rich and poor in such quantities that stocks dwindled and by the 1850s they had become a luxury. Fortunately the first artificial oyster beds were already being prepared, otherwise oysters may have disappeared altogether from British waters.

Distribution   Live on firm ground in shallow coastal waters in many parts of Britain, but the main supplies come from south-east England, especially around Colchester and Whitstable. The River Helford, Cornwall, is also known for its oysters and new beds are being created in Scotland (John Noble's beds on Loch Fyne are making the news at the moment.) There are also oysters off South Wales and Southern Ireland.

Availability   Native British oysters are on the increase again, thanks to research into breeding and farming.

In season: September – April.

Guidelines   Oysters are always sold raw, so the best bet is to get them from a reputable supplier. They must be eaten very fresh, as soon as possible after they have been opened. (If opening oysters causes you problems, leave the task to your fishmonger.)

Don't be put off by the irregular, distorted shape of the oyster's shell or the variations in colour. Both are quite natural.

At the moment you are likely to pay more for home-grown native oysters than for, say, imported Portuguese ones, but it is worth it in terms of freshness and flavour.

Cookery   Oysters are first and foremost raw food, eaten straight from the shell and moistened with a drop or two of lemon juice. Oyster soup is sometimes made and oysters once kept company with steak and kidney in savoury pies.

Prawn

These have rapidly become the most popular and well-known of all shellfish, and they are eaten in vast numbers.

Distribution   Most are caught in deep waters off Norway and Iceland, although a small catch is taken from British waters, especially in the north.

Availability   Very common.
In season: all year round.

Guidelines   Many species appear under the general heading of prawns, the two most common being *Palaemon serratus*, which is the prawn of inshore waters, and *Pandalus borealis*, the northern or deep-water prawn. All species of prawn (and their close relatives the shrimps) are scavengers, combing the waters for any kind of edible debris. In a curious way, this is what makes them so nutritious and full of flavour (think of a free-range chicken).

Prawn are always sold boiled, either whole or peeled. On average there are about 40 whole prawns to a pint (that is how they are sold) and about 110 peeled. Buying peeled prawns is convenient if you want to save time, but there's nothing to beat the fresh flavour of a newly shelled whole prawn.

When buying prawns look for a good pink colour and for firmness of the body and tail. If the prawns look limp, tired and watery they are stale and have probably been hauled in and out of a freezer or refrigerator. Also make sure they are not damaged.

AVOID frozen prawns which, in general, have precious little flavour.

Cookery Prawns have innumerable uses: they are delicious picked straight from the shell, they can be made into curries and spicy oriental dishes, used as garnishes for fish, turned into sauces, soups and paste.

Also look out for smoked prawns.

Also see Shrimp on page 182.

<u>Scallop</u>

The most instantly recognisable of all molluscs because it has a classic shell, whose shape has inspired painters, designers and architects and has even been used to sell oil.

Distribution Scallops are dredged up in vast numbers from sandy seabeds off the Atlantic coast of Britain and in the English Channel.

In season: all year round; best January – June.

Guidelines You will recognise a scallop first of all by its famous shell, which actually has two distinct parts, one curved, the other flat. Fresh scallops are normally displayed in the half shell, so that you can see what you are buying. The scallop itself has a solid meaty adductor muscle with which it opens and closes its shell and propels itself through the water, also an orange female roe and a whitish testis (most scallops are hermaphrodite). These are the parts that are eaten.

Scallops should be bought very fresh, they should look fresh and should smell of the sea. Ones that are damaged, watery or off-colour should be avoided. Frozen scallops are increasingly common, and deep-freezing is one reason why they can be caught and sold right through the year. Like all frozen shellfish, they are disappointing, tasteless and lacking in texture.

The price of scallops is exorbitant. Perhaps if fewer were exported they would become cheaper and more plentiful on British fishmongers slabs.

Cookery Scallops should not be overcooked otherwise they become chewy. They can be gently poached in white wine, grilled on skewers with bacon, or served with a light cheese sauce.

Note: **Queenies**, or queen scallops are smaller and have both shells curved. They live in very deep water off the Isle of Man where they are a great local delicacy. Treat them like scallops.

Scampi

The very word scampi conjures up fearful images of deep-fried nuggets of tasteless fish served with chips in the basket. Which is a pity, because the Dublin Bay prawn (or Norway lobster, to give it its correct name) is one of the finest of all crustacea, and doesn't deserve such treatment.

Distribution   Lives on the sea bottom in waters off the south and west coast of Ireland and around the Scottish coast. Caught mainly in trawls and seine nets.

Availability   Disembodied scampi frozen into little lumps seems to be universal nowadays. It's much rarer to find the whole creature offered for sale, although some local fishmongers in Scotland and Ireland, as well as some enterprising English merchants, do sell it.
   In season: all year round.

Guidelines   First of all the name needs some explanation. Scampi is actually the plural of the Italian name, and it was the Italians who first made this shellfish popular (there's a vast colony in the Adriatic). Dublin Bay prawn derives from the fact that Irish fishing boats coming into Dublin Bay in the 19th century often had these prawns on board, and they were hawked round the city streets.
   It's hard to believe that 30 years ago British fishermen were tossing back any scampi they caught; it's equally hard for many people to believe that scampi is anything other than a piece of white flesh unconnected with any living creature.
   Although the scampi we eat is simply the tail of the Dublin Bay prawn, the whole creature, cooked and pink is a welcome sight when it does appear. Its long straight claws and fanned tail are easily recognised, although the tail holds the meaty prize. (In fact you can extract some flesh from the claws if you crack them open).
   Frozen scampi or, even worse, frozen *breaded* scampi coated in nasty synthetic crumbs, is something very different and will give no pleasure to lovers of real food.

AVOID it.

Cookery   It must be said that the French understand the Dublin Bay prawn better than we do, and have many superb recipes for cooking it. They can be served whole as part of a shellfish celebration with all kinds of fruits of the sea accompanied by sharp mayonnaise tinged with lemon; they can be split open and grilled with garlic butter, served with spicy sauces and used to garnish fish soups and other dishes.

Shrimp

Despite the fact that prawns have stolen the limelight in recent years, the common brown shrimp of British waters is a splendid little creature, very tasty if fresh and excellent for sauces and high teas. They are available all year round. Morcambe Bay was once the site of the great shrimp fishery and potted shrimps form the town still bear witness to the old trade.

Follow guidelines and details for Prawns.

Whelk

The big coiled shell of *Buccinum undatum* is unmistakable, and so is its bizarre-looking edible body.

Distribution   Inhabits deep waters in many parts of Britain, although about 80% of the British catch comes from north Norfolk, around Wells-next-the-sea and Brancaster. The whelks are lured with bait into special iron pots which are shot against the tide.

Availability   Much of the catch finds its way to holiday resorts such as Blackpool, although seafood stalls in many parts of the land sell them.

In season: all year round.

Guidelines   Whelks are always boiled and usually shelled before being sold. A big fresh whelk is a mighty mouthful that should be eaten absolutely fresh otherwise it will be tough. Compared with cockles and winkles their flavour is quite strong and their texture varies from succulent to rubbery.

Cookery   Nowadays whelks have a limited usefulness. They are always eaten with vinegar and brown bread. (Not so in the 16th century, when 4,000 whelks were used to garnish salted sturgeon at the enthronement feast for the Archbishop of Canterbury in 1504!)

> *Enjoy real food. It's one of the greatest pleasures we have.*

Winkle

A tiny and rather despised little mollusc which has recently found favour in fashionable European restaurants where it is served as an amusing luxury.

Distribution Widely distributed round all British coasts on stretches of rocky or weedy shore between high and low tide-marks.

Availability Commonly sold on seaside shellfish stalls and in many fish shops throughout the land.
In season: all year round.

Guidelines Sometimes known as periwinkles, these tiny molluscs have sharply pointed shells, spiralled like little whelks and are normally grey or dark brown in colour.
  They are sold ready cooked, in their shells, and generally bought by the pint.
  Winkles are hardly worth bothering with if your're looking for a quick source of sustenance, but the whole point about them is the leisurely ritual of extracting them from their shells with a pin. It's something of a challenge to extricate the little creatures from their twisted tortuous homes. The whole thing is edible apart from the little mica plate at the mouth of the shell, which needs to be removed before you can get at the winkle.

Cookery Almost always eaten as they are on little saucers with pepper and vinegar handy.

Shellfish suppliers

Most fishmongers have some fresh shellfish for sale; there are also a few who specialise and sell nothing else. The list below features some of the specialist dealers, fisheries and suppliers of particular shellfish.

Crab

R. C. Davies
1 The Gangway, Cromer,
Norfolk

Crayfish

K. J. Richards
Riversdale Farm,
Stour Provost, Gillingham,
Dorset
Tel: (074 785) 495

Oyster

The Butley-Orford
Oysterage
Market Hill, <u>Orford</u>,
Suffolk
Tel: (039 45) 277

D. & M. Mussett
The Oyster Sheds,
96 Coast Road,
<u>West Mersea</u>,
Essex
Tel: (020 638) 2871

Loch Fyne Oysters
Ardkinglas Estate,
<u>Cairndow</u>, Argyll,
Scotland
Tel: (049 96) 217   M.

Pembroke Oyster Fishery
(Captain Cook)
The Delicatessen,
Bush Street,
<u>Pembroke Dock</u> Dyfed,
Wales
Tel: (064 63) 2652

Shrimps (potted)

Baxters Ltd
Poulton Square,
<u>Morecambe</u>, Lancashire

Vegetables

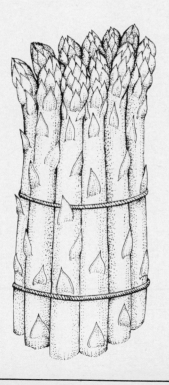

Vegetables are perhaps the most difficult of all our foods to pin down and define. Everyone knows what you mean, but how to put it into words? It wasn't until the 1760s that 'vegetable' was used specifically to mean 'herbs and roots grown for food', but that is obviously too narrow a definition. We have swollen tubers like potatoes and Jerusalem artichokes, simple roots such as carrots and parsnips, stems like celery, leaves from a whole range of plants including cabbages, lettuces and spinach. The immature flower heads of globe artichokes are vegetables and so are tomatoes, which botanically are berries. So our definition has to be more subjective: vegetables as plant products (sometimes the whole plant, sometimes part of it) which have predominantly savoury uses and can be eaten on their own or as an accompaniment to other dishes.

All our cultivated vegetables derive from wild plants, most of which were introduced from abroad. We do have one or two native vegetables like seakale, but most are adopted foreigners, although they grow and thrive quite happily here.

Different ages have their favourite vegetables and nowadays we have a bigger choice than ever before, not only of home-grown varieties but of imported exotic vegtables too. The vegetables listed in the following pages have been selected because they are the main ones with a distinct home-grown season; they are the most characteristic British vegetables. To the list of commonly *eaten* vegetables in Britain you would need to add aubergines, avocados, peppers, endive, chicory, salisify, celeriac, kohl-rabi and many more.

Vegetables in our diet The simple message, endorsed by the NANCE report (see page 14), is that fresh vegetables are good and we should eat more of them. Although most contain around 80% water they are also good sources of natural sugars, protein and vitamins. 'Sweet' vegetables such as parsnips and carrots are useful sources of natural sugar, while potatoes as well as containing a lot of starch also have 2% protein. But the best sources of vegetable protein are leguminous plants such as beans and peas which can have as much as 8% (plus fibre as well). And a great many vegetables are rich in vitamins, especially A, B and C.

The way vegetables are prepared is important because it can affect how nutritious they are. Vitamins are particularly sensitive and can disappear rapidly after the vegetable has been picked. Spinach, for instance, can lose up to 50% of its vitamin C within 24 hours, in fact it's a general rule that vegetables are at their best, both in terms of flavour and nourishment when freshly gathered. Vitamins are usually found just under the skin or in the outer leaves of vegetables so careful preparation is important. Peel thinly, don't waste indiscriminately, cook lightly and try to avoid too much cutting or shredding which proves an easy way out for nutrients. Also try to eat more raw vegetables.

Organic vegetables and growing your own Today's vegetable crops are at the mercy of the chemical industry, and as production grows more intensive, so the pesticides and fertilisers increase too. It's common practice for commercially grown crops like leeks and lettuce to get a standard eight or nine doses of spray, and this is happening to almost all our vegetables, not simply when they are growing but also when they are stored. And it's been shown that many of these vegetables contain significant levels of chemical residue of one kind or another, which the consumer can't detect. It's time we cleaned up our vegetables, particularly as we are not short of them and over-produce anyway.

We need vegetable growers who are prepared to produce safe, wholesome food, and that is beginning to happen. Interest in organically grown vegetables is growing all the time and people are getting wise to the activities of the chemists, the plant breeders and the commercial growers, and are increasingly worried about consuming quantities of toxic residues with their food.

Of course one way round this is to reject commercially produced vegetables altogether and grow you own. No wonder there's been an explosion in the demand for allotments in recent years. However this is only an improvement if you don't imitate the practices of the commercial growers.

Organic gardening has found its champion in Lawrence D. Hills of the Henry Doubleday Research Association (see page 000). which now has over 6,000 members in the UK alone. Hills and his team have done more than anyone to make organic gardening a practical reality.

Varieties Today's plant breeders have an obsession with colour, appearance and yield which has all but ruined most of our vegetables. They now look too good to be true: perfectly shaped, unblemished, standardised – not a misshapen tomato or a less than perfect carrot in sight – but where is the flavour? It has been systematically bred out in favour of cosmetic qualities and profitability. There's also an insidious levelling process at work which tries to iron out precisely those qualities which make particular varieties of vegetable different and interesting. It's a problem that now affects all our food: bread is all the same, cheese is all the same, and the breeders are trying to give us potatoes that are all the same too.

Varieties do tend to change over the years, old-established names being replaced by new cross-breeds or hybrids. That's part of the business of agriculture, but it shouldn't mean ditching all of our most interesting old vegetables simply because they don't fit into the plant breeders scheme of things. We need to know more about varieties because that is what makes vegetables interesting; we need to know more about growing and eating them. We should keep up the pressure for better, more varied vegetables and let it be known that we would prefer vegetables which are less-than-perfect but useful, disease-resistant and full of flavour, to bland, uninteresting types whose only virtue is that they produce a high yield.

Vegetables are likely to become even more important in our diet in the coming years, so we will need more not fewer different varieties: vegetables that can be grown in a whole range of different soils, vegetables that will thrive in town gardens as well as country allotments. Vegetables that will be resistant to disease and will offer lots of possibilities for the cook.

At present the EEC dictates that all vegetables in commercial cultivation be registered, which involves expensive field trials and testing. As a result only a small number of 'desirable' varieties with a broad appeal tend to be registered. But that doesn't mean that you cannot *grow* old, rare or interesting varieties yourself. And to help there are now what have been called 'vegetable sanctuaries' and seed banks, particularly at the Henry Doubleday Research Association and The National Vegetable Research Station, Wellesbourne, Warwickshire, which aims to have a stock of 15,000 varieties.

Guidelines for buying vegetables (i) Get your vegetables from a shop, market stall or supermarket where there is a high turnover and where there's a good display of fresh vegetables, preferably not pre-packed.

(ii) Fresh is always best and you should avoid tinned vegetables and also most frozen ones unless you are really desperate. Freezing is fine if you have a glut of home-grown produce that otherwise might go to waste, but there's little point in buying packet after packet of frozen stuff where there are good vegetables to be had fresh.

(iii) Always keep your eyes open and try to select or inspect the goods before you pay your money. Many supermarkets have 'help-yourself' vegetable sections where you can pick and choose, but it might need more cunning if you are dealing with a shrewd market trader.

(iv) Follow the general guidelines given under specific vegetables and always try out new types or varieties when you see them.

Artichoke, Globe

An edible thistle, prized by the Greeks and the Romans and the great luxury vegetable of the Italian Renaissance. In Britian it flourishes well, even in the far north and is grown as much for its floral beauty as for its virtues as a food. Although gardeners cultivate it, most commercial varieties come from Europe.

In season: (home-grown) June – September; (imported) all year round.

Guidelines   In Britain varieties are generally listed as 'green' or 'purple', although many named varieties come from abroad.

The immature globe-like flower heads are the part that is eaten, and they should be tightly packed, green fleshy scales with no signs of browned edges. The smaller the globe the younger the artichoke; very young ones are not really worth buying as they have little flavour.

AVOID canned artichokes or artichoke hearts. They have a poor flavour and can be sharp and stringy. Many cans labeelled 'artichoke bottoms' are in fact very small whole artichokes.

Cookery   Boiled whole and eaten, leaf by leaf with hot melted butter, hollandaise sauce or vinagrette. The central 'heart' surrounded by its hairy 'choke' is particularly delicious.

Artichoke, Jerusalem

These are not artichokes and they have nothing to do with Jerusalem. They are actually members of the sunflower family introduced to England from France in the early years of the 17th century, although they came originally from North America. The name 'Jerusalem' is a corruption of the Italian *girasole*, meaning that its flowers would turn with the sun.

In season: (home-grown) November – March.

Guidelines   The knobbly underground tubers, which have something of the flavour and character of sweet potatoes are the part which is eaten. Try to buy ones that are not too knobbly otherwise you will end up with a great deal of waste; and always buy more than you need to allow for this. Nicely formed specimens are also easier to peel. They should feel hard as rocks and be crisp when cut open. One warning: they are great provokers of wind in some individuals!

Cookery   Need to be scrubbed well and thinly peeled. Can be boiled, steamed and served with sauces or made into a purée. Jerusalem artichokes can also be turned into the splendid Palestine soup.

Asparagus

One of our most treasured vegetables, partly because of its exquisite flavour, partly because its English season is over in a few brief weeks. Asparagus was highly rated by the Romans but it didn't establish itself in Britain until the 16th century. Asparagus is a member of the lily family and in the wild grows as a shoreline plant. It was known as 'sparrow grass' back in the 17th and 18th centuries.

In season: (home-grown) May – June.

Guidelines   Above all else, asparagus needs to be fresh and eaten on the day it is picked. Of course, the chances of this are quite slim unless you buy English asparagus direct from a local grower or frequent a very reliable stockist. Most English asparagus now comes from Norfolk, Suffolk, Essex and Worcestershire, although some is grown as far north as Lancashire. The further it has travelled the less chance there is of it being really fresh.

Asparagus is actually the young shoot of a tuberous root, and the key to buying it is to look for youth and tenderness. The spears should be firm and not at all droopy (which is a sure sign that they are old); avoid those with thin, wrinkled, woody stems. The proportion of green to white normally depends on the variety (the white part is simply that which has been underground). Finally the tips should be closely packed and succulent.

Always try to choose spears of even thickenss and look out for the different grades: jumbo is the largest, followed by extra selected, selected and choice. 'Sprue' are thin, bent and straggly spears, which may look unappealing but are actually good to eat and quite cheap.

Cookery   Tie a bundle together, making sure the spears are all the same length. Cook by standing upright in boiling water. Traditionally served with melted butter or hollandaise sauce. Good for soups and decorating quiches too.

Bean, Broad

One of our most ancient, satisfying and nutritious beans and a staple vegetable since the Iron Age. For centuries it was Europe's only bean (until varieties were introduced from the New World) and had the added advantage that it could be dried very successfully and stored through the winter. It is also extremely hardy, and many varieties are now planted in the autumn or at the turn of the year for picking in May or early June.

In season: (home-grown) May – July; (imported) April – June.

Guidelines Always choose young pods that feel full. These are the most tender. Tiny pods (only two or three inches long) can be picked and cooked whole, but in most cases the beans are shelled. If the pods are very bumpy the beans inside will be very large, tough-skinned and floury.

Broad beans are as nutritious as wheat and contain a high percentage of vegetable or second-class protein as well as fibre.

Cookery Should be cooked in the minimum of lightly salted water with a sprig of thyme or savory. Young ones need delicate treatment; old ones can be skinned and made into a hearty purée or thick soup. Excellent with boiled bacon or ham.

Beans, French

A whole family of new beans came to Europe and eventually to England from South America during the 16th and 17th centuries, and the variety we now call the French bean is perhaps the finest of all. One of the advantages of these beans is that they come into season as the stalwart broad beans are fading.

In season: (home-grown) June – September; (imported) all year round.

Guidelines Pencil-thin French beans (the *haricots verts* of French cookery) need to be eaten very young and very fresh. They are sometimes known as 'snap beans' and if a bean snaps crisply between the fingers it is ideal for cooking. Avoid those that are large, limp or bumpy, as well as any that are damaged or brown. Like asparagus, French beans need to be in perfect, unblemished condition.

Cookery Need to be boiled fast and quickly. They should retain more than a hint of crispness. Garlic and parsley are all that is needed to finish off the dish. Cold French beans are delicious in salads.

Use the response form on page 287 to send us your suggestions and information.

Bean, Runner

In Britain, scarlet runners are the favourite gardener's bean, and every summer, trellises and frameworks of wooden poles and twine are erected on vegetable plots throughout the land. Like French beans, runners derive from plants brought over from the New World.

In season: (home-grown) July – October.

Guidelines The problem with runner beans is stringiness, and there are a number of ways of spotting 'string' beans. Stringiness comes with age, so you should avoid beans that are dark green (as opposed to the fresh light green of young specimens), knobbly and full of big seeds. Like French beans they should snap crisply between the fingers.

Good runner beans should be succulent and juicy. The whole pod is eaten (top, tailed and thinly sliced).

Runner beans freeze well, although they lose their freshness and flavour in the process. I've never eaten a frozen runner bean that was anything but watery and tasteless.

Cookery Should be boiled or steamed until tender but still crisp. Huge heaps of freshly cooked runner beans are one of the great delights of Sunday lunches in the summer. Runner beans also make a pleasant soup and can be transformed into an unusual chutney.

Beetroot

Related to the sugar beet and mangold, beetroot naturally has a high sugar content, but it is the colour of its flesh that is its main feature and perhaps the reason why it has never been very popular – at least in Britain.

In season: (home-grown) all year round.

Guidelines Vary considerably in shape, size and quality. The best are young, small, round ones; once they reach tennis-ball size, or larger, they can be coarse and woody. Make sure that the roots aren't damaged and that all the whiskery roots are intact. Beetroot should also have some stalk attached. All of this is to ensure that they don't bleed.

Many greengrocers sell freshly cooked beetroot. Always pick one that has been newly cooked and is still steaming; if it is cold it may also be old, and cooked beetroot goes mouldy very quickly. If you are buying pre-packed beetroot (not recommended) make sure you double check the date stamp for the same reason.

Cookery   Boil (without peeling) until they are tender but not mushy. The skin will rub off easily when it is cooked. Allow to get cold and slice up for salads, eat hot with plenty of herbs, or follow the European way and make soup out of it. Harsh, vinegary pickled beetroot is generally awful unless you make it yourself and eat it young.

Broccoli (Sprouting Broccoli)

Various kinds of broccoli are all members of the cabbage family which are valued for their flowering shoots. Broccoli was first popularised in the 1720s, although it has been eaten in Italy since Roman times (the word *brocco* means 'sprout').

In season: all year round depending on variety.

Guidelines   Sprouting broccoli comes in different colours, purple, white and green. Purple sprouting broccoli is by far the most popular and its colour is due to the presence of anthocyanin, as well as chlorophyll, in the sprouting head. Anthocyanin is water-soluble, so the purple colour disappears during cooking. Limp, yellowing sprouts which are mostly stem and leaf are not worth buying. Look for firm stalks and good heads. White broccoli is occasionally seen in England, although it's more common in gardens than shops. Green broccoli has recently found favour under the name of 'Calabrese' and is a much larger, closely packed head. Supermarkets often sell them trimmed and wrapped together, a few at a time, in cellophane. The quality is generally worth the high price you will be asked to pay. Most frozen broccoli is of the calabrese type, but it doesn't bear comparison with the fresh vegetable.

Cookery   Can be cooked in bundles upright, like asparagus. Broccoli is also excellent stir-fried, especially when it is very young and tender.

Brussels Sprout

An excellent vegetable whose reputation has been ruined by generations of careless cooks who have overcooked it and allowed it to stew for hours in huge pans of water. There's a hint that they may have actually been grown near Brussels in the Middle Ages, but it's a rather tenuous connection.

In season: September – March.

Guidelines   Sprouts are actually miniature cabbages that cling to the thick stalk of the plant under an umbrella of large, cabbage-like leaves. (Many plant breeders have now succeeded in producing sprout plants that are virtually leafless, which is a pity because 'sprout tops' are a good useful vegetable in their own right if cooked like spring cabbage.)

Wait until the first frosts of autumn before you buy sprouts; early in the season they can be anaemic and lacklustre. Choose smallish, evenly sized sprouts that are closely packed, tight, firm and a nice green colour. Avoid those with yellowing wilted leaves or any that are loose-leafed.

Cookery   Generally cooked in a minimum of boiling water until soft but still crisp. Traditionally served with chestnuts as an accompaniment to Christmas turkey, but can be excellent with any kind of roast meat, poultry or game.

Cabbage

The very word cabbage seems to strike terror into the heart of many unfortunate souls who have had to endure rank overboiled mush masquerading as a vegetable. In fact cabbage – and that includes a whole family of plants – is one of our oldest vegetables and can be splendid if cooked and handled with a little consideration.

We have come a long way from the tough, rubbery-leaved wild cabbage picked and eaten by our Celtic ancestors. Now we have cabbages to suit every season of the year, from the loose-leafed spring cabbage to the savoys and red cabbages of winter.

In season: (home-grown) all year round, depending on the variety.

Guidelines   Different cabbages have different qualities, but you should always look for freshness and crispness. Spring cabbages, or spring greens as they are often called, have only the suggestion of a heart, but the leaves should be a good green colour with no signs of wilting, limpness or yellowing.

If you are buying a hard cabbage with a heart, it's often best to pick one with the outer leaves intact, as it's likely to be fresher than the little 'footballs' which seem to decrease in size each day as the greengrocer peels off another layer of wilting leaves. In this case, appearances can be deceptive.

Late in the year there is the monster Dutch white cabbage, often cut into chunks for easy selling, although it's a vegetable that will keep for months in a cool airy place. White cabbages are always sold trimmed and, once again, should be rock-hard, an attractive greenish-white colour and fresh looking. Red cabbages, with their distinctive colour (due to the presence of anthocyanin pigment) are usually trimmed too. Savoy cabbage, on the other hand, has beautiful dark green crinkly leaves and if properly handled has a deliciously mild flavour (although it's often fatally waterlogged during cooking).

Cookery Cabbages have as many uses as there are varieties. They can be chopped and eaten raw in salads, stuffed, braised in soups and stews, pickled or simply boiled or steamed for a short while and served with meat or fish.

Carrot

Looking at a wild carrot with its tough, pale-fleshed root, it's hard to believe it bears any resemblance to the cultivated varieties now grown all over the world. But that is the way with most of the wild ancestors of our common vegetables.

In season: all year round.

Guidelines Young carrots sold in bunches in the early summer should look fresh, and smooth-skinned. If they still have their tops they are likely to be in good condition and worth buying. Those without tops or in packets can be weeks old and lacking in flavour. As the year progresses, carrots get bigger, more rough looking and more robust in every way. Try to avoid those that have been badly damaged during harvesting and ones that are full of worm holes or show signs of rotting. By winter carrots will be at their largest and may become too woody for decent eating – although with careful peeling and trimming they can still add flavour to hearty stews and casseroles.

Raw carrots are a good source of vitamin A, as well as vitamin C, fibre and minerals. (The redder they are the more vitamin A they contain).

Cookery Young carrots are delicious eaten raw in salads or lightly stir-fried; older ones have many uses from cakes and casseroles to soups.

Cauliflower

'Cauliflower is but a cabbage with a college education'. These disdainful words uttered by Mark Twain do make a point that cauliflowers are cabbages with a difference, but they don't deserve such severe criticism.

In season: all year round (may be imported during the winter months).

Guidelines A cauliflower should be judged by its 'curd' or its mass of creamy-white flower buds. If this is tightly packed, fresh-looking and firm it should eat well. Cauliflowers which still have their protective outer leaves intact are the best of all as the leaves serve to shield and protect the curd from damage.

AVOID cauliflowers that have yellowing leaves, a nasty smell or a mould-infested curd pitted with black holes.

Selected 'florets' or pieces of curd, neatly trimmed, are sometimes sold at an inflated price. Both their quality and freshness can vary a great deal, especially as they may come from different cauliflowers.

Don't be too surprised to see purple cauliflower occasionally. These are simply big brothers to purple sprouting broccoli.

Celery

Cultivated celery didn't appear in Britain until the 17th century, so it's quite a recent crop. Before that, cooks and herbalists relied on the strong pungent flavour of 'smallage' or wild celery as a flavouring and as a cure against the bite of wild beasts.

In season: all year round (best during the winter).

Guidelines Celery was once a winter vegetable, but nowadays it's available right through the year, even in the height of summer. Modern varieties of green celery, spotlessly clean and packed in long plastic bags are now a familiar sight, and there's no denying that they are useful. But for the real thing, the true celery, you will have to wait until the frosts of autumn. This is when white celery appears, blanched and covered in soot. The stems may be stringy sometimes and the dirt may be a nuisance – although there's no better way of reminding yourself that vegetables do actually grow in the earth, and that they don't appear spontaneously, pristine and packaged ready for use. It's worth thinking about when you are scrubbing the soot off your celery. The virtues of good winter celery are its crispness and its full flavour, but all celery should be firm rather than limp and it should not have discoloured tops (a sign of age) or rotten brown patches.

Cookery   Eat it raw, make it into soup, stir-fry it, braise it and serve it with game. The possibilities are endless.

Cucumber

The cucumber is an ancient vegetable. It was being eaten in the Middle East many thousands of years ago and gained high reputation in classical times; it is said that the Roman Emperor Tiberius ate cucumber every day of the year. In recent years, growers have striven to provide us with a daily supply of this most useful member of the gourd family.

In season: (home-grown) March – October; (imported) all year round.

Guidelines   Cucumbers now come in all shapes and sizes, long, fat, smooth-skinned, warty, but there's one sure way of deciding whether they are fresh or not. Feel them and press them gently. If they seem firm and taught, 'bursting with juiciness', they are in their prime. Don't be put off by the rugged appearance of ridged cucumbers; they are just as good as their glossy, smooth-skinned cousins.

Peeling cucumber is always a point of contention; in the end it's a matter of personal taste. Today's so-called 'burpless' cucumbers don't have the windy reputation of their forebears and it is generally agreed that the skin is the cause of all that flatulence!

Cookery   Cucumber is first and foremost a salad vegetable, but it makes the most refreshing soup, is perfect with yoghurt and can be turned into a superb sauce to go with fresh salmon or turbot.

Hamburg Parsley

Most parsley is grown for its leaves, but Hamburg parsley is actually treated as a root vegetable. It was well-known and common in the 18th century but seems to have gone out of fashion in Britian since then.

Description   Above ground it has feathery green leaves not unlike turnip tops, while below ground it has a long white edible root.

Guidelines   Not a common vegetable in shops, but worth growing as a garden vegetable. The root has a flavour which has been described as a cross between parsley and celeriac.

Uses   Particularly useful as a flavouring for soups and stews.

Leek

Worn by the Welsh as an emblem of national identity, grown to monstrous size by gardeners in Northumberland, the leek is a colourful vegetable with even a touch of country wisdom in its pedigree. One old saying proclaims: 'Eate leekes in Lide (March) and ransins (wild garlic) in May And all the years after physitians may play.'

In season: (home-grown) August – May.

Guidelines At the very beginning of their season, in late summer, leeks might be mistaken for large spring onions, while at the end they can be huge – certainly emblematic, but hardly edible. In between, they are excellent. The leaves should be a good green colour, not at all yellow or wilting and there shouldn't be too much waste on them. Neatly trimmed leeks may be convenient, but for freshness it's best to buy the whole thing, soil, roots and all.

Towards the end of the season beware of leeks that have started to form a hard core in the centre. This has a curious texture of cooked, but its presence is a good indicator that the rest of the leek will be tough and stringy.

Cookery Because leeks are very mucilaginous, they turn up in a lot of soup recipes, and this is an ideal way of using old specimens. There are leek pies in the West Country, and leek puddings with a suet crust in the North-East. While for exponents of the new cookery there are delicate leek purées to go with fish.

Lettuce

There are now hundreds of different varieties of lettuce, all stemming from the bitter wild lettuce. In the Ancient World it had several very contrasting uses: at first the Romans ate it at the end of a feast so that its milky soporific juice would send the reveller quietly to sleep, but later it appeared at the begining of the meal, with radishes, to stimulate the appetite – as a little salad in fact.

In season: all year round (depending on the variety).

Guidelines Although there are many, many types of lettuce only a handful seem to appear in the shops: there are the heartless, cabbage-type varieties (the proverbial rabbit food), upright cos lettuce, thick leaved succulent Webb's Wonder and the Iceberg, which is as tightly packed and crisp a lettuce as you are likely to find. There are others too, like the jagged

Oak Leaf lettuce and the blanched Batavian endive with its bitter frilly leaves.

A lettuce pulled straight from the ground is the freshest you can get, and most sold in the shops can't really compare. But your best bet is to go for locally grown ones which are generally dirty and untrimmed, although that doesn't matter at all: it is the quality and firmness of the leaves and the crispness of the heart which is important. It's almost impossible to revive very tired floppy lettuces.

Cookery It's hard to imagine that there was ever a salad without lettuce, the two are forever linked together. While that is the prime use of lettuces of all kinds – and the more you can vary them the better – they can also be turned into soup, lightly fried or braised.

Marrow/Courgette

The huge vegetable marrow, a regular showstopper at village shows and fêtes, has in recent years been outsted by the delicate little courgette, a diminutive version that needs none of the peeling and scooping of the old monster.

In season: (marrow) August – October; (courgette) June – October.

Guidelines There's no virtue in buying monster marrows; they may look like fun, but they are no fun to eat – stringy and watery with a skin as tough as tree bark. But they can be pleasant and useful if young and carefully chosen. The solid, woody feel of an old marrow is an unmistakable warning.

Courgettes are a different matter altogether. They should be small (only 2–3 inches long) with a good green colour, a firm feel, not squashy, and a soft outer skin. Shop courgettes can vary in size a great deal, but if you select carefully you can pick out ones that are roughly the same size for cooking. Signs of mould on the hard rounded end of a courgette will tell you that it has been hanging around and has got damp.

Cookery Marrows are for stuffing with savoury mixtures, for making wine and for turning into chutneys and jams. Courgettes call out for more delicate treatment: they too can be stuffed, as well as being lightly boiled, deep-fried as fritters or used as part of colourful Mediterranean dishes like ratatouille.

Fresh is always best.

Mushroom

Think of mushrooms these days and you imagine anaemic white buttons, the all-pervading products of the mushroom farm. It's easy to forget that mushrooms grow in the wild and that there are scores of superb fungi which are for the most part ignored in this country.

In season: (cultivated) all year round; (wild) mainly in the autumn.

Guidelines Cultivated mushrooms come in three main sizes: tiny buttons, which are unopened 'buds', cups which have begun to open and large 'flats' which are opened right out and have a darker colour. All have different uses, although button mushrooms are virtually without flavour. Their only redeeming feature is that they can be used whole and add a certain texture to some dishes. Cups can be used in all kinds of ways and are the most commonly sold. Big, blackened flats should be more readily available because in many ways they are the best of the lot – their rich, dark flavour is perfect for enriching stews, casseroles and so on.

Mushrooms should look fresh. Moisture is the big enemy: it turns them quickly to a putrefying mass; on the other hand mushrooms that are a little dry can still be used, as they swell up again when cooked. Don't buy old brown mushrooms which have no texture and little flavour and may possibly be suspect.

If you are contemplating picking and using wild mushrooms you should make use of an identification guide, but it's worth pursuing puffballs, parasols, inky caps as well as common field mushrooms.

Some shops now sell a range of fungi, including chanterelles, ceps (boletus), morels and quite a number of others. In most cases these are dried – and very expensive. Consult *The Mushroom Feast* by Jane Grigson for more details.

From a nutritional point of view, mushrooms contain more protein per 100 grams than almost any other vegetable, and are also rich in B vitamins.

Cookery Extremely versatile. Can be sliced and eaten raw in salads, stir-fried, made into soup, stuffed, added to stews and casseroles and so on.

Onion

It's hard to imagine cooking without onions, and they have been a vital vegetable in one form or another for thousands of years. Central Asian in origin, their descendants are now found in almost every kitchen in almost every country in the world.

In season: all year round.

Guidelines   The main quality of a good onion, apart from its flavour, should be its hardness and crispness. Don't buy onions that feel soft or squashy, or indeed any that are beginning to sprout, which suggests they are past their best.

There are all kinds of onions these days: big, mildly flavoured Spanish ones and pungent little red ones from Egypt, as well as our standard home-grown varieties. Then there are shallots, which grown and multiply in clumps and are the best onions for pickling and adding whole to dishes.

Spring onions are generally eaten raw in salads should be firm and fresh, without any signs of sliminess or unpleasant odour. Very large ones can be wickedly strong.

It's worth buying onions in bulk or keeping a string or two hung up in a dry airy spot, because they store well and there's nothing more infuriating than running out of onions or having to buy them every other day.

Cookery   Onions add flavour, richness and body to almost any dish you care to name. Sometimes they are chopped or grated, sometimes they are cooked whole in their skins.

Parsnip

Before the days of sugar, parsnips were valued for their sweetness and a dish of mashed parsnips was a common sight on the medieval table, although by the 16th century they were being used to feed pigs rather than humans.

In season: August – March.

Guidelines   Like carrots, parsnips are now scrubbed, trimmed and cellophane-wrapped and they are a sorry sight. By-pass them and head straight for a big box containing unwashed, untrimmed roots which have a better flavour and are likely to be fresher too, especially if they have been grown locally. Select the ones you want, try to get all roughly the same size, so that they cook evenly; you will also want to avoid parsnips that are very scabby (this can mean a lot of waste) as well as ones with a deep hard crown at the top, which also has to be cut out.

Cookery   Can be boiled or steamed, are delicious baked and make an excellent soup. Herbs and butter suit them well.

Pea

The fate of the pea was sealed in 1929, when a new technique for freezing different foods was developed. Since then the frozen pea has become the most clichéd vegetable we have and the end result has been that fresh peas are often the dregs of the harvest, what is left after the frozen food manufacturers have got their hands on the pick of the crop.

In season: June – September.

Guidelines   The quality of most peas sold in shops is enough to send you scampering towards the freezer cabinet. Most are too hard, too large and too old. Peas should be small, sweet and green – exactly what the frozen pea claims to offer.

Apart from the fact that freezing has deprived us of good fresh peas – unless we grow our own – it also subtly changes the peas themselves. They are certainly sweet – often too sweet – and they are undeniably tender, but they have no character. There's no pleasure in eating them.

Cookery   Peas soup with fresh mint is a great delicacy, green peas have found their natural home alongside duck, they can be made into purées, dried for the winter, or simply cooked and served dotted with a little melted butter.

Potato

Undoubtedly one of the most famous vegetables in the world. Two thousand years ago the South American Incas were eating them, although they have only been in our kitchens and gardens for a few centuries. Potatoes are now so important and even commonplace that they were often separated from other vegetables and tend to maintain their own singular identity. How often have you seen in pubs and restaurants dishes advertised 'with potatoes and vegetables'?

In season: all year round (depending on the variety).

Guidelines   More than any other vegetable the pleasure and interest in potatoes come from the scores of different varieties that can be grown in our soil. And yet some of our finest potatoes are dying out, neglected by growers and retailers, either because they are too individual, inconsistent, light croppers or simply unusual. We should be able to enjoy more not less varieties. We shouldn't simply select and breed for resistance to blight, high yield or even shape. But that is what is happening. The list is being whittled down to a handful of well-known varieties which have to serve for all our needs.

So the first rule of buying potatoes is to check the variety or varieties on offer. After that you need to distinguish between new potatoes, which are a great treat during the late spring and early summer, and maincrop which appear virtually throughout the year in most places.

Always buy potatoes loose. It's common to see them scrubbed and packed in plastic bags, which does them no good. There's no way of telling how long they have been hanging around or what condition they are in. Potatoes should be hard, there should be no signs of greening (which means they have been exposed to the light for too long and have developed toxic alkaloids) and the 'eyes' should be hardly showing (these are the points where the potato puts out shoots). They should also be free of mould or rot.

New potatoes are really at their best straight from the ground, but if you have to buy them, make sure the skins can be rubbed easily as this indicates that they have been recently dug. Small ones look and taste the best. New potatoes lose their flavour quickly, so buy in small quantities as you need them.

If you want to discover more about potatoes and grow unusual varieties, the man to approach is Donald MacLean at Dornock Farm, Crieff, Perthshire, Scotland. He has a tuber bank of some 200 different varieties.

Cookery   Each variety of potato has its uses: some are good for baking, others make excellent chips; some are perfect for mashing, while others are best served whole. There are potatoes for salads and potatoes for soups, potatoes that can be roasted or added to stews and hot pots.

Radish

There's something of a mystery about radishes. They are unknown in the wild yet were being cultivated and eaten in Egypt 2,000 years ago. The Greeks and Romans loved them, and we once valued them more highly that we do today, when they are very much the poor relations of the salad bowl. (The peppery beaked seed pods were put into pickles back in the 18th century).

In season: all year round, most common during the summer.

Guidelines   Salad radishes come in several forms: little red globes, red and white globes or red and white cylindrical roots (the well-known French Breakfast variety). Their essential quality is crispness. They should not be too large, spongy or woody within, so eat them young.

Cookery   Almost always eaten raw, often chopped up in salads, but much better nibbled whole.

Spinach

The Arabs had the right idea when they named spinach 'the prince of vegetables'. It came originally from Persia, and in its original state it must have looked like a spiky bolted lettuce. Succulent leafy varieties developed when the plant settled in colder climates.

In season: (home-grown) April – November; (imported) November – April.

Guidelines Spinach has a famous reputation as healthy nourishing food, and is rich in vitamins A and C as well as in calcium and has more protein than most other leaf vegetables.

There are actually two types: the true spinach and so-called 'perpetual spinach' or spinach beet. There's little difference in taste or appearance between the two.

Spinach should have a freshly-picked look; the leaves should be bright green and crisp. Don't buy yellow, wilting spinach or leaves that have been stuffed into plastic bags and have become sweaty and slimy. Also you won't want to pay for large quantities of tough stringy stalk.

Cookery Very young spinach leaves can be eaten raw in salads, but usually it is cooked with no extra water other than that clinging to its leaves after washing. It has innumerable uses from soufflés, quiches and tarts to soup and a host of spicy oriental and Middle Eastern combinations.

Swede

You may not think that the swede is worthy of verse, yet it has been described mysteriously by the poet Edward Thomas in a poem called simply *Swedes*. This rather ungainly orange root did indeed come to us from Sweden in 1781, and it's still sometimes known as the Swedish turnip.

In season: September – May.

Guidelines Despite its name, the swede has little in common with the turnip, except perhaps a certain basic similarity in character. Swedes can vary in colour from purple to yellow and they can vary in size too: some are no bigger than tennis balls, others are massive knarled specimens. Always go for smaller swedes and pick out those that are unblemished. Large, old swedes have very thick tough skin and coarse woody flesh.

Cookery Mashed and buttered swede calls out for haggis and malt whisky, or any kind of strongly flavoured meat or game. Very useful chopped and added to stews and casseroles.

Sweetcorn

When we think of sweetcorn, or maize, we think of sunshine, America and cornflakes, and rightly so because this plant has an ancient transatlantic pedigree dating back thousands of years. Maize is now grown extensively as food for animals, as cereal crop and as a vegetable.

In season: (home-grown) August – October; (imported) November – February.

Guidelines A ripe corn-on-the-cob should be golden in colour, the grains should be plump and look as if they will burst when pricked with a pin, and there should be a silky tassle at the tip. If the weather is unpredictable, fresh Englaish cobs can be badly and unevenly formed, dry and barely ripe. In such cases you may be better off with a good quality frozen cob. Canned sweetcorn is convenient – nothing more – while bags of frozen corn grains are generally chewy and tasteless.

Cookery Whole cobs are normally boiled and chewed. Sweetcorn can be made into soup, fritters or served as a side vegetable colourfully mixed with red and green pepers.

Tomato

The tomato reached Europe from South America sometime in the 16th century and came to England around 1580, but it was centuries before it was trusted as food. It was grown as a decorative curiosity, but no one dared actually eat it. There was talk of its poisonous, unwholesome nature (it is in fact a relative of the deadly nightshade) and of its power to liberate the sexual appetite; added to that it looked too colourful and unnatural to be used as food. Eventually 'love apples', as they were nicknamed, crept into the kitchen and since then they have never looked back.

In season: (home-grown) April – October; (imported) all year.

Guidelines Home-grown tomatoes represent everything that is unsatisfactory and wrong with plant breeding. They look perfect, an even red colour, round, unblemished and all the same size. But where is the taste? Breeding has sacrificed flavour for appearance and high yields. I also suspect that the lack of decent nutrients is partly responsible for their dismal blandness. And there's also the lurking threat of pesticide and spray residues in the fruit themselves. All of which should point you in the direction of an organic grower or a nurseryman who can provide you with plants to grow yourself.

Buy fresh tomatoes as you need them rather than stockpiling them and allowing them to get over ripe.

Cookery Tomatoes makes marvellous soups, they are perfect sliced with fresh basil as a salad and lend an essential colour and flavour to many dishes, especially those from the Mediterranean.

Turnip

Like the swede (see page 204), the turnip has acquired a bad reputation from years of careless cooking, and it's a vegetable we tend to put very low down the league table of favourites.

In season: all year round.

Guidelines   To be successful, turnips need to be chosen with care. They should be on the small side, firm and unblemished. You will get no joy out of massive winter turnips with their tough skins, squashy fibrous flesh and acrid pungent flavour. They should smell 'sweetly peppery'. When young – in the spring – you can also make good use of their green leafy tops.

Turnips also vary in shape and colour: some are broad and flat, others are round and there are also some long, while their colours range from red, through white, yellow and even grey.

Cookery   Small ones are delicious cooked whole. Larger ones can be chopped and added to stews and casseroles or turned into soup.

Watercress

Originally one of the great wild vegetables, growing in unpolluted running water in many parts of Britain, watercress is now an important commercial crop and has been since the end of the 18th century. Much of our watercress now comes from Hampshire and, to a lesser extent, Hertfordshire.

In season: all year round.

Guidelines   Watercress can be bought loose in bunches or vacuum-packed. The latter is rather expensive but it is usually good quality and there's little or no waste. Don't buy watercress that is yellow or slimy.

Apart from its superb biting flavour, watercress is also a good source of iron and has a very high vitamin C content.

Cookery Think of watercress as much more than a garnish or an afterthought on steaks. It makes a lovely purée or delicate sauce to go with fish; watercress soup is delicious and watercress sandwiches are delightful.

Suppliers of vegetables

Greengrocers, farm shops, market stalls and 'pick your own' outlets are the main sources of vegetables. If you want to find a source of organically grown vegetables consult *The Organic Food Guide*.

Useful Organisations

Good Gardeners Association
Arkley Manor Farm, Rowley Lane, Arkley, Barnet, Hertfordshire
Tel: (01) 449 7944

Henry Doubleday Research Association
Convent Lane, Bocking, Braintree, Essex

National Vegetable Research Station
Wellesbourne, Warwickshire
Tel: (0789) 840382

Organic Farm Foods
Unit 7, Ellerslie Square, Lyham Road,
London SW2
Tel: (01) 274 0234
(All kinds of organic produce including vegetables).

Seaweeds

Seaweeds belong to one of the most primitive of all groups in the plant kingdom, the algae. They have no true stems, roots or leaves, although they do have hold-fasts, by which they cling to rocks and stones, and from which the 'stipe' or stem-like part emerges. Like land plants they also have a seasonal cycle, budding in the spring, growing rapidly in the summer and dying off during the winter. And they are harvested too, the best time being during early summer when they are at their most luxuriant.

Seaweed is an ancient food, probably one of Man's earliest forms of sustenance, and it was prized by the Chinese, Greeks and Romans as food, medicine and fertiliser. In the Far East its potential is realised and seaweed is an important industry. Elsewhere, particularly in Britain, it is almost ignored. Wild food enthusiasts seek it out and in Ireland and Wales some seaweed is gathered and used commercially, but generally it is a valuable resource that goes unnoticed.

Nutritional value of seaweed Seaweeds vary, but the nutritional content of most of them is very high. They contain large amounts of vitamins, especially thiamin, B2, B12, A, C, and D, as well as important quantities of valuable trace elements and minerals, particularly iodine.

The Greeks used seaweed to treat goitre and it is still valuable for some glandular and deficiency complaints.

Uses of seaweeds Most seaweeds have a curious flavour, which can be off-putting at first, but the taste for them is soon acquired and they make an interesting and useful vegetable. Their medicinal value is proven and they are particularly useful for vitamin and mineral deficiency.

Seaweed is also food for other plants and is one of the finest natural manures and fertilisers for vegetables such as asparagus and sea kale.

They also yield extracts and chemical derivatives such as alginates (vegetable proteins) which have a host of uses.

Carrageen (Irish Moss)

Not only a valuable and nutritious seaweed in its own right, but also an important source of alginates – vegetable gelatines which have a great many commercial uses.

Availability Common on stones and rocks on the western and southern shores of Ireland and England. Best gathered fresh in April and May.

Guidelines The purple fronds of carrageen (*Chondrus crispus* and *Gigartina stellata*) are easily recognised because they branch repeatedly into a fan shape.

Carrageen can be collected and used fresh, in which case it needs to be cleaned and simmered with milk and sugar until it disintegrates and forms 'Irish moss blancmange'. It can also be dried, when it takes on a bleached, creamy-white colour and is stored in bags. Prepared carrageen is often found in health food shops.

Uses The alginates in carrageen can be extracted and used as emulsifiers in table jellies, ice creams, confectionery and syrups. Also made into thin durable films for edible sausage skins and have been recommended for the treatment of coughs. There were many other uses, too, listed by Dorothy Hartley in *Food in England*: 'it prepares paper, surfaces, coloured printings, marbles, endpapers, prints leather and silver surfaces, fills plaster pores, makes wallpaper dressings, is used in printing fabrics, and fixes false teeth.' Not a bad record for a humble seaweed!

Dulse

A tough, resilient, unco-operative plant that must have its origins in the hardy diet of early coastal settlers. Despite the fact that it is very common, it is rarely eaten nowadays.

Availability Found on stony shores in many parts of Britain. Mainly used in the west of Ireland and a few remote areas of Scotland.

Guidelines Reddish-purple in colour with long leathery fronds. Has been eaten raw in salads, although it really needs up to five hours' slow simmering to make it edible.
  Also called 'dillisk' or 'dellesk'.

Uses One traditional Irish dish is 'dulse champ', in which the cooked seaweed is mixed with butter and mashed potato. In New England it has been dried and eaten as a relish, and it has also been used as a kind of tough, salty chewing gum.

Laver

'There is a charm about the weed which ought to have kept it in the front as one of the distinctions of English cookery'. So wrote E. S. Dallas in *Kettner's Book of the Table*, published in 1877. He added: 'That it should fall into neglect is one of the unfortunate results of modern civilisation, which produces uniformity of fashion – the same cookery and the same dishes all over the world.' Fortunately laver has clung on and is still a great delicacy; there are no longer large drying houses along the South Wales coast and organised picking is very much a thing of the past, but laver can still be gathered or purchased locally by those with an appetite for the unexpected.

Availability   Common all round Britain, but especially on exposed Western shores, including parts of South Pembrokeshire and around Pen-clawdd, the last village of north Gower before the peninsula joins the mainland. Markets and fish shops in towns on both sides of the Bristol Channel sell it. You will see great buckets of it as well as little packets dotted with oatmeal and wrapped in cellophane; laver bread also comes in cans.

Guidelines   Recognised by its thin, wavy fronds, which are rosy-purple, turning to olive green at the edges. The name laver was introduced by 17th century botanists, although in Scotland and Ireland it is still called by its old names – 'slouk' and 'sloke' respectively.

Preparing laver is a long business, so it is always sold ready cleaned and cooked to form a rough purée, known as laverbread. This looks a bit like suspect cooked spinach, and the first taste can be very disconcerting. But persevere, give it a chance, and you may end up really enjoying it.

Uses   Laverbread is traditionally rolled in oatmeal, fried in bacon fat and eaten for breakfast. It is also turned into a sauce for serving with Welsh lamb or mutton. The seaweed purée is combined with the juice of a Seville orange, some butter and a little stock, and is eaten hot with the roast meat. But real laver fans prefer to eat their laverbread 'neat and strong'.

Herbs

Strictly speaking a herb is any kind of non-woody flowering plant, but in practice the word has come to mean a plant that is useful or beneficial to man – or indeed animals. We tend to think of herbs as culinary ingredients, but they have also been revered as medicines, and since ancient times have been endowed with great power and magical properties; sometimes even their mere presence was sufficient to ward off the powers of evil or create a feeling of happiness.

The therapeutic, religious and magical virtues of herbs were celebrated in herbals, vast encyclopedias of knowledge about the action and uses of various plants. The famous English herbalists of the 16th and 17th centuries, men like John Parkinson, Nicholas Culpeper and John Gerard, wrote epic tomes on the subject, and as well as detailed information about cures and treatments, they also gave clues to the old culinary uses of herbs. Gradually herbs became all-purpose plants, equally useful for the cook and the physician. And even with the advent of synthetic pharmaceuticals, many people still put their trust in herbs, as well as keep a good stock of them in the kitchen and garden.

It's no wonder that herbs have found favour in recent years, for they have come to symbolise all that is wholesome and natural. In an age increasingly suspicious of artificial flavourings, additives and drugs, they offer a perfect way out. They can provide food and flavouring, fragrance and decoration; they can be home-grown, they are attractive and each one is quite distinctive. Herbs are fascinating because they seem to embody ancient virtues and have a real flavour of history about them.

The plants listed on the following pages are those which are best known and most useful in the kitchen. Some do have recognised therapeutic qualities too, but the choice is aimed more at the cook, rather than the herablist. Of course there are many more that could be mentioned, herbs that have been dormant for centuries, but have literally sprung up again in recent years: rocket, southernwood, soapwort, verbena, woodruff. All have their uses and are worth growing just for the sheer fun of it.

Buying fresh herbs   Herb-growing is now a booming cottage industry, and herb farms are appearing everywhere. As a result it is now easy to buy a whole range of interesting and unusual varieties from these suppliers or from stores which are beginning to stock both seeds and plants from some of the more adventurous growers. Not so long ago it was difficult even to buy a sprig of fresh parsley from a shop; nowadays all kinds are sold by greengrocers, delicatessens and supermarkets.

Sprigs of fresh herbs should *look* fresh, not dried out or wilted. There should also be plenty of green leaves (some pre-packed sprigs of herbs are 90% unusable stalks and stems). If you are buying a whole plant, buy at the right time of year for planting out and choose a specimen that is healthy-looking and stocky, rather than one that is thin and straggly.

Growing your own There's no substitute for a sprig of herbs picked fresh from the growing plant, and to achieve this you have to be both cook and gardener. But this is a very practical and sensible state of affairs. Herbs have the advantage that they can be grown just as well in window boxes in high-rise flats as in spacious country gardens; many of them are also quite happy to live indoors.

Specific details on planting and cultivation are outside the scope of this book, but readers can easily consult one of the many book on the subject. (See Bibliography page 275-76). Suppliers of herbs are always ready to help and advise, and often provide leaflets or instructions on the subject.

Dried herbs Fresh herbs are the best because they have the most distinctive scent and flavour. But some can also be dried quite successfully, and this is a useful way of ensuring a stock of those herbs that die down in winter. Mints, bay leaves, thyme, lemon balm, rosemary and others can be dried; parsley, chervil, chives and tarragon don't dry well. Once again, specific details of drying herbs at home can be found in any herb book.

Always be wary of buying dried herbs from shops, because they may be very old and consist of little more than flavourless dust. But if you do have to buy them, always purchase small quantities at a time and use them quickly.

If you buy little sealed packets or sachets, then you hve to take pot luck; if however you buy from a shop that sells dried herbs loose, you can at least smell and examine the quality before you pay your money.

Remember that dried herbs are much more concentrated than fresh ones. Every teaspoon of dried herbs is roughly equivalent in flavour to three teaspoons of fresh.

Angelica (*Angelica archangelica*)

Legend has it that St. Michael the Archangel revealed the qualities of this herb in a dream during the time of plague, and a piece of the root held in the mouth was supposed to banish the 'pestilentiall aire'.

Description A giant member of the parsley family, growing up to 7 ft tall in rich, moist, well-shaded soil. Easily recognised by its hollow stems, umbels of flowers tinged pink, and broad, toothed leaves. Hardy annual, biennial or triennial.

Uses Its young candied stems are used for decorating cakes; it is added to marmalades and preserves of marrow and rhubarb, and its roots give a distinctive flavour to many liqueurs and aperitifs. The raw blanched shoots can be eaten in salads.

Medicinally it has stimulant and tonic properties, aids digestion and relieves troublesome coughs. It is a popular ingredient of herb teas.

Basil Sweet basil (*Ocimum basilicum*)
Bush basil (*Ocimum minimum*)

One of the great culinary herbs that reached England from India and the Middle East in the 16th century.

Description Delicate and fragrant, basil likes warmth and has an unmistakable Mediterranean character. It's a sturdy, erect plant, whose leaves give off the most seductive aroma. Annual.

Uses Basil was used to flavour the famous Fetter Lane sausages in the 17th century, and still goes well with sausage and minced meat mixtures. It is *the* herb with tomatoes, and can be put into salads and rice dishes. It is also the essential ingredient of Italian pesto, a thick garlic and herb sauce.

Medicinally its camphor-based oil is highly aromatic and digestive; it is said to calm the nerves and has definite cooling properties.

Always buy a pot of fresh basil to give you a supply of leaves right through the summer.

Bay (*Laurus nobilis*)

Sometimes known as the bay laurel or sweet bay, this is one of the most widely used of all herbs. A crown of bay leaves was the symbol of victors and emperors in the ancient world.

Description A small tree or large bush, normally growing to about 10 ft, although perfect specimens may reach 60 ft in ideal conditions. The leaves are pointed, glossy and dark green. Perennial.

Uses The leaves, which can be picked fresh from the tree or used dried, are essential in many English, French and Mediterranean dishes. Fresh bay leaves have a slighty more bitter flavour, while very old dried leaves are no use at all.

They are part of bouquet garni, are added to marinades and pickles, decorate pâtés and are put into every conceivable kind of meat and fish dish. Soups and stews are flavoured with bay leaves and even sweet milk puddings and custards benefit from them.

The oil in bay leaves has a powerful invigorating effect, thought to lift depression and give a feeling of elation. It also promotes perspiration and so aids feverish colds.

Borage (*Borago officinalis*)

Originally from the Middle East and introduced into this country by the Romans, borage is a lovely herb in every sense. You have only to look at it to believe, as the old herbalists did, that it was a plant to make you merry and glad.

Description Can grow up to 3 ft high. The stems and leaves are covered with coarse hairs, but it is the delightful, five-pointed sky-blue flowers that catch the eye. It has been described as 'growing demurely with its blue head slightly bowed like that of some medieval lady'. Annual.

Uses Borage is a herb for using fresh in the summer. Float the leaves into fruit drinks and 'Pimms' where they provide a cooling taste of cucumber. The leaves can also be finely chopped and put into salads or mixed with yoghurt or cream cheese, while the flowers have been candied, although this form of preservation hardly does them justice.

Borage leaves have been used as a cosmetic bath to cleanse and strengthen the body and beautify the skin. Borage is also a good bee plant when in full flower.

Chamomile (*Chamaemelum nobile*)

Sweet chamomile and its relative the wild or German Chamomile (*Matricaria chamomilla*) are herbs with a long history. Indeed chamomile was listed as one of the nine sacred herbs of the Anglo-Saxons.

Description Sweet chamomile has feathery, apple-scented foliage and white daisy-like flowers. It is a perennial (unlike the wild chamomile which is an annual).

Uses Chamomile tea, made from an infusion of the flower heads is an age-old remedy still much in demand as a mild sedative and a settler of upset stomachs. Body and hair lotions were prepared from it, and it was a maker of lawns. (The prostrate non-flowering variety *C nobile* Treneague can be used to emulate the famous scented lawn at Buckingham Palace which is pure chamomile.)

Chervil (*Anthriscus cerefolium*)

A close relative of the common cow parsley, the first white umbelliferate to bloom in the spring along hedgerows and road-sides. Chervil is a native of southern Russia and the Middle East, and came to Britain with the Romans.

Description It grows to about 1 ft high with delicate fern-like, grassy green leaves and umbels of tiny white flowers. Biennial.

Uses Always use the leaves very fresh and pick from the outside of the plant. Chervil can be chopped and tossed into soups and salads. just before serving; it is a good herb for omelettes and scambled egg and can be used to flavour wine vinegar. Its virtues are only appreciated when it is raw and freshly gathered.

Chive (*Allium schoenoprasum*)

Introduced into China some 2,000 years ago, but not cultivated in Britain till the Middle Ages, chives have long been valued for both their delicate onion flavour and for their health-giving properties.

Description Hollow, thin, grass-like stems with almost no bulb. They grow in clumps and produce attractive purple flower heads. Perennial.

Uses Because they contain a high proportion of volatile oil, chives don't dry well, indeed it's not worth buying or using them unless they are fresh. Chives have a great affinity with cheese of various kinds, from cream cheese and cottage cheese to Cotswold cheese (otherwise known as Double Gloucester with chives (see page 44)). Chives can be chopped and added to potato salad, mashed potatoes and omelettes, and a delicate chive sauce is excellent with trout or fillet of pork.

Medicinally chives are rich in sulphur and have antiseptic qualities as well as aiding the digestion.

> *Buy locally. Support your local producers and suppliers, but always check the true origins of your purchases.*

Comfrey (*Symphytum officinale*)

Common comfrey was one of the wonders of the herbalist's medicine cupboard: it was highly prized by the Greeks and Romans and was used for everything from drawing splinters and setting bones to soothing internal organs.

In 1870, a Quaker farmer named Henry Doubleday began to import a fine variety of comfrey from Russia and planted it on his farm in Bocking, Essex. It was the beginning of what was to become the Henry Doubleday Research Association founded by the pioneer of organic gardening Lawrence D. Hills.

Description A relative of the borage (see page 217) with hairy, spear-shaped leaves and clusters of pinkish, mauve and white bell-like flowers. The valuable roots can extend 10 ft into the soil.

Uses Comfrey's medicinal properties are well-known and its composition actually bears out its therapeutic claims. It is rich in B vitamins, especially B12, also vitamins C and E, plus elements such as iron, calcium, manganese and phosphorus, and it contains allantoin, an invaluable compound for healing tissues.

The leaves can be cooked and eaten like a kind of glutinous spinach or dipped in batter and deep-fried. The young shoots have also been eaten like a coarse version of asparagus.

Comfrey tablets and ointment are available, you can buy packets of the leaves dried to make into an infusion or tea (they are hygroscopic and draw moisture from the air, so make sure the packets are well sealed); there's also comfrey flour – actually dried leaves crushed to a greenish powder. Or you can order plants of Russian comfrey direct from the Henry Doubleday Research Association (see page 207).

Coriander (*Coriandrum sativum*)

One of the oldest herbs known to man; the ancient Chinese believed it bestowed immortality. It's a native of southern Europe and the Near East, but is now cultivated in many parts of the world, and was brought to Britain by the Romans.

Description Coriander is both a herb and a spice. It's a strong-smelling, green leaved plant easily recognised because the lower leaves are fan-like and the upper ones are feathery. The little ripe spherical seeds are very aromatic, but completely different in character to the herb. A hardy annual growing up to 3 ft high.

Uses As a herb, coriander is an indispensible ingredient in Indian cooking, for garnishing curries and flavouring chutneys. The seeds, ground up, have a spiciness that also makes them a curry spice, while the whole seeds can be tossed into soups, casseroles and the like and have a pleasing affinity with lamb. Nearer home, coriander is an essential pickling spice and may well have found its way into old traditional dishes like steak, kidney and oyster pie.

Costmary (*Chrysanthemum balsamita*)

Grown in English gardens since the 16th century, costmary was also known as 'alecost' because is was used to flavour ale, and its common nickname 'bibleleaf' derived form the fact that its long leaves were used as book-marks by bible-reading American colonists.

Description A member of the chrysanthemum family, with yellow, button-like flowers, growing to a height of about 3 ft. Perennial.

Uses The leaves can be used fresh or dried and have a characteristic spicy-mint flavour. Put them in soups, game and poultry dishes, stuffings and even cakes.

Dandelion (*Taraxacum officinale*)

Wild dandelions have been eaten since earlist times, but we in Britain have shunned them as a crop since the 19th century. The French have more wisdom, and produce several cultivated varieties.

Description A widespread and unmistakable plant, often discarded as a weed in British gardens. It has thick, dark green leaves growing from the base and bright yellow flowers borne on a long hollow stem. Perennial.

Uses Dandelion leaves are extremely nutritious – they are high in vitamin A, have more iron than spinach and four times as much vitamin C as lettuce. They can be quite bitter when raw, but lose this if blanched and cooked with a knob of butter. Add them to salads, or serve as a dish with pieces of crisp fried bacon. Dandelion roots can be turned into a caffeine-free coffee substitute, while the yellow flowers go to make dandelion wine.

While dandelions are common enough to be found and used at almost any time of the year, you can also get seeds for special cultivated varieties which have particularly thick succulent leaves.

Dill (*Anethum graveolens*)

Dill gets its name from the Norse *dilla* meaning to lull to sleep, and its powers as a soothing potion were understood by the Greeks and later the Anglo-Saxons used it for quieting babies and as part of a cure-all magic salve for various afflictions.

Description A yellow-flowered umbelliferate, similar to fennel, with feathery fern-like leaves and little buff coloured seeds. Dill is a smaller, more delicate plant in every way to fennel. Annual.

Uses Dill 'weed', as the freshly chopped leaves are called, makes a sauce for fish, especially salmon, and a sprig of the plant is essential in pickled cucumbers. Dill seeds are sprinkled on breads and rolls, are delicious added to apple pie and give an extra dimension to vegetables like cabbage and cauliflower.

Dill contains the volatile oils limonene and carvone; in the form of gripe water it aids digestion and soothes upset stomachs; it is also rich in mineral oils and is recommended as a milk stimulant for nursing mothers.

Garlic

One of the most ancient and highly regarded of all herbs and flavourings, garlic has been an essential ingredient of many national cuisines since the days of the Pharoahs. We don't think of it as a truly English food, although it was very common in all kinds of recipes, especially during the 17th and 18th centuries. It has had a revival in recent years with the opening up of our gastronomic horizons, but many people still have a deep-rooted prejudice against it.

Description A member of the lily family grown for its swollen bulbs which are divided up into a number of different 'cloves'. Thee are many varieties: some are mild and sweet in flavour, others strong and pungent; some are small, others grow to giant size: there are also species with white skin and others coloured mauve or purple.

Uses Garlic is probably the most valuable of all flavourings and appears in literally thousands of different dishes from countries as far apart as France and China. Its great virtue is that it blends with almost any kind of meat, fish and game, not to mention vegetbles and other herbs.

In addition to that, garlic is also extremely healthy. It contains antiseptic substances that help the digestion and it has been eaten as a stimulant. It is also known to reduce blood pressure and relieve bronchitis.

Fennel (*Foeniculum vulgare*)

One of the most highly esteemed of all herbs, popularised by the Greeks and Romans and revered by the Anglo-Saxons who proclaimed that 'Thyme and fennel' were 'a pair great in power'. Fennel had a host of uses, from sharpening the eyesight and 'making those more lean that are too fat' to warding off the tricks of the elves and demons.

Description Very similar in appearance to dill, with umbels of yellow flowers and feathery green foliage. But fennel is more robust, growing up to 6 ft high. It is cultivated and also grows wild along roadsides and wasteground, especially in south and east England. Perennial.

Uses Fennel leaves are the perfect accompaniment to fish, from a delicate sauce or mayonnaise to the sprigs which are used as a base for grilling red mullet or sea bass. Like dill, fennel has natural oils and acids which aid the digestion and make a good foil to rich foods like pork. Chopped fresh fennel leaves are excellent tossed into salads; the seeds can be used like dill seeds and have a nutty, aniseed flavour. Fennel can be dried, although it is at its best fresh and aromatic.

Horseradish (*Armoracia rusticana*)

Horseradish has been grown and cultivated in northern Europe for centuries and is a tough customer; once established it's almost impossible to eradicate and will spring up in the wild in almost any conditions.

Description Large, crinkly, palm-like leaves, resembling the dock, will show you where horseradish is growing. However, it is the knobbly white roots that yield the highly prized condiment. Perennial.

Uses Freshly grated horseradish root has a pungent volatile oil that makes the eyes stream and the nose run. For hundreds of years it has been served freshly grated or as a sauce with roast beef (although in the 17th and 18th centuries it accompanied almost every kind of roast meat). It also goes well with fish and can be macerated to produce horseradish vinegar.

Horseradish has high levels of vitamin C, contains a natural antibiotic and has useful antiseptic elements which kill many germs; it stimulates the digestion and the kidneys and is therefore not only delicious with rich fatty foods but therapeutic too.

You can buy jars of grated horseradish, which can be excellent or too old and stale to be of any real use.

Hyssop (*Hyssopus officinalis*)

A herb of purification since ancient times. 'Purge me with hyssop and I shall be clean', said the psalmist in the Bible. More favoured as a medicinal and decorative herb, rather than one for the kitchen, but worth investigating.

Description A pretty shrubby plant about 18 inches high, with dark-green pointed leaves and royal blue flowers. Doesn't grow wild in Britain. Perennial.

Uses Both the leaves and the flowers are used, fresh or dried. Add the leaves to cranberry sauce or rich duck pâté, or use them with dishes of lentils and other pulses.

Medicinally hyssop is useful for its antiseptic qualities; it is given for coughs and upset stomach and is used as a poultice for bruises and rheumatism.

Juniper (*Juniperus communis*)

The fruit (berries) of the juniper were once highly valued in English and Scottish cooking, but have fallen into neglect in recent years. Juniper is now most readily recognised as the essential flavouring for gin.

Description The juniper bush is a small, prickly evergreen, now largely confined to moors and pine woods in Scotland, although it's easily cultivated in the garden and is still widespread in many European countries from Spain to Sweden. The berries begin as little green cones which turn to black in the second and third year, when they are picked.

Uses The strong aromatic oil in juniper has elements of turpentine, and it is this which gives it its character. Its resinous and slightly sweet flavour is perfect with game dishes (venison, grouse, hare, etc.); it has been used to flavour hams and makes a good stuffing for goose or turkey.

Lavender (*Lavandula* spec.)

The scent of lavender is one of the most seductive of all in the English garden and it's understandable that this little shrub has retained its popularity for centuries; it is one of the few herbs that is cultivated and harvested on a commercial scale for its natural oils.

Description There are many varieties in cultivation; the most common being *Lavandula dentata* (French lavender) and *Lavandula vera* (English lavender). French lavender is a large bushy shrub with grey serrated leaves and spikes of pale mauve blossoms; English lavender is smaller, with pointed grey leaves and deep-mauve blossoms. There's also *Lavandula stoechas*, a dwarf with rich purple flowers, and a white flowering variety, *Lavandula officinalis alba*. These and other varieties are rare.

Uses Mainly valued for the oil and scent in its flowers, especially in lavender bottles, pot pourri and for making cooling lotions. But lavender was once a culinary herb, too, and the flowers can be used dried in cakes, or in herby mixtures with oregano and rosemary. Lavender sauce with fish is making a comeback in some enterprising English restaurants.

Lemon balm (*Melissa officinalis*)

Melissa is the Greek for bee, and the Greeks grew lemon balm close to their hives because bees loved it and it was thought to enhance the value of the honey. It was indispensable in old herb gardens; even so, it's now given little attention.

Description Related to the mints, indeed it looks at first glance as if it might be a mint of some kind. It grows about 2 ft tall, spreads with abandon and has oval, yellowish leaves with serrated edges and little whitish flowers. It also has an unmistakable lemon scent. Perennial.

Uses Lemon balm should be more popular than it is. Use it whenever you can. Chop it into omelettes and salads, put the leaves into iced drinks and fruit cups; add it to rice dishes and stuffings for fish and poultry. It also goes well with cooked apple.

As a medicinal herb, lemon balm curbs flatulence, and creates mild perspiration (so it is useful against feverish colds). The old herbalists believed it could lift depressions and renew vigour.

Lemon balm dries quite successfully but is best used fresh. It is worth noting that its flavour is far less strong than its scent.

Lovage (*Levisticum officinale*)

Sometimes known as 'love-ache' or love parsley, lovage was once an important herb, but it seems to have gone out of fashion since Elizabethan times. A revival of this splendid, but neglected, herb is long overdue.

Description   All parts of the plant are used – leaves, stems, seeds and roots. Its curious scent and flavour – somewhat musky, with a hint of celery and lemon – can provide new contrasts if the leaves are chopped and added to potato or tomato salads; the seeds can be added to breads and used on biscuits, but its great use is as a delicious and distinctively flavoured soup.

Lovage contains a volatile oil called angelic acid, which is antiseptic. Its resins and oils are also said to act on the kidneys and bladder.

Lovage is also part of a traditional West Country cordial of the same name.

Marjoram (*Origanum majorana*)

Marjoram does grow wild in Britain, but it is the sweet or knotted marjoram (*O. majorana*) that is most commonly used in the kitchen. It has been cultivated as a flowering herb since ancient times, when it was regarded as the herb of happiness and was also used for preserving ale before the advent of hops.

Description   A strongly perfumed member of the mint family, growing to a healthy shrub-like plant, some 2 ft high. It has oval greyish-green leaves and white or pale pinkish flowers in clusters or knots. Perennial, although it ought to be treated as a half-hardy annual in Britain, where the winters are cold.

Uses   A very important kitchen herb, equally useful fresh or dried. Use the leaves fresh in herb scones, omelettes, salads and sauces; add to soups and stews, particularly with red meat. Also try making brown bread sandwiches filled with marjoram leaves spread with cream cheese. Its aromatic qualities make it ideal for pot pourri and sweet muslin bags to go in bath water; it was once valued as a herb to be strewn on the floors of houses.

Marjoram is an antiseptic and stimulant; it also appears to aid healing by increasing the number of white blood cells to fight infection.

Mint (*Mentha* spec.)

Perhaps the most widely used and cultivated of all herbs in Britain. The Romans appreciated its culinary and medicinal virtues; it flourished in Medieval monastery gardens and was beloved of the great English herbalists: Nicholas Culpeper listed no fewer than 40 ailments for which mint was beneficial!

Description Mints abound and there are many different varieities and hybrids, all with slightly different qualities and characteristics. The best known is the Spearmint (*Mentha spicata*), the common commercial and garden variety, but even this has variations; Applemint (*Mentha rotundifola*) is the finest of the round-leaved mints with its distinctive furry leaves; Eau-de-Cologne mint (*Mentha piperita citrata*) has dark purplish leaves and a distinctive scent; Peppermint (*Mentha piperita officinalis*) is grown commercially for the extraction of peppermint oil, and there are many others worth cultivating.

Uses Different mints have different uses. Applemint is the best for cooking; use it for making mint sauce for lamb or mutton, add it to green peas or new potatoes, turn it into mint jelly. It also forms the basis of oriental chutneys, with chillis, coconut and yoghurt; it can be added to salads of lentils, mushrooms, tomatoes and so on, and it blends well with apples and gooseberries. It is also used for fruit cups, mint julep and makes a refreshing iced tea. All its uses are redolent of summer.

Mint can be used equally well fresh or dried: the best variety for drying is the spearmint.

Medicinally mint has cooling and digestive properties, stimulating the appetite, settling the stomach and counteracting wind.

Parsley (*Petroselinum crispum*)

An indispensable herb known throughout the world for centuries and the subject of innumerable superstitions and legends. Its native home is the Mediterranean and it was highly valued by the Greeks and the Romans, who probably brought it to Britain.

Description   There are several varieties, the most common in Britain being curled parsley (*Petroselinum crispum*). Plain-leaved variety (*Petroselinum crispum filicinum*) is less attractive to look at, but is hardier. One advantage of curled parsley, especially in gardens, is that it cannot be confused with poisonous fool's parsley (*Aethusa cynapium*), a wild plant that often finds its way into parsley beds. Biennial.

Uses   Best used fresh, although it can be dried. It's the universal garnish and the chopped leaves go to make parsley butter and parsley sauce; it is also used as a vegetable – lightly fried and served with fish.

Parsley is also a highly nutritious herb, containing as much vitamin A as cod liver oil and three times as much vitamin C as oranges. It's a rich source of vitamins B, D and E, as well as iron, sulphur, calcium, potassium and phosphorus. It has been used as a diuretic and is said to be helpful in kidney and bladder disorders. And it contains the volatile oil, apiol, which has been used to treat malaria.

Hamburg parlsey see page 197

Rosemary (*Rosmarinus officinalis*)

Innumerable sacred legends have grown up around this important and popular herb: it was regarded as a defence against evil, as a herb of friendship and – most well-known of all – as a symbol of remembrance.

Although it was mentioned in Anglo-Saxon medico-magical works, it didn't become popular in Britain until the Middle Ages.

Description   A sweet-scented bush growing up to 6 ft high with tiny pale-Blue flowers and grey-green spiky leaves. Grows wild on mediterranean hillsides, but is easily cultivated in Britain. Perennial.

Uses   Sprigs of Fresh rosemary have a pungent, aromatic quality and should be used sparingly. The dried leaves are quite useful but can be even stronger and are less aromatic, so they too should be used with care. Since rosemary is an evergreen, it can be picked fresh at any time of year.

Very good with roast joints, especially lamb and pork. The leaves can be crumbled or chopped and added to soups, casseroles and stews. The natural oils in the plant make it useful for lotions, toilet waters and pot pourri and it is good as a tonic for the hair and scalp. Rosemary wood was once used for making lutes and carpenters' rules.

Sage (*Salvia officinalis*)

A great, all-purpose healing herb since ancient times: indeed an ancient proverb asked the question 'Why should a man die while sage grows in his garden?'. Its natural home is the north Mediterranean coast, but it has long been cultivated in Britain, although it didn't become popular as a culinary herb until the 16th century.

Description A relative of the mints. Although by far the most common and popular is the garden sage (*S. officinalis*), there are numerous other varieties: red sage, pineapple sage, clary sage and so on. Garden sage is the easiest to grow and best suited to English gardens. It has pointed greyish leaves with purplish or white flowers, and can grow into a thick shrubby bush after a few years. Perennial.

Uses Fresh sage leaves have a powerful flavour, go well with pork or veal, and make the classic sage and onion stuffing for roast duck. They can be chopped and added to spinach, potatoes or split peas, and also form part of the usual 'mixed herbs'. Sage is also the most popular flavouring for good butcher's sausages, while Sage Derby cheese gets its colour and flavour from the herb (see page 42). Sage leaves dry well.

Sage tea, sage cream, sage wine and even sage tobacco were favourites with country people in the past.

Salad burnet (*Poterium sanguisorba*)

Known to the Anglo-Saxons, but reached the height of its popularity as a kitchen herb during Elizabethan times. It is a native of Europe, grows wild on chalky soil in southern England and is easily cultivated.

Description A delightful plant with little toothed leaves growing in pairs, which have a smell of cucumber when crushed. The flower head is a kind of greenish 'bobble' borne on a long stem. Perennial.

Uses The young fresh leaves can be used to perfume and flavour cooling drinks. They can be infused to make burnet vinegar and are important in some classical French sauces and herb butters. But when young they are at their best when added to mixed green salads, where their flavour and texture provides a good contrast to the other green leaves.

Savory
Summer savory (*Satureia hortensis*)
Winter savory (*Satureia montana*)

Species of savory arrived in Britain from the Mediterranean with the Romans, and were so popular that they were taken to America by early settlers. Summer savory is the most widely used for cooking and for its medicinal value; winter savory does have culinary uses, although in the past it was liked because of its decorative qualities and was used to make low hedges for herb gardens and dwarf shrub mazes in Tudor times.

Description Summer savory grows to about a foot high, has narrow elongated leaves and plain pinkish-mauve flowers. It tends to straggle. Annual.

Winter savory is a sturdy shrub-like plant with bluish-purple flowers. Perennial.

Uses Both have a strong powerful flavour, somewhat peppery and aromatic, and should be used sparingly. Equally good fresh or dried. Summer savory can be put into sausages and stuffings and traditionally goes with peas and broad beans. Medicinally it has been used to soothe sore eyes, ease colic and help coughs and catarrh. It is also claimed that rubbing a leaf on a bee sting will ease the pain.

Winter savory is less popular in the kitchen, although it is good with trout and gives a new flavour to tripe.

Sorrel (*Rumex scutatus*)

The word sorrel is based on an old Teutonic word meaning 'sour' and in fact all the true sorrels are 'sour docks'. Although we think of it primarily as a French herb, it can be easily cultivated in Britain, and is a relative of the well-known wild sorrel (*Rumex acetosa*) which is one of the first green plants to appear in spring.

Description Its dark-green, arrow-shaped leaves and spikes of red and green flowers are easily recognisable. When cultivated, sorrel can grow up to 2 ft tall. Perennial.

Uses Has the character of both a herb and a vegetable, and its sharp, acid leaves, picked young, have a wide range of splendid uses. In Elizabethan times it made a green sauce for fish, and currently today's chefs match salmon with delicate sorrel sauce; it can be turned into a delicious refreshing soup, added to omelettes or made into a purée to go with veal. The leaves can also be cooked like spinach, although the two are very different in character. It can also be used raw in salads, provided the leaves are very young. Old sorrel leaves can be tough, coarse and very acidic.

Fresh sorrel should be more commonly available in shops, but it is easily grown in the garden, so it is always on hand when you need it.

Note: never cook sorrel in an iron pan and only chop it with a stainless steel knife, since the acid in the leaves may attack the metal, turning it black.

Sweet cicely (*Myrrhis odorata*)

Sometimes called sweet chervil, sweet ciss or simply 'sweets', all of which refer to its distinctly sugary overtones. It is an old-fashioned herb, popular in Britain during the 16th and 17th centuries, and still growing wild in parts of northern England and Scotland. It can also be cultivated from seed.

Description Similar to chervil in appearance (see page 218), with delicate, feathery leaves and umbels of white flowers. It normally grows to about 3 ft in height. Perennial.

Uses Sweet cicely's sugary character means that it can be used as a substitute for sugar and it gives a subtle aniseed flavour to stewed fruits like plums and gooseberries which can be sharp and acidic. It also goes well with cabbage and parsnips. The roots can be boiled and eaten as a vegetable like parsnips or chopped into salads. The seeds (once blended into a wax polish to perfume wooden floors and furniture) can be tossed into stews and soups.

Sweet cicely has been prescribed for many ailments: distilled cicely water acts on the kidneys, while the ointment is recommended for gout.

Tansy (*Chrysanthemum vulgare/ Tanacetum vulgare*)

In the Middle Ages and up to the 17th century, tansy was one of the most important of all cottage garden herbs, with an extraordinary range of culinary and medicinal uses. All of which is bewildering to us, because the plant tastes bitter, smells unpleasant, and is positively dangerous if used in excess.

Description A member of the compositae with fern-like leaves and golden, button-shaped flowers. Usually grows 2–3 ft tall. Annual.

Uses Most of tansy's old uses were associated with Easter, when the leaves were chopped and added to cakes, puddings and omelettes. Indeed a 'tansy' was a kind of baked or boiled custard flavoured with tansy leaves. It may also be used in stuffings, meat pies and fish dishes. (Izaak Walton in his 17th century classic *The Compleat Angler* includes it in a recipe for cooking minnows.)

Tansy is well worth investigating, but proceed with caution!

Tarragon
French tarragon (*Artemisia dracunculus*)
Russian tarragon (*Artemisia dracunculoides*)

One of the finest of all culinary herbs, tarragon was first mentioned in Europe in the 12th century. It was originally prescribed as a remedy for toothache and to cure the bites of mad dogs, but it now reigns supreme in the kitchen.

Description It is important to distinguish between true French tarragon and Russian or false tarragon. Both are bushy perennials with smooth, slender leaves and little grey-green flowers, but Russian tarragon is paler and has none of the delicacy or flavour of its French relative. French tarragon is difficult to cultivate, and has to be grown from cuttings or root division; Russian tarragon, on the other hand, grows easily from seed.

Uses Always use tarragon fresh; dried tarragon quickly loses its flavour and becomes musty. Make sure you are buying the French, rather than the Russian variety, as the difference in flavour and aroma is enormous.

Tarragon is one of the classic herbs for French cooking: it is an essential ingredient of béarnaise sauce; it makes a lovely sauce to go with chicken, sole and eggs and can be used to garnish delicate cream soups. Freshly chopped leaves transform omelettes, flavour mustard, and can be used to make herb vinegar. Tarragon-flavoured butter is served with asparagus, artichokes and broccoli spears.

Eat with the seasons.

Thyme (*Thymus vulgaris*)

One of the greatest compliments you could pay an ancient Greek was to tell him he smelled of thyme; it was the herb of courage, elegance and grace in those days and was also known for its antiseptic, purifying properties: its name in Greek means to fumigate or 'burn sacrifice'. Garden thyme (*Thymus vulgaris*) has been cultivated and valued as a kitchen herb for hundreds of years, and even bees like it; indeed honey made from it is one of the most fragrant of all.

Description There are countless species of thyme: in addition to the common garden thyme, there's lemon thyme (*Thymus citriodorus*), a great favourite with cooks; variegated thyme (*T. citriodorus variegatus*) is similar to lemon thyme but has golden variegated leaves; caraway thyme (*T. herba-barona*) is known for its distinctive caraway scent; there's also *T. nitidus*, *T. pauciflorus*, *T. serpyllum* and many others, as well as the wild thyme (*T. drucei*) which grows on chalk and limestone in many parts of Britain.

All have very characteristic scents, flavours and form, although most grow as creeping shrubs, with small leaves and tiny flowers which can be any colour from white or pink to reddish-purple. Perennial.

Uses Choose thyme for its scent and flavour. Garden thyme is vry strong and pungent, compared with the subtle, heady and aromatic scent of wild thyme.

Thyme is one of the most useful kitchen herbs, at its best fresh but still very effective when dried, with none of the mustiness of some dried herbs. Add it to meaty casseroles and stews, with beef, chicken, oxtail, mutton or rabbit, where it mingles well with onions, garlic and wine. Use it with parsley to make stuffing and include it in bouquet garni; it also goes with vegetables like courgettes, potatoes and peppers and is good in pâtés and terrines.

Thyme's volatile oil, thymol, is an antiseptic and can be used as a medication for coughs and catarrh if made into a gargle or tea.

Herb growers

Most herb growers supply fresh plants in pots; some also sell seeds and cut herbs. Telephone or write for further details and catalogues (always enclose s.a.e.). If you want to visit a herb grower at times other than those listed, it's wise to telephone in advance.

Thornbury Herbs
Elm Grove, Thornbury,
Bromyard,
Hereford & Worcester
Tel: (088 854) 204
Open: 9.30 am – 5 pm
Monday – Saturday

Foliage, Scented &
Herb Plants
Ranmore Common,
Dorking, Surrey
Tel: (048 65) 2273/4731
Open: March – September
10 am – 5 pm Wednesday,
Saturday & Sunday

Thornham Herbs
The Walled Garden,
Thornham Magna, Eye,
Suffolk
Tel: (037 983) 510
Open: 10 am – 5 pm   M.

Cornish Herbs
Trelowarren,
Mawgan-in-Menage,
Helston, Cornwall
Tel: (032 622) 374
Open: April – September
noon – 5 pm
(except Mondays)   M.

Lomond Herb Garden
Lomond, Horsehill,
Hookwood, Horley,
Surrey
Tel: (0293) 862318
Open: April – September
9.30 am – 5 pm Monday –
Wednesday; 9.30 am – 1 pm
Saturday   M.

Old Rectory Herb Garden
Rectory Lane, Ightham,
Kent
Tel: (0732) 882608
Open: 9 am – 4 pm Monday
– Friday; 9 am – noon
Saturday

Herbs in Stock
Whites Hill, Stock,
Ingatestone, Essex
Tel: (0277) 841130
Open: April – September
10 am – 5 pm

Norfolk Lavender Ltd
Caley Mill, Heacham,
King's Lynn, Norfolk
Tel: (0485) 70384
Open end May – end
September 10 am – 6 pm;
end September – end May
9 am – 4 pm (Monday –
Friday)   M.

Greenways Herb Farm
Church House, Lyonshall,
Kington,
Hereford & Worcester
Tel: (05448) 350
Open 10 am – 6 pm
(except Wednesdays)

Doria Herbs
The Garden Flat,
72 Maida Vale, London W9
Tel: (01) 624 3589
Open: telephone before
calling

Wells & Winter Ltd
Mere House, Mereworth,
Maidstone, Kent
Tel: (0622) 812491
Open: 10 am – 5 pm

Netherfield Herbs
The Thatched Cottage,
37 Nether Street, Rougham,
Suffolk
Tel: (0359) 70452
Open: 10.30 am – 5.30 pm
most days

Green Earth Nurseries
Draycote Lane, Draycote,
Rugby, Warwickshire
Tel: (0926) 663195
Open: May – October
Saturday & Sunday
(telephone first)

Mary Webb Herbs
Hilcrest, Astley,
Shrewsbury, Shropshire
Tel: (09397) 339
Open: telephone before
calling M.

Arne Herbs
Old Tavern,
Compton Dundon,
Somerton, Somerset
Tel: (0458) 42347
Open: daily M.

Candlesby Herbs
Cross Keys, Candlesby,
Spilsby, Lincolnshire
Tel: (075 485) 211
Open: 9 am – 5 pm
Tuesday – Sunday M.

Iden Croft Herbs
Frittenden Road,
Staplehurst, Kent
Tel: (0580) 891432
Open: 9 am – 4 pm

Selsley Herb & Goat Farm
Waterlane, Selsley,
Stroud, Gloucestershire
Tel: (045 36) 6682
Open: 2 pm – 5 pm
Tuesday – Sunday M.

Suffolk Herbs
Sawyers Farm,
Little Cornard, Sudbury,
Suffolk
Tel: (0787) 227247
Open: Saturday only M.

Foxhollow Nursery
73 Lower Pillory Down,
Little Woodecote,
Wallington, Surrey
Tel: (01) 660 0991
Open: daily

Hollington Nurseries Ltd
Woolton Hill, Newbury,
Berkshire
Tel: (0635) 253908
Open: April – September
10 am – 1 pm, 2 pm – 5 pm
(except Mondays) M.

Daphne-Ffiske Herb
Nursery
2 Station New Road,
Brundall, Norwich, Norflok
Tel: (0603) 712137
Open: 10 am – 4 pm
Thursday – Sunday M.

Wilton Park Nursery
Park Lane,
Old Beaconsfield,
Buckinghamshire
Tel: (04946) 3418
Open: April – September
M.

Yorkshire Herbs
The Herb Centre,
Middleton Tyas, Richmond,
N. Yorkshire
Tel: (032 577) 686
Open: 2 pm – 5 pm
(except Fridays) M.

Herb shops

Dried herbs can be found in every supermarket, delicatessen and food store, but fresh herbs in pots are more difficult to track down. One very useful source of supply is Culpeper the Herbalist, which has a chain of shops in major cities. (New branches are due to open in Chester, Liverpool and Lincoln.)

28 Milsom Street,
Bath, Avon
Tel: (0225) 25875

12d Meeting House Lane,
Brighton, Sussex
Tel: (0273) 27939

25 Lion Yard, Cambridge
Tel: (0223) 67370

10 Swan Lane, Guildford,
Surrey
Tel: (0483) 60008

21 Burton Street,
London W1
Tel: (01) 629 4559

9 Flask Walk, Hampstead,
London NW3
Tel: (01) 794 7263

The Market,
Covent Garden,
London WC1
Tel: (01) 379 6698

14 Bridwell Alley,
Norwich, Norfolk
Tel: (0603) 618911

7 New Inn Hall Street,
Oxford
Tel: (0865) 49754

33 High Street,
Salisbury, Wiltshire
Tel: (0722) 26159

4 Market Street,
Winchester, Hampshire
Tel: (0962) 2866

43 Low Petergate, York
Tel: (0904) 51654

Open: 9.30 am – 5.30 pm Monday – Saturday (all shops)
For Mail Order write to Culpeper the Herbalist, Hadstock Road, Linton, Cambridge.

Useful organisations

The British Herb Trade
Association
2 Manor Farm Cottages,
Cothelstone, Taunton,
Somerset
Tel: (0823) 433322/433215

The Herb Society
34 Boscobel Place,
London SW1
Tel: (01) 235 1530

Fruit

Fruits remained part of the wild harvest long after cereals were being grown in early Britain, and our ancestors made good use of crab apples, sloes, wild cherries, elderberries and the like. The trees took many years to mature, and once established could be relied on to yield up their annual crop without much encouragement from the farmer.

Cultivation really got under way in Roman times, when new varieties were introduced and systematic planting and grafting were the order of the day. More and more varieties started to appear from abroad during the Middle Ages, and by the 16th century horticulture, gardening and growing all kinds of fruit and vegetables was very much the fashion. It was the age of improvement, when the whole of the south-east corner of England was transformed into one huge garden.

Many of today's fruits are relative newcomers, brought from many parts of the world, bred and cultivated to suit our soil and climate, but we still have our old favourites, everything from apples and pears to the wild blackberries and elderberries gathered on autumn forays.

Much of what I said about vegetables (see page 186–88) also applies to fruit: growers today have the same obsession with yield and appearance at the expense of flavour and real quality; large amounts of commercially produced fruit are tainted with sprays and pesticides of one kind or another, and organically grown produce is still relatively hard to come by unless you live near to a farm; there's also a tendency to concentrate on only a handful of commercially desirable varieties, while ignoring some of our most interesting types. All of this suggests that we could greatly improve our fruit, both in terms of quality and variety. And we will need to, because fruit – like vegetables – may well form a much more important part of our diet in the foreseeable future.

Guidelines for buying fruit (i) Always buy fresh fruit, rather than frozen or tinned because it is nicer to eat and generally more nutritious.

(ii) You can buy fresh fruit from good greengrocers, market stalls, farm shops and so on. You can also 'pick your own' in more and more places. This has the advantage tht you can guarantee the freshness of the crop and select exactly what you want. The produce is always good value too. If possible buy your fruit locally and at the peak of its season for best results.

(iii) The qualities to look for in fruit are plumpness, firmness and fragrance. Unless you are going to eat the fruit straight away, buy it a little underripe. And don't be tempted to buy vast quantities at a time, unless you can handle them. Fruit spoils rapidly and you may find that half your purchase is ruined by the time you come to use it.

(iv) Try to inspect or ask for a sample of fruit you intend to buy.

(v) Don't accept fruit that is mushy or bruised.

(vi) Always be ready to try out new varieties, particularly if they are home-grown.

Apple

First cultivated over 3,000 years ago, apples have long been our most important fruit, and there are now something like 3,000 named varieties, although the choice offered in most shops could be counted on the fingers of one hand. Their range is enormous from smooth or striped sour-green fruit to shiny red-skins and and russets.

In season: desserts: (home-grown) September–May; (imported) all year round.

culinary: (home-grown) September–June.

Guidelines Like potatoes in the vegetable kingdom, apples are dominated by varieties, and it's worth getting to know their names. Fortunately most shops advertise and label different kinds, so you don't need to be an expert on apple identification. Always try out a new variety when you see it.

Apples fall into two main groups. Desserts apples for eating fresh including famous names like Cox's Orange Pippins, Worcester Pearmain, Laxton's Superb, Egremont Russet, James Grieve, Discovery, Crispin and Spartan. Culinary or cooking apples (most of which are home-grown) include Bramley's Seedling, Grenadier, Lord Derby and Newton Wonder among others.

Apart from these home-grown varieties, a lot of apples are now imported, especially from France as well as the USA, Canada, New Zeland and South Africa. The ubiquitous French Golden Delicious now dominates the scene, and I have a theory that people buy it for the same reason they buy keg cider or keg beer, because they know what to expect. Every pint the same, every apple the same. But how consistent, how dull. If that is what you like, fair enough, but it's a pity not to try out some of the more unusual home-grown varieties, although finding them might be a problem. Such is the competition from abroad that British growers are being encouraged to uproot and disregard their interesting trees and concentrate on a few commercially desirable, high-yielding varieties. A sad, but familiar story.

Nowadays apples are grown for size and appearance rather than flavour, so you can be easily disappointed if you are looking for decent, tasty fruit. Try a small greengrocer or market stall, where the fruit may well be more local in origin. You can normally tell a good ripe apple by its fragrance.

Uses Eating apples are normally consumed as they are, from hand to mouth, but they are also good for salads of various kinds. Cookers can be used to make soup, sauces and all sorts of desserts from pies to charlottes.

Apples can also be transformed into various beverages.

Apple juice is increasing in popularity all the time. Some of the best comes from cider-maker John Chevallier Guild, The Aspall Cyder House, near Stowmarket, Suffolk, who produces both cider and apple juice from organically grown fruit, and so must come top of the list. Other cider-makers, including Merrydown of Horam, Sussex and Biddenden Vineyards in Kent also make apple juice as part of their operation. Among the apple juice specialists, Devorah Peake at Hill Farm, near Colchester, Essex produces large quantities of juice from Cox's Orange Pippins, sold under the name of Copella.

Blackcurrant

First cultivated in England during the 17th century, blackcurrants are now an important commercial crop, largely due to the fact that they are a particularly rich source of vitamin C.

In season: July–August.

Guidelines Blackcurrants are less common in shops than they used to be, as most farms now have contracts with firms producing fruit syrups and the like. However if you do find some look for punnets containing large ripe berries, with only a few turning from green to black. Some will be loose, some will be on their stalks, but they should be firm and not squashed. You won't want containers full of leaves either, or currants that are wet and starting to rot.

Uses Turned into a famous syrup, but also used for pies, jams and jellies. Blackcurrant sauce is now a popular accompaniment to duck.

Even less common in the shops are shiny redcurrants and their albio relatives, whitecurrants. The same guidelines apply to both.

Cherry

Clusters of pinkish white cherry blossom give us the foretaste of summer, and the fruit until recently had its own fairs when great festive gatherings were held in the orchards.

In season: June–August, depending on the variety.

Guidelines Cherries come in three main groups. Sour or acid cherries are best for cooking, and the most widely known is the Morello with its dark flesh and juice. Sweet dessert cherries can range in colour from yellow to dark red (you can tell them from Morellos by tasting them). There are also hybrid varieties known as Dukes or Royals, which have the qualities of both sweet and sour cherries and are equally suitable for cooking or eating fresh.

Always buy firm, dry fruit without bruises or blemishes, and steer clear of containers with too many leaves and not enough fruit.

Uses Soups, sauces, cakes, liqueurs, the cherry finds its way into all of them.

Damson

This ancestor of many of today's cultivated plums has remained virtually unchanged for something like 2,000 years. Damsons are found in some gardens and in the wild, but the most highly prized of all come from plantations in the Lyth Valley in the Lake District.

In season: September–October.

Guidelines Smaller than most of today's cultivated varieties with blue-black skins. Don't buy squashy or bruised specimens.

Although they may appear in some greengrocers they are often sold locally at farm shops and on roadside stalls.

Uses An excellent fruit for preserving. Can be turned into a splendid jam with apples, made into a sweet pickle (for eating with cold meat and game) and also transformed into a solid fruit cheese. Damson pies and tarts are also worth making.

Gooseberry

Originally a little sharp wild berry, the goseberry blossomed under cultivation, and by the beginning of this century there were some 200 different varieties. They were the favourite cottager's fruit and gooseberry shows are still a feature of life in the north of England, especially in a number of Cheshire villages.

In season: end April–End August.

Guidelines In general use little green gooseberries for cooking and ripe yellow or red ones for eating fresh. Cooking gooseberries can be safely used underripe, although dessert gooseberries need to be fully ripe. Make sure the berries are firm, not squashed or split.

Uses Gooseberries make a splendid traditional sauce for oily fish lke mackerel as well as for richly flavoured goose. They make delicious jams and jellies (often flavoured with elderflowers), not to mention gooseberry fool and a famous raised gooseberry pie from Oldbury-on-Severn (actually called an Oldbury tart).

Greengage

Sir Thomas Gage brought back some round green plums from France in 1724, and so this delicious fruit became known as the 'green Gage plum'. And ever since, its relatives have been rated as some of the finest members of the plum family.
   In season: around August.

Guidelines It's a pity that greengages are not more widely available in shops, as they are marvellous fruit with beautifully scented, sweet-flavoured flesh and delicious skins. As with other members of the plum family, avoid bruised or squashy specimens. The skins of greengages are less troublesome that those of other plums.

Uses Makes excellent jam and chutney. Try substituting greengages for plums in various recipes.

Loganberry

First raised by Judge J.H. Logan in Santa Cruz, California in 1881, the loganberry was first thought to be a natural cross between a blackberry and a raspberry, although it may simply be a natural variety of the Pacific blackberry.
   In season: early July–late August.

Guidelines Grown commercially in southern and eastern England, as well as Hereford & Worcester. They are tangy fruits looking rather like large, wine-coloured raspberries. Excellent for cooking. Watch out for signs of squashiness, especially at the bottom of punnets where the fruit is under pressure and stains the wood or cardboard.

Uses Particularly good for jam, but can be substituted for raspberries in quite a number of recipes.

Pear

Cultivated pears are all descended from *Pyrus communis*, the wild pear, and have a reputation for prodigious age, indeed some may live for as long as three centuries. France has always been the great country for pears, although there are some famous English varieties such as Conference.

In season: (home-grown) August–March; (imported) all year round.

Guidelines Pears are perfectly ripe for only a short time, so the trick is to buy them just before they are ready and then kept in the house until their moment arrives. They are ready when the stalk end is just beginning to feel soft, but they should not be squashy.

Dessert pears should have a strong scent with juicy almost buttery flesh. Stewing pears, which keep very well, are very hard and lacking in flavour and juice. Slow cooking greatly improves them.

Uses Pears can be stewed or puréed, they are also delicious when spicily pickled. Good when added to fruit salads and excellent with cheese.

Plum

Many of our best plums began life in woods and hedgerows, like the yellow Pershore plum discovered in the Vale of Evesham. Some came over from France, while the famous Victoria was discovered in a Sussex garden.

In season: (home-grown) August–October; (imported) December–April & June–October.

Guidelines Eating or dessert plums should be firm without being squashy, their skins should be smooth and glossy with a slight 'bloom'. Cooking plums – most of which have blue-black skins – are often sold under-ripe.

Don't buy bruised, mouldy or damaged plums.

Although we tend to think first of Victoria plums, these are by no means the best plums around; their place is in the can.

Uses Can be stewed or bottled or made into chutney or jam. Dried plums are known as 'prunes'.

> *Remember that real food means making better use of our skills and resources*

Quince

Cultivated since ancient times and loved by the Romans, the quince is a marvellous fruit with the most heavenly perfume.

In season: September–October.

Guidelines If you see some quinces for sale in a shop or on a market, buy them, for you may not get another chance. When ripe they have tough golden skins, firm rather acidic flesh and that marvellous aroma. Buy them when ripe, although they are not eaten raw, but always cooked.

Uses Excellent for jams and jellies. Also for mixing with applies and pears in fruit pies and tarts.

Raspberry

When the Greek gods tired of nectar and ambrosia it's claimed that they feasted on raspberries picked from Mount Ida. Wonderful fruit indeed, although most of our memories of them are more down to earth. The delicious little wild raspberries of Yorkshire and Scotland are quite rare but sublime, and Scotland has now become the home of the cultivated raspberry with acre upon acre of canes on the east coast of the Lowlands around Dundee and Perth.

In season: July–September.

Guidelines Need to be eaten very fresh. Although they are less juicy than some other soft fruit, raspberries are normally sold hulled (with the central plug removed) so they need delicate handling and packing othewise they can easily become squashed. If they are cracked or pitted near the top they are not at their best.

There's no need to wash raspberries, simply pick through them and sort them out, discarding any that are in poor condition.

Uses At their very best eaten raw. Wild raspberries accompany grouse from the moors and the fruit has even been matched with skate. Also good for summer pudding and jam and makes a nice sauce to go with desserts.

Rhubarb

Not strictly a fruit like apples or strawberries, although its uses are mainly fruity. The ancient Chinese and later the

Greeks used the powdered root medicinally, but it wasn't until the end of the 18th century that the stems and stalks found their way into English kitchens.

In season: December–July.

Guidelines At the beginning of its season (from December until early March), rhubarb is forced. It is thin, pale pink with yellowish leaves, and most of it comes from Yorkshire. Maincrop rhubarb is in season from March onwards; it is larger, darker and generally more coarse and stringy although it has plenty of flavour. Forced rhubarb won't need to be peeled but large maincrop sticks will.

Always remove the leaves from the sticks as they contain poisonous oxalic acid.

Don't use sticks that are limp or split.

Uses Rhubarb is stewed, put into pies and tarts, made into jam with ginger or turned into a fool.

Strawberry

The wild scarlet strawberry of Virginia was brought from its native America at the beginning of the 17th century. Since then it has developed a great deal and its descendants are now, for us, the very essence of summer in England.

In season: (home-grown) May–October; (imported) September–June.

Guidelines Freshness is all, so you should patronise a reputable trader who does good business and has a fast turnover. Strawberries are immensely popular and quite a lot of second-rate fruit can appear on the market especially early in the season before the fruit is really ripe. They are over-priced and virtually tasteless.

Try to inspect the strawberries packed into punnets, and look out for squashed or mouldy specimens that can easily taint their neighbours. And make sure you are not being offered a heap of under-ripe fruit which are pale and patchy in colour.

In the end the quality of English strawberries always depends on the weather. Wet days at the wrong time can ruin the crop.

Uses Traditionally it's strawberries and cream, but you might also try the fruit moistened with red wine. Large quantities of fruit can be turned into jam, or used for fools, mousses and even a soup.

> *Look hard at labels and packaging. Learn the language and learn to read between the lines.*

Some Wild Fruits

As well as cultivated fruit there are scores of different wild fruits that food hunters can enjoy. Most have to be gathered from the countryside, although a few do appear occasionally, espeially in farm shops and on roadside stalls. For more information consult *Food for Free* by Richard Mabey.

Bilberry

Abundant on heaths and moors, particularly in the north of Britain. The plant grows low amid dense heather, so picking can be a laborious business. The juicy black berries appear from July–September. Good for crumbles, pancakes, jams and jellies.

Blackberry

The familiar 'bramble' is the most widespread and commonly gathered of all our wild fruit, and blackberrying is a popular autumn pastime. The prickly shrub grows in all kinds of woods, hedges and waste places and the juicy berries are ready betwen August and early October. Can be turned into jams and jellies, as well as pies and puddings.

Bullace

One of our early types of domestic plum, before more sweet and succulent varieties were produced. The fruits are rather like monster sloes (see later) of vaiable colours, and they appear in both gardens and hedgerows. Best for liqueurs, jams and jellies.

Elder

A splendidly versatile plant whose two main virtues are its muscat-scented flowers and clusters of reddish-black berries.

These appear in profusion between August and October, and while they are quite astringent on their own, they can be added to a number of dishes including james and jelies or turned into a most unusual sauce.

Medlar

A strange tree, with even stranger looking fruit. It grows in gardens and some hedgerows and bears odd fruit that look like giant brown rose hips. These stay rock-hard until the winter, in fact they can only be eaten when they are semi-rotten or 'bletted'. Medlars can be turned into jelly, baked whole or eaten by scraping flesh out of the skin.

Rose Hip

The fruit of the wild rose – the hip – has one great advantage: it is loaded with more vitamin C than any other fruit or vegetable, four times as much as blackcurrants and twenty times more than oranges. Rose hips are inedible as they are, since they contain masses of prickly hairs, so they have to be converted into the famous syrup or a jelly, which filters out the nasty bits.

Rowan/Mountain Ash

Well known as a town tree, planted along highways and in parks, but also common in the wild, where its clusters of bright orange berries are easily recognised between August and October. They make a particularly good jelly (mixed with apples) to serve with all kinds of game.

Sloe/Blackthorn

The ancestor of all our cultivated plums, but the most tart and acidic fruit you are likely to taste. The dark-blue berries, or sloes, appear in the spike-laden bushes in the autumn, and are best picked after the first frosts have softened and mellowed them. Can be turned into chutney or jelly, but are most famously used to produce sloe gin.

Nuts

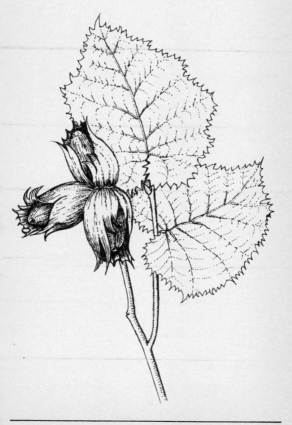

Strictly speaking nuts are single-seeded, hard-shelled fruits that need to be cracked open, however the word is used quite freely to include legumes like peanuts, as well as almonds and coconut – anything in fact that has an edible kernel inside an inedible shell.

Nuts have been gathered since prehistoric times and have been valued both as a source of concentrated, high-protein, vegtble food and also for their oil. Many, like hazelnuts and chestnuts, can be gleaned from the wild, although others are grown systematically in plantations.

The choice of nuts is enormous. I have concentrated on those that are – or have been – part of British cookery and can be obtained from home-grown sources. But there are many others: Brazil nuts, cashew nuts, coconuts, macadamia nuts, peanuts, pecan nuts and pistachio nuts, to name but a few, although we are unlikely to find acorns and beechmast – two great wild food stand-bys – in the shops these days.

Nutritional value of nuts   The greatest virtue of nuts is as an unequalled source of second-class vegetable protein; not other food can match them. Black walnuts, for instance, contain an impressive 28% protein, more than even herrings or lean beef, and other nuts are not far behind. No wonder that they are high on the list of every vegtarian diet.

Most nuts also contain useful amounts of vitamins – especially B group and C – as well as minerals and good quantities of valuable fibre.

However, if there is a fly in this particular ointment, it is the fact that nuts also contain prodigious amoutns of fat and are extremely calorific. Much of this fat is often unsaturated, even so the overall level is very high – something like 60% – which results in an energy value of almost 3,000 calories per pound of nuts. So it's worth remembering that you are taking in fat as well as protein when you eat them.

Buying nuts   The is quite straightforward if you are buying whole, unshelled nuts from a reliable source. Nuts in their shells are designed to keep, but out of their protective casing, the fatty kernels can quickly go rancid unless treated. So many pre-packed, shelled nuts have preservatives and anti-oxidants added to them, while others, such as peanuts, are often fried in saturated fats and coated with salt – both of which are undesirable.

Almond

A native of Morocco and the Near East, the almond was brought to Britain by the Romans, and almonds were an important ingredient in Medieval cooking, providing thickness and 'whiteness' to sauces and dishes, as well as adding their own distinctive flavour. They were once cultivated on quite a large scale, but are much less common now.

Availability Almost all are imported from Italy, Spain, France and California.

Guidelines There are actually two species, very different in character: the sweet almond (*Prunus dulcis*) and the bitter almond (*Prunus dulcis var. amara*). Sweet almonds are grown for their edible nuts, which are oval, light brown and have shells pitted with holes.

Bitter almonds are never eaten raw as they contain traces of prussic acid (HCN). But you are unlikely to be poisoned, or indeed eat the nuts at all, because they are extremely pungent. However, the acid is highly volatile and evaporates when the almonds are cooked. Bitter almonds are much broader in shape than sweet almonds.

Uses Sweet almonds can be used whole for baking and confectionery; they can be purchased ground to make into almond paste, also chopped, and they can be roasted. Bitter almonds are used to produce almond essence as well as almond oil, which has been prized as a cosmetic for moisturising the skin since Roman times.

Chestnut

The sweet chestnut (*Castanea sativa*) is a native of the Mediterranean, where hundreds of different varieties grow wild. It came to Britain with the Romans, although its other name 'Spanish chestnut' refers to the traditional source of the supply.

Availability Widely available. English chestnuts can be bought or gathered from the wild during October and November.

Guidelines Wild English chestnuts should not be confused with horse chestnuts – the familiar 'conkers' which come from an unrelated tree and are not edible. The shiny brown nuts are coverd in a distinctive spiny husk.

Chestnuts brought from the shops are already husked and most come from Southern Europe. The finest of all are the exclusive, large *marrons* from France; most however are less impressive and vary in quality a great deal. The nuts should look fresh, with shiny skins, and should feel firm. They don't keep well at room temperature.

Uses Because chestnuts have more starch and less oil than other nuts, they are used extensively as a vegetble; a dish of whole chestnuts and Brussels sprouts goes perfectly with Christmas roast turkey; chestnuts can also be boiled, steamed, turned into a purée and, of course, roasted in the embers of a fire. And in many parts of Europe they are ground to make a sweet flour which is turned into bread.

Hazelnut (Cobnut, Filbert)

There's great confusion about the difference between 'cobnuts' and 'filberts', both of which are classed as hazelnuts. The most popular commercial variety is called the Kentish Cob *or* Lambert's Filbert and was first raised by Mr. Lambert of Goudhurst in Kent around 1830. In fact it is, botanically speaking, a filbert.

Both cobs and filberts are related closely to the wild hazelnut (*Corylus avellana*), which has been gathered and eaten since prehistoric times.

Availability Wild hazelnuts are abundant throughout the British Isles. Commercial cobs and filberts are grown mainly in Kent. They are sold in greengrocers as well as farm shops and roadside stalls during September and October.

Guidelines The name hazelnut derives from the Anglo-Saxon *haesil*, meaning a head-dress, an apt description for the way in which the husk or cupule covers the nut. Cobs and filberts are normally picked and sold with their husk intact, so you can easily tell which is which: cobs are small and round, filberts are larger, more oval and have an enveloping husk.

The shells should be woody-brown in colour (if they have a greenish tinge they are not fully ripe) and the nuts inside should be firm and full-flavoured.

Keep well if stored in a warm, dry place.

Uses Very versatile: can be used to make hazelnut bread or the renowned nut cutlets; also chopped and added to a soup of Jerusalem artichokes, put whole into pâtés, and turned into a stuffing for turkey. Vast quantities are also needed for confectionery – so much so that tons have to be imported from abroad.

Walnut

Juglans regia, known to the Greeks as the Persian tree, was introduced into England from the Middle East more than 400 years ago and has firmly established itself as the classic English nut. The tree is magnificent and beautiful, its timber has been treasured by furniture makers for hundreds of years and its fruit is impessively nutritious – high in protein, fibre, minerals and vitamins (including vitamin C).

Availability Native British walnut trees are sadly in decline; the old trees have been used for timber and they haven't been systematically replanted. Some indigenous trees do still bear fruit, but most for sale come from France, Italy, Rumania and China. Fully ripe during late October and November.

Guidelines Young walnuts can be fairly tasteless, but if you gather them when they are green and their shells are still soft, they can be pickled in vinegar or preserved in syrup.

Ripe walnuts should be competely dry and should have a distinctive pale brown colour with convolutions on the shell that echo the curious appearance of the nut wihin. The Greeks described the nut as *karyon* (*kara* meaning head) because it resembled the human brain in appearance.

Uses Ripe walnuts can be used for cakes and confectionery; they are added to sauces and garnishes for meat dishes, put into salads and included in a whole range of vegetarian specialities. Walnut oil has a very pronounced flavour and is used for salad dressings.

Condiments, Pickles and Preserves

Salt

Salt, or sodium chloride, to give it its correct chemical name, has been part of our diet since prehistoric times and it was already being deliberately and systematically exploited in neolithic times. The custom of eating salt may have started as a whim, although there was also a physiological need to keep the body topped up with essential chemical.

Most salt either comes from sea water or from mined deposits left by primeval seas. Brine springs, rivers and lakes were also sources of this vital substance in the past.

Uses of salt   Salt's main function is to ensure that our bodies work properly (see below), but it has also become the most all-pervading of seasonings particularly in the West. It is also widely used as a preservative for all kinds of food from bacon to kippers, cheese and butter. (Salt works by osmosis, that is water is drawn out of the cell membranes into the salt or brine solution; with less water in the food, bacteria cannot develop and so the food is preserved.)

Salt in the diet   Salt is one chemical we cannot do without: muscles wouldn't function, nerves wouldn't carry messages and food would remain undigested. This is because over half the body consists of fluids containing salt. The important point is to keep a very delicate balance within the body, not too little, not too much.

In recent years, however, our diet has become increasingly loaded with salt. We can opeate and survive quite happily on 4–5 grams each day, depending what we do and where we live, but many of us now consume anything up to 20 grams daily in various forms. Most nutritionists now agree that this kind of salt intake can lead to high blood pressure which in turn can increase the risk of heart attacks in people predisposed towards them.

The problem is that much of the time we don't know that we are eating salt at all. but it's an essential ingredient of a vast number of processed foods including breakfast cereals, bread and all kinds of tinned vegetables; it's the main ingredient of stock cubes and it's found in preserved meat like bacon, smoked fish, some butter, cheese and pickles.

We also deliberately salt our food. I'm not convinced by the argument that we should eat completely unseasoned vegetables. Apart from the fact that it's bad cookery (skilful seasoning is one of the marks of a good chef) it's actually quite a small contributory factor since much of the salt remains in the cooking liquid. Worse is the habit of indiscriminately sprinkling salt onto cooked food. This is not only an insult to a carefully prepared dish but can significantly increase the amount of salt we take in each day.

So the message must be cut down on salt (NACNE (see page 14) at least a 25% cut), season very carefully, don't lace your food with it and steer clear of highly processed items that have a lot of added salt (although if you are a real food fan you will be avoiding most of these things anyway).

Rock Salt

Salt mines were discovered near Northwich in Cheshire around 1670 and subsequently other centres such as Nantwich and Droitwich proved fruitful. To begin with the rock salt was hewn out manually like coal, but later it was dissolved and pumped out of the pits as brine, which was then evaporated in iron pans. Rock salt can be bought as unrefined crystals or, in a more refined state but without any additives, as 'block' or 'kitchen' salt.

Thompson's rock salt, produced at the Lion Salt Works, Marston, near Northwich (the sole-surviving open-pan slat works in the country) is justly famous.

Sea Salt

Obtained by the evaporation of sea water using artificial heat. There were important salt workings along the East Anglian and South coasts in the early Middle Ages, in fact the Domesday Book lists no fewer than 45 'pans' in the region. These East Anglian works played an important part in the development of the medieval herring industry, which relied on salt for preserving and curing the fish.

If you have a choice always go for sea salt: it has the best and most pronounced flavour (which means you can use less of it for cooking, and, because it comes from sea water it also contains valuable trace elements such as iodine.

The most renowned sea salt comes from the Maldon Crystal Salt Company of Maldon in Essex, which stands on the site of a Medieval salt works and is actually part of a tradition dating back some 2,000 years.

Table Salt

A highly refined salt produced from the old salt workings of Cheshire and Worcestershire. It is ground very fine and has magnesium carbonate added to it to make it 'free-running'. (This is because salt is hygroscopic and absorbs moisture in damp weather; as a result it cakes and becomes heavy and unmanageable). Nowadays manufacturers may treat the salt with sodium ferrocyanide which cause little tentacles to form on the crystals, thus preventing them from sticking together.

Table salt may be cheap but in every other respect it comes bottom of the salt league table.

Vinegar

The word vinegar is derived from the French *vin aigre*, meaning sour wine, and is a by-product of fermentation. Originally all vinegar was made from wine and this remained popular right up to the 19th century when it was gradually superseded in this country by brown, pungent malt vinegar. This was often very dubious in quality and composed of diluted sulphuric acid coloured with burnt sugar or infusions of oak chips, consequently most discerning cooks continued to use wine vinegar or to make their own from safe ingredients.

The starting point for vinegar can be any kind of raw material containing starch or sugar, such as malted barley, mollasses, applies or grapes. The sugar is fermented to give alcohol, which in turn is fermented again to produce acetic acid, the main component of vinegar. Natural vinegar yeasts will convert alcohol into acetic acid (as anyone who has left a bottle of wine open for too long will know), but most commercial manufacturers add special yeasts to ensure that the fermentation goes according to plan.

The strength of different vivegars varies a great deal. Commercial spirit vinegars can be 10–13% acetic acid, while the minimum for wine vinegar is 6% and for malt and other vinegars 4% is the required acidity.

Cider Vinegar

This vinegar is endowed with remarkable therapeutic and health giving properties, thanks largely to the work of one Dr. DeForest Clinton Jarvis, whose books *Folk Medicine* and *arthritis and Folk Medicine* became world bestsellers in the 1960s. Jarvis preached a new theory of natural medicine which had cider vinegar – and honey – as its cornerstones. It has been proposed as a cure for evrything from arthritis, obesity and kidney troubles to headaches and hiccups. It also seems to be a useful way of keeping the body in good working order, thereby preventing disease in the first place.

Cider vinegar is normally made from cider and the three main brands on sale here come from cider-producers: Aspall 'cyder' vinegar from Suffolk is perhaps the best because it is made from organically-grown fruit. The other two worth mentioning are Merrydown in Sussex (who market cider vinegar under the trade name Martlet) and Whiteways of Wimple, Devon. No additives or preservatives are included.

Uses Cider vinegar's effectivness is due largely to its high concentration of minerals (especially potassium) and organic acids, but it's equally useful in the kitchen as a condiment and flavouring. It can be used for pickling, salad dressings and for making mustard and sauces. I is also good for marinading meat and fish.

Distilled vinegar

Simply made by distilling malt vinegar to produce a very strong colourless liquid high in acetic acid.

Uses The common alternative to malt vinegar in most home-made pickles. It is useful because it is colourless and is not as pungent as malt vinegar.

Herb Vinegar

Made by steeping fresh herbs in wine vinegar. The most common are tarragon, rosemary, thyme and horseradish, although almost any herb can be used. A sprig of the herb is usually left in the bottle when it is sold, which improves both the flavour and the look of the vinegar.

Uses Particularly good for salad dressings. Tarragon is also suitable for béarnaise sauce.

Malt vinegar

The common English vinegar, made by fermenting malted barley into a rough kind of beer, then transforming it into vinegar. It is matured in oak casks and coloured with caramel. It is the cheapest and most widely used of all vinegars.

AVOID very cheap, inferior brands which can be quite unpleasant. They may be made directly from acetic acid which is diluted and coloured, or they may use cheap starting materials such as wood pulp. Unless the vinegar is carefully purified it may contain traces of harmful chemicals.

Uses Good malt vinegar is the most common vinegar for pickles, sauces and chutneys, and although it can be used for cooking in robust dishes, its flavour tends to be much too pungent.

Spirit vinegar

The starting point for this vinegar is often molasses or sugar beet, which is turned into alcohol and then distilled. It is very strong, 10–13% acetic acid, and is greatly favoured by commercial pickle manufacturers, which is why their products are so harsh and acidic.

Uses Not normally sold in shops.

Wine vinegar

Although wine vinegar is generally regarded as the finest of all vinegars, don't assume that simply because the label says 'wine vinegar' that the product will be good. All wine vinegar should be made from wine, but sometimes it is made sloppily from poor wine and the results are very rough indeed. Good wine vinegar needs to be made slowly and patiently in oak vats so that its aromatic qualities are concentrated (the Orléans and Boerhaave processes are the most famous).

Wine vinegar can be red, white or rosé, and there is an excellent sherry vinegar in a similar style too.

Uses Its characteristic delicate flavour makes it ideal for salad dressings and sauces as well as for subtly flavoured pickles.

Mustard

Our ancestors, the hunter-gatherers of prehistory enjoyed chewing wild mustard seeds for their pleasant stimulating effect, but it wasn't until the arrival of the Romans that mustard-making came into its own. At first it was ground in little stone mills and mixed with vinegar, but by the 17th century it was being pressed into hard compact tablets that could be blended with anything from cider and cherry juice to buttermilk.

Around 1720, however, all that changed when a certain Mrs Clements from Durham perfected a way of producing fine ground mustard flour free from bits of husk. Then in 1814, a Norfolk miller named Jeremiah Colman moved into the water mill at Stoke Holy Cross near Norwich and set up his own mustard-making business, and even today Colman's mustard dominates the market. Much of their mustard now comes in a smooth prepared form, and this is perhaps how we know it best. However, there has been a change of fashion since the mid-1970s with the rise of many small enterprises and cottage industries producing a whole range of English coarse-grained mustards which have injected a real breath of fresh air into the mustard market.

Guidelines People who like English mustard now have a choice of three main types. First of all there's mustard powder. Colman's Genuine Double Superfine is renowned although it's usually available only at Colman's very own Mustard Shop in Norwich. One or two of the smaller firms such as Wiltshire Tracklements also produce mustard powder although theirs is slightly different because it is pure mustard without the usual addition of wheat flour. Mixed with water and allowed to bloom these make traditional English mustard at its best.

It's more common to find the mustard prepared or ready-mixed in the jar. Here again Colman's lead the field, although Taylor's mustard from Newport Pagnell is worth seeking out. Some of these mustards may be coloured naturally (with turmeric) or artificially.

But the real excitement comes from the new range of whole-grain mustards produced by many of the newer firms. Although these were inspired by the French-style of mustard, they do have a thoroughly English character. The mustard seed is barely crushed or sometimes stone-ground, so that the whole grain remains and very little of the important volatile oil that gives the mustard its flavour and aroma is lost. These mustards are usually vinegar-based (either wine vinegar or cider vinegar) and are imaginatively seasoned with various herbs and spices; some contain beer, others cider, while to satisfy Welsh and Scottish appetites there are a number of locally made honey mustards.

William Tullberg of Wiltshire Tracklements, Calne, produces the superb range of Urchfont mustards, while Charles Gordon operates just as impressively from Peaslake in Surrey. Also look out for the Dorset Preserving Company, Wilsons, Crabtree & Evelyn and St Elven from Cornwall, all of whom produce worthwhile mustards in the new style.

The main point to remember when buying any mustard is to look at the label to ensure that the product has no additives in the way of artificial preservatives, colouring and flavouring etc. Today's new breed of mustard-makers are committed men who are prepared to make their mustard without recourse to additives.

Uses Mustard is the classic condiment and is at its best on the side of the plate, although it can be used for sauces, salad dressings and in a number of prepared dishes. Mustard also has the advantage that it is an emulsifying agent which can help in the digestion of fatty foods like pork pies and sausages. It is also a powerful preservative and a useful weapon against unfriendly bacteria.

Pickles

Pickling is an ancient form of preserving vegetables and fruit (as well as meat and fish) and it was practised with great skill and imagination by the Greeks and Romans, who made all kinds of pickles from herbs, roots, flowers and vegetables – everything from pickled asparagus and fennel to lettuce leaves and turnips, which were preserved in a mixture of honey, myrtle berries and vinegar.

The traditions of pickling continued without a break right up to the 19th century when a significant change began to take place. This was the age of the first commercial pickle-makers, whose products were regarded with gret suspicion by cooks such as Eliza Acton. She noted that: 'In numerous instances those (pickles) which are commonly sold to the public have been found of so deadly a nature as to be eminently dangerous to persons who parttake of them often and largely'. Her advice was 'to have them prepared at home'. In 1899 there was a special government enquiry into food adulteration which helped to alleviate the problem, and as the food industry grew it tended to discourage the unscrupulous back-street manufacturer.

Today's pickles and today's pickle-makers are the descendants of many of these original firms.

Guidelines The range of pickles on offer these days is quite limited – onions, red cabbage, gherkins, walnuts – although a few smaller enterprises may offer things like damsons and figs. Most of the large firms use spirit vinegar and large quantities of salt so that their pickles will keep for a long time. As a result most of them are very salty and very acidic; also if they are beginning to show their age they will be soft and squashy, rather than crisp. Unless you find a small firm using perhaps cider vinegar, it is far better to follow Eliza Acton's advice and make your own.

Chutneys, Relishes & Sauces

Both chutneys and ketchups have an oriental ring to them: the word chutney comes from the Hindustani *chatni*, meaning a strong sweet relish, which ketchup derives from the Chinese *koe-chiap*, a pickled fish sauce. Neither appeared in England until the 17th century. Piccalilli was one of the earliest and consisted of a vinegar-based sauce flavoured with garlic, ginger, mustard seed, pepper and turmeric in which were pieces of fruit and vegetables such as cabbage, cauliflower and plums.

The first ketchups were indeed vinegary and fishy (often flavoured with anchovies); they were also dark, pungent and spicy. By the 19th century things had become more exotic, new ingredients appeared on the scene – particularly tomatoes – the old fishy flavours disappeared and the range of chutneys and ketchups became much thicker, more pulpy and had sugar included in them.

Guidelines Today's chutneys and ketchups are bland compared with their 19th-century predecessors, judging by the lists of ingredients. They are generally far too sweet (often sugar beet is their main constituent) but they also have the harsh tang of spirit vinegar and their texture is gummy and glutinous due to the quantities of tragacanth and gum arabic added to them. Artificial colouring and preservatives also figure in quite a number of them. So, if you are buying one of these commercially produced chutneys or ketchups, always read the label first to see what you are getting.

There are however some admirable exceptions to this rule. One that deserves a mention is the firm of Cartwright & Butler, based in Wells-next-the-Sea, Norfolk. They are a good example of a real thriving cottage industry, their range of chutneys, and relishes is made from wholesome ingredients (they use cider vinegar and raw sugar). The recipes are interesting and unusual – anything from tomato and red pepper relish to sweet and sour celery pickle – and they are presented in a most appealing fashion.

Jams, jellies & marmalades

The problem with all these fruity preserves is sugar, because that is the way in which the fruit is actually preserved. The word jam first appeared in cookery books about 1718 and both the name itself and the pulpy preserve quickly replaced for elegant old-fashioned methods of preserving whole fruit in syrup. Commercial jam-making got under way during the agricultural depression of the 1870s and 1880s, when farmers were anxious to find new markets for unwanted fruit. At first these preserves were cheap, unwholesome concoctions of fruit and vegetable pulp with sugar, colouring and extra flavouring added.

Marmalades, originally made with quinces, but always now associated with oranges, lemon and other citrus fruit, didn't suffer quite so badly at the hands of the commercial manufacturers, and earned a high reputation in Victorian times before they became the standard feature on breakfast tables throughout the land.

Guidelines Today's jams, fruit jellies and marmalades are all high in sugar and most commercial varieties also contain colouring, gelling agents and stabilisers. So they tend to be very sweet, gaudy in colour and quite solid in texture. Their ingredients alone would make them not worth recommending, but most also have an inferior flavour.

Watch out for the low-sugar jams offered by some shops. These might seem like a good idea, but the lack of sugar means that the jam won't keep so well, consquently preservatives have to be added; less sugar also means a thinner sloppier jam, so extra gelling agents and stabilisers are needed.

There are however some jams made without sugar – the Whole Earth brand is one to look out for. They rely on apple juice for sweetness, have a really natural fruit flavour and because they are free of colouring and other additives they look natural too. Of course they don't keep as long, but will survive quite well in a refrigerator.

Similar alternatives exist for marmalade.

Producers of condiments and preserves

Salt

Maldon Crystal Salt
Company Ltd
The Downs, <u>Maldon</u>, Essex
Tel: (0621) 53315

Lion Salt Works
(Thompson's Salt)
<u>Marston</u>, near Northwich,
Cheshire
Tel: (0606) 2066

Mustard

Wiltshire Tracklements
(Urchfont Mustard)
44 Church Street, <u>Calne</u>,
Wiltshire
Tel: (0249) 812634

Colman's Mustard Shop
3 Bridewell Alley, <u>Norwich</u>,
Norfolk
Tel: (0603) 27889

Charles Gordon Associates
Ltd
Hoe House, Peaslake,
<u>Guildford</u>, Surrey
Tel: (0306) 73776

Cider venegar

Merrydown Wine Company
Horam Manor, Horam,
<u>Heathfield</u>, East Sussex
Tel: (043 53) 2254

Whiteways of Whimple Ltd
Whimple, <u>Exeter</u>, Devon
Tel: (0404) 822332

J. M. Chevallier Guild
The Cyder House,
Aspall Hall, <u>Stowmarket</u>,
Suffolk
Tel: (0728) 860510

Preserves

Dartington Farm Foods
<u>Dartington</u>, near Totnes,
Devon

Cartwright & Butler Ltd
The Spice Mill,
<u>Wells-next-the-Sea</u>, Norfolk

Honey

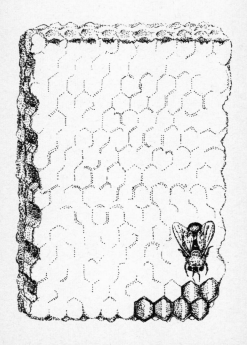

Long before sugar started to blacken Elizabeth I's teeth, honey was the universal sweetener. And it had been that way for thousands of years. Of course bees were making honey before man arrived on the scene, but once our ancestors started to hunt for their food, honey must have been one of their very first forms of nourishment. At first they simply plundered the hives, but later they began to keep bees deliberately and to harvest the fruit of the hive. There are records of beekeeping in Acient Egypt as early as 2400 BC.

The story of honey is a fascinating and amazing one: it takes in the secretion of nectar by flowers, the foraging of bees to collect the nectar (which involves a flight path of three orbits round the earth for a single jar of honey). The transformation of nectar into honey in the complex community of the hive, and the final splendid harvest.

The honey bee is unique in the natural world and no other creature has built around itself such a wealth of folklore, superstition and symbolism. Bees were sacred – even divine – in many early civilisations and their extraordinary way of life made them appropriate symbols of prosperity and fruitful activity. Even now their social organisation is often seen as a mirror of our own society.

A great deal has changed since the days when the Ancient Britons named their native land 'the honey isle'. Eva Crane summed it up this way in *A Book of Honey*: 'Honey, the food that bees have produced for twenty million years, is now handled by machine and transported across the world.'

Making honey Bees make honey from the nectar they collect from a whole host of flowering plants and trees. Nectar consists of a very weak solution of various sugars, but each species of plant prduces nectar that is completely individual and it is this which gives each particular type of honey its character and flavour.

Bees carry the nectar to their hives in their honey stomachs, where enzymes begin to convert the sucrose in the nectar into laevulose and dextrose. Once in the hive, the nectar is deposited in the honeycomb, where the trasformation continues. In the warmth of the hive, water evaporates and the honey becomes concentrated. When it is ripe the bees cap it with wax.

After that, technology usually takes over. The combs are uncapped by machine and the honey extracted from them by centrifugal force. It may also be heated to make it easier to extract. Finally it is pumped into a strainer, filtered and packed.

The nutritional value of honey Honey is natural, nourishing and delicious, each type with its own subtle fragrance and flavour. The actual constituents of different honeys vary depending on the nectar from which they are derived, but an average one will contain about 38% fruit sugar, 31% glucose and 7% maltose as well as some others. In addition to that, all honeys are rich in minerals, especially sodium, potassium, magnesium, manganese and iron, along with vitamins (mainly B group and C) plus proteins and amino acids.

Because it contains simple sugars, honey is very easily assimilated by the body and can be absorbed directly into the blood stream without any shock to the system (unlike complex refined sugars). It is also a natural antiseptic and antibiotic useful for treating anything from coughs to burns (bees, it seems, actually manufacture antibiotics which they inject into the honey and comb).

Uses of honey Honey is the perfect sweetener, the ideal alternative to refined sugar. It blends well with wholefoods of all kinds and can be used to make lots of different cakes, breads and to flavour new kinds of confectionery. It is also useful for glazing ham and chicken, preserving fruit and has a host of other applications.

As well as being a valuable natural medication, honey is also the basis for many cosmetic preparations.

Guidelines for buying honey (i) Honey comes in two forms, runny and granulated. The runny types, which are the most popular, and are actually made by heating granulated honey. Once this has turned runny it doesn't readily revert to its original state. Honey that is high in glucose tends to granulate easily, and most honey becomes granular with age.

(ii) The flavour, colour and consistency of honey depend on the source of the nectar, water content and the way it has been produced. There are pale golden honeys, brown ones, red, black and even sea-green and they come from literally hundreds of different plants throughout the world.

(iii) Some cheaper brands of honey come from bees that are fed on a sugar solution which is placed outside the hive. This means that they honey tends to lack vitamins and minerals as well as being poor quality. Don't be taken in by the statement 'Guaranteed pure': this simply means that nothing has been added to the honey *after* extraction from the comb.

(iv) Always seek out 'pure' honey from a single source, rather than low-quality blends that are labelled 'produce of more than one country'.

(v) If the jar of honey you buy smells or looks as if it is beginning to ferment, send it back. Whatever else is wrong it will definitely have too much water in it.

(vi) Don't be put off by cloudy honey. This is due largely to pollen grains, which are valuable nutrients in their own right.

(vii) One new threat to the quality of honey is the adulteration with high fructose syrup (HFS). This is already widespread in the USA and I am reliably informed that it has been tried in this country too. It is a way of making a little real honey go a long way by bulking it out with syrup that has never been hear a hive.

(viii) A word about British honey. We consume a great deal, but because of our unpredictable climate and short flowering season, only about 12% of the honey we eat is home-produced. But it does have advantages: the flavour is good because it does not need the heat processing which ensures that no granulation takes place en route. In Britain we also have a more varied floral source than some other countries which gives our honey a particular flavour.

Honey producers and suppliers

There are at least 500 producers and suppliers of British honey, most of which belong to the Bee Farmers' Association. Look out for their products in health food shops and delicatessens.

Chain Bridge Honey Farm
Horncliffe,
Berwick-on-Tweed,
Northumberland

Gillbrow Apiaries
Kirkandres-on-Eden,
Carlisle, Cumbria
Tel: (022 876) 523

Orchard Farm
High Common,
North Lopham, Diss,
Norfolk
Tel: (095 381) 707

Haldon Honey Farm
Doddiscombsleigh, Exeter,
Devon
Tel: (0647) 52312

MG Apiaries
19 Westfield Avenue, Goole,
North Humberside
Tel: (0405) 3801

Broadland Apiary
High Road, Burgh Castle,
Great Yarmouth, Norfolk
Tel: (0493) 780230

Vivian's Honey Farm
Hatherleigh, Devon

Jasmine Apiaries
Polyphant, Launceston,
Cornwall

Cobham Apiaries (Kent)
152 Addison Gardens,
London W14
Tel: (01) 603 5950

Great Bradwins Apiaries
11 Sherwoods Road, Oxhey,
Watford, Hertfordshire
Tel: (0923) 42016

Rauseby Apiaries
St Martin's Way, Ancaster,
Grantham, Lincolnshire
Tel: (0400) 30271

South Coast Honey Farms
42 Priory Road,
West Moore, Wimborne,
Dorset
Tel: (0202) 872547

Useful organisations

Bee Farmers' Association
Orchard Farm,
High Common,
North Lopham, Diss,
Norfolk
Tel: (095 381) 707

International Bee Research
Association
Hill House, Gerrards Cross,
Buckinghamshire
Tel: (0753) 885011

Appendix

Useful organisations

Apart from specific organisations and bodies listed in various sections of the book, there are a number of more general organisations which are concerned with the promotion of better food in one way or another. Readers should get in touch with them if they are interested.

The Farm and Food Society
4 Willifield Way,
London NW11 7XT
Tel: (01) 455 0634

A very active organisation dedicated to the promotion of farming that is 'humane to animals, wholesome for consumers, fair to farmers'.

Friends of the Earth
337 City Road,
London EC1V 1NA
Tel: (01) 837 0731

Environmental action and the protection of our natural resources are the main themes of this leading international organisation.

The McCarrison Society
23 Stanley Court,
Worcester Road,
Sutton
Surrey
Tel: (01) 643 2812

Inspired by the work and teachings of Dr Robert McCarrison who pioneered ideas about the relationship between diet and health. The Society says 'His work was unique in that it showed how human health is related to the wholeness of food'.

Organic Farmers and
Growers Ltd
9 Station Approach,
Needham Market,
Ipswich,
Suffolk
Tel: (0449) 720838

One of its main functions is as a cooperative and clearing house for organic produce. It believes in 'biological husbandry' and the use of traditional farming methods which are brought up to date when necessary.

Orgnic Food Service
Ashe, Churston Ferrers,
Brixham, South Devon

Promotes organically produced food and compiles a directory of organic growers and producers.

The Soil Association
Walnut Tree Manor,
Haughley,
Stowmarket,
Suffolk
Tel: (044 970) 235

Britain's oldest organic organisation, increasingly outspoken and committed to the cause of better food. Had great success in 1983 countering the launch of the Government's 'Food from Britain' campaign.

Bibliography

Arlott, John. *English Cheeses of the South and West*. Harrap, 1960

Ayrton, Elisabeth. *The Cookery of England*. Andre Deutsch, 1974

Ayrton, Elisabeth. *English Provincial Cooking*. Mitchell Beazley, 1976

Bailey, Adrian. *The Cooking of the British Isles*. Time Life, 1969

Beech, Anne. *The Gourmet's Directory*. Croom Helm, 1975

Boyd, Lizzie (ed). *British Cookery*. Croom Helm, 1976

Burdett, Osbert. *A Little Book of Cheese*. Howe, 1935

Campbell, Susan. *Guide to Good Food Shops*. Macmillan, 1981

Cannon, Geoffrey and Walker, Caroline. *The Food Scandal*. Century, 1984

Chapman, V. J. *Seaweeds and their Uses*. Methuen, 1970.

Cheke, Val. *The Story of Cheesemaking in Britain*. RKP, 1959

Crane, Eva. *A Book of Honey*. Oxford University Press, 1980

Crane, Eva (ed). *Honey: A Comprehensive Survey*. Heinemann, 1975

Cutting, C. L. *Fish Saving*. Leonard Hill, 1955

David, Elizabeth. *English Bread and Yeast Cookery*. Allen Lane, 1977

Davidson, Alan. *North Atlantic Seafood*. Macmillan, 1979

Dowell, Philip and Bailey, Adrian. *The Book of Ingredients*. Michael Joseph, 1980

Drummond, J. C. and Wilbraham, Anne. *The Englishman's Food*. Johnathan Cape, 1958

Fish Handling and Processing. HMSO, 1965

Fitzgibbon, Theodora. *The Food of the Western World*. Hutchinson, 1976

Gear, Alan (ed). *The Organic Food Guide*. Henry Doubleday Research Association, 1983

Gerrard, Frank. *Sausage and Small Goods Production*. Northwood, 1976

Grigson, Jane. *English Food*. Macmillan, 1974

Grigson, Jane. *Jane Grigson's Fruit Book*. Michael Joseph, 1982

Grigson, Jane. *Jane Grigson's Vegetable Book*. Michael Joseph, 1978

Grigson, Jane. *The Mushroom Feast*. Michael Joseph, 1975

Hartley, Dorothy. *Food in England*. Macdonald, 1954

Heath, Ambrose. *English Cheeses of the North*. Harrap, 1960

Hemphill, Rosemary. *Herbs for All Seasons*. Angus & Robertson, 1972

Hills, Lawrence D. *Organic Gardening*. Penguin 1877

Hogan, William. *The Complete Book of Bacon*. Northwood, 1978

Hutchins, Shelia. *English Recipes*. Methuen, 1967

Hutchins, Shelia. *Good Cooking*. Collins, 1978

Idyll, C. P. *The Sea against Hunger*. Apollo Editions, 1978

Look at the Label. Ministry of Agriculture, Fisheries and Food, 1984

Lovelock, Yann. *The Vegetable Book*. George Allen & Unwin, 1972

Lowenfeld, Claire. *Nuts*. Faber & Faber, 1957

Mabey, David and Richard. *In Search of Food*. Macdonald & Janes, 1978

Mabey, Richard. *Food for Free*. Collins, 1972

Mabey, Richard. and Greenoak, Francesca. *Back to the Roots*. Arrow, 1983

Oddy, Derek J. and Miller, Derek S. *The Making of the Modern British Diet*. Croom Helm, 1976

Peterson, Vicki. *The Natural Food Catalogue*. Macdonald, 1978

Rance, Patrick. *The Great British Cheese Book*. Macmillan, 1982

Stobart, Tom. *Herbs, Spices and Flavourings*. Penguin, 1977

Tannahill, Reay. *Food in History*. Eyre Methuen, 1973

Wallis, M. et al. *The Oxford Book of Food Plants*. Oxford University Press, 1969

Wilson, C. Anne. *Food and Drink in Britain*. Constable, 1973

Index

Real food recommendations

Please use this form to recommend any shop, market stall, producer, farm etc. which produces or sells real food of one kind or another. Also use it to comment on and criticise existing recommendations and listings.

To: Jordans Real Food Guide
Quiller Press Ltd
50 Albemarle Street
London W1X 4BD

Name of establishment ....

Address ....

....

Telephone No. (if known) ....

Type of establishment, eg. shop, farm, market ....

....

Type(s) of real food produced/sold ....

....

General comments ....

....

....

....

....

....

....

....

Name and address of sender ....

....

....